Frank Eckardt, Javier Ruiz Sánchez (eds.)
City of Crisis

Urban Studies

Frank Eckardt, Javier Ruiz Sánchez (eds.)
City of Crisis
The Multiple Contestation of Southern European Cities

[transcript]

This publication has been realized with the generous support by the Deutscher Akademischer Austauschdienst (DAAD).

Bibliographic information published by the Deutsche Nationalbibliothek
The Deutsche Nationalbibliothek lists this publication in the Deutsche Nationalbibliografie; detailed bibliographic data are available in the Internet at http://dnb.d-nb.de

© 2015 transcript Verlag, Bielefeld

All rights reserved. No part of this book may be reprinted or reproduced or utilized in any form or by any electronic, mechanical, or other means, now known or hereafter invented, including photocopying and recording, or in any information storage or retrieval system, without permission in writing from the publisher.

Cover layout: Kordula Röckenhaus, Bielefeld
Cover illustration: john krempl / photocase.de
Typeset by Mark-Sebastian Schneider, Bielefeld
Printed and bound in Great Britain by Marston Book Services Ltd, Oxfordshire
Print-ISBN 978-3-8376-2842-5
PDF-ISBN 978-3-8394-2842-9

Content

City of crisis (Preface)
Frank Eckardt and Javier Ruiz Sánchez | 7

City and Crisis: Learning from urban theory
Frank Eckardt | 11

Crisis and the city
Neoliberalism, austerity planning and the production of space
Álvaro Sevilla-Buitrago | 31

Madrid
A tale of an ambitious city that failed to fulfil its global vision
José Miguel Fernández-Güell | 53

**Contest Discourses of Austerity in the Urban Margins
(A Vision from Barcelona)**
Nuria Benach | 71

Urban crisis or urban decay?
Italian cities facing the effects of a long wave towards privatization of urban policies and planning
Maria Cristina Gibelli | 89

The city and its crises
Francesco Indovina | 109

When it rains, it pours
Urban poverty in a metropolitan suburb during the crisis period
Alberto Violante | 123

Greek Spatial Planning and the Crisis
Maria Zifou | 155

"The right to the city" in Athens during a crisis era
Between inversion, assimilation and going beyond
Vaso Makrygianni and Charalampos Tsavdaroglou | 179

State repression, social resistance and the politicization of public space in Greece under fiscal adjustment
Maria Markantonatou | 199

Planning and governance in the Portuguese cities in times of European crisis
João Seixas and José Carlos Mota | 215

Authors | 257

City of crisis (Preface)

Frank Eckardt and Javier Ruiz Sánchez

The crisis continues. The accumulated debts of the European states is rising steadily. Despite the undertaken efforts, economy of the member states of the European Union has not regained its path of development. The consequences of this crisis are numerous, profound and difficult to oversee (Bitzenis, 2015). Only sketching the 'maybe worst' social aspects of these consequences, one has to think of the remaining high youth unemployment and the effects on the individuals (Antonucci, 2014). This clearly means that the effects of the crisis will last longer than the hoped for economic recovery and might create a generation of young adults with the experience of devalued biographies and social exclusion (cp. Friedrich and Schreiner, 2013, Dølvik, 2015).

In political terms, the crisis has led to a vague emergence/ revival of nationalist, revanchist and populist movements, which in turn profoundly challenges the legitimacy of the European project (Macartney, 2013, Champeau, 2015; Dēmētriou, 2015; Scicluna, 2015). The political landscape in Europe has dramatically changed even in countries where the economic crisis is not as dramatic as in the Southern European countries, which this book intends to highlight.

Instead of defining any kind of theoretical starting point, the editors and authors of the book are trying to make sense of the current crisis by being both academic scholars and observers of the crisis, at the same time. Explanations for the current crisis might be formulated either in a more abstract manner or in a way that contextualizes the crisis with historical terms. Although contributions to this book are not restrained from heading towards these directions, the main direction of this work is to research on the interferences of the local, social and political contexts with the more global levels of the crisis. In this regard, the focus shifts naturally from the global and national dimensions to local situations where coping with the impact of the crisis has to be realized. Cities are the place of vulnerability in this crisis (Ranci, 2014).

Being urban scholars, the contributors are giving an insightful view at the local situations in Italy, Greece, Portugal and Spain. They are trying to use their findings to contribute to the analysis of the crisis in general and for the respective countries in particular. As the author are following theoretical approaches, different ways of academic discourse deriving from the local case studies are represented in this book. This is because – at least at this moment – no single narrative seems to exist that can cover all the aspects which are worked out in the following chapters. In the eyes of the editors, one part of the crisis lies exactly here: There are no strong explanations and narratives available, which could counterbalance the omnipresent simplifications of the populist movements. The public's inability to reflect on the crisis undoubtedly worsens the situation. This book is therefore motivated by the will to demonstrate that academia needs to face this dangerous lack of multifold narratives. As engaged academics, the sterilized form of reflection exposed cannot be the form of discussing the crisis where we are in. In contrast, the awareness of the incompleteness and temporality of the reflections represented on the next pages is taken up with a sense that voicing insights which admit turbulent changes might be the only way for a re-orientation.

Despite the fact that the urban level of society is the most vulnerable and therefore the most important area of people's life, there has been little attention paid by political and social studies on the question 'how the crisis impacts local societies'. Moreover, even in urban studies the crisis has so far gained little reflection. With a critical note, austerity has been identified as the main political ideology (Thompson, 2013) that has fostered the European crisis. While there is a good argument for this criticism, the complexity of the phenomena, which we subsume under the vague term of "crisis", needs to be kept upright if we want to understand its full outcome and its causes (Griggs, 2014; Tabb, 2014). One aspect that has been neglected in this discourse on city and austerity politics is the role of intermediate institutions. Coming from fields of architecture and urban planning, most contributions in this book are especially looking at their programs, actions and rooms to manoeuver.

To find out what planning and architecture has to do with the generation of crisis, in particular by following neoliberal mindsets, and to what extent planers, practitioners, academics and architects can react on this today, was the initial idea that brought the editors together. In a joint study program of the Bauhaus-University Weimar and the Politecnico de Madrid, students worked together to get an understanding of the role and impact of urban planning in the context of the European crisis. While Madrid was the obvious case for the Spanish students, the German team had to notice that austerity politics have a severe impact on social and financial affairs in German cities as well. Very soon, it became evident, that in the Spanish and German cases more is at stake: Processes of deindustrialisation, regional inequalities, contested welfare states, post-fordist modes of economy, increasing precariousness of work relations, and increasing hardship due to social exclusion cannot be left out when trying to understand the immense dynamics which are sometimes obscured by the discourse of "crisis".

Thanks to the generosity of the German Academic Exchange Organisation (DAAD), this common learning process was financially supported. This also allowed us to invite scholars from other Southern European countries to exchange ideas on the topic of the "city of crisis" for a two-day seminar in Weimar, back in December 2013. This book is based mainly on the results of our debates and the shared feeling, which is that, it is most urgent to continue exchanging and reflecting on the crisis in the European cities, which is the final objective of this publication.

References

Antonucci, L. (2014) Young people and social policy in Europe: dealing with risk, inequality and precarity in times of crisis. Basingstoke: Palgrave Macmillan

Bitzenis, A. (2015) Europe in crisis: problems, challenges, and alternative perspectives. New York: Palgrave

Champeau, S. (2015) The future of Europe: democracy, legitimacy and justice after the euro crisis. London: Rowman and Littlefield

Dēmētriou, K. N. (2015) The European Union in crisis: explorations in representation and democratic legitimacy. Cham: Springer

Dølvik, J. E. (2015) European social models from crisis to crisis: employment and inequality in the era of monetary integration. Oxford: Oxford Univ. Press

Friedrich, S. and P. Schreiner (eds) (2013) Nation – Ausgrenzung – Krise. Kritische Perspektiven auf Europa. Münster : edition assemblage

Griggs, S. (2014) Landscapes of antagonism: Local governance, neoliberalism and austerity. In: Urban studies, 51/15, 3290-3305

Macartney, H. (2013) The debt crisis and European democratic legitimacy. Basingstoke: Palgrave

Ranci, C. (2014) Social vulnerability in European cities: the role of local welfare in times of crisis. Basingstoke: Palgrave

Scicluna, N. (2015) European Union constitutionalism in crisis. London: Routledge

Tabb, William K (2014)The wider context of austerity urbanism. In: City, 18/2, 87-100

Thompson, H. (2013) Austerity as ideology: The bait and switch of the banking crisis. In: Comparative European politics, 11/6, 729-736

City and Crisis: Learning from urban theory

Frank Eckardt

Georg Simmel has become famous in urban studies for his essay "Die Großstädte und das Geistesleben" on the mental effects of living in the metropolis (1995/1903). In this classical text, he is drawing conclusions from his life in Berlin at the turn of the century. The German capital at that time exploded because of an unknown flux of migrants into the city. The population density was higher than ever before and equaled that of Chicago and New York. Simmel asked himself on his daily walks through the overcrowded city, in what way people orient themselves and how do they come into contact which each other. In line with psychological discussion at that time, he described the urban dweller as a person who is overcharged by stimuli and thus developing a kind of nervousness. To protect against the massive flux of unfiltered stimulations, the urbanite hides behind a kind of defensive system (being blasé) and controls interaction by a process of directed intention. Simmel (Junge, 2012) saw this as a crucial socio-psychological competence by which to avoid outbursts of aggression between strangers and enable the necessary distances to unknown people. This profound insight, one can say, is one of the most influential ideas about why urban segregation is occurring and why cities are as unequal as they are even today. But Simmel has not worked out a theory on urban inequalities or any kind of theory on the development of cities in general. Rather on the contrary, Georg Simmel understood himself as a philosopher in the first place. Despite him being a founding member of the German Sociological Association and entitling a book comprising a series of his essays as "Sociology", Simmel is often misunderstood as an "easy to take" reference for the urban social scientist in need of an ancestral thinker to help in making their point more than one-hundred years later.

It is no surprise that European intellectuals (Fontana, 2013; Händler, 2014, Maggioni, 2012) are returning to Georg Simmel and his view on the city. His basic text on mental life in the metropolis has been reinterpreted in many ways before the current crisis reached the level of academic reflection. In their edited volume, Mieg, Sundsboe and Bieniok (2012) have discussed Simmel's elementary idea of the metropolis in relation to various subjects like ethnic segregation, urban poverty, gentrification, architecture, marginalization, creative class, or postindustrial change. Apparently, the basic concept of Simmel remains powerful for enabling an analytical view on the city. While it is not here the place to review these attempts to give Simmel's text an actual meaning in the current situation, one can draw a rough conclusion from these readings what the "actual Simmel" is and thereby avoid unfruitful debates about who has "really understood" him or what the better reading might be. It needs to be said, in the first place, that Simmel's style of writing an essay provokes a rather "postmodern" and fragmented reading of his article on the city, as his works are not put into any overarching theoretical framework, although lines to other articles and to his major philosophical ideas can certainly be worked out (cp. Frisby, 2013). Most of the references in urban studies do not take full account of related perspectives in Simmel's work but concentrate on his view of spatial sociology and are often missing the emphasis that he puts on the aesthetic dimension of the urban. This is particularly problematic, as it is with his view on aesthetics and perception that Simmel develops a theory of modernity. The following short interpretation of these three aspects of Simmel's early reflection on the chaotic city of Berlin, with its immense suffering, estrangement and alienation, provides a starting point for discussion of the urban dimension of the contemporary crisis and possible alternatives.

1. Money and the city

As a philosopher, Simmel was more interested in explaining particular phenomena he observed by linking them to a consideration of how we can perceive the world rather than following an empirical research paradigm. The latter was more realized by the Chicago School of Sociology whose charismatic leader Robert Park had the chance to listen to Simmel's lecture during his time in Germany. While Park and his colleagues had been engaged in research that not only shared the academic interest in how the city develops but also wanted to explore the empirical reality as if the city was a laboratory, Simmel worked out his argument for such an explorative sociological research agenda. Simmel and the Chicago School shared a moment in time and opened the development of science to the inclusion of society in a naturalistic manner (cp. Hooker, 2013). While the Chicago School saw itself as part of a movement, still inspired by the Progressive Era and American Pragmatism, Simmel aimed at the predominance of some kind of European philosophy that blockades a view on the empirical reality of modernity. His major argument, working from the classical concepts of perception by Immanuel Kant, in short, lays the fundaments for a larger theorization of society based on the reflection of strangers and poor people and on modernity in general.

Modernity in the eyes of Georg Simmel is based on the same principal assumption that he worked out with regard to encounters and their mental effects in the metropolis. As referred to above, the main theoretical problem Simmel wants to clarify is the establishment of society by the thin lines between individuals. He assumes the city as worked up from below, in contrast to ideas where the city is the place of abstract social structures or in which the differentiation of society is only mirrored or reproduced in space without reflecting the effects of space on society. Nevertheless, it is modernity, as such, that interests him in the first place, not so much the city. The city however is characterized as being a describable unity with a clear distinction from the country-side and rural life. And it is part of a modern life style that differs from the life on the countryside in a particular tension between closeness and distance. Above all, the reflection on the city needs to be framed in a more general understanding of a modernity that is shaped by exchange. The nervous encounters in the city are of the same kind of exchange as are all affairs transacted in modernity. In this way, the city is a part of the "philosophy of money" which is by no coincidence the most important work of Simmel, as he himself saw it, and elaborates the character of exchange relations (cp. Rammstedt, 2003). It is all about money in the city as this is the major driver of exchange. Money however is not a morally estimated goal in itself but an expression and a creation of value. While the stranger in the city seeks to find relationships valued for supporting a lifestyle similar to his own, money is a means to express values for objects. The interference of strangers can work out to create a common understanding and in its most optimistic end point: love. Money undergoes changes as well. First it is an expression of a valued object (as for the stranger: a desired person), then the money becomes an object of estimation by itself. Turning into a value, money becomes exchangeable. The exchange of money, the urban lifestyle and the appearance of a modern individualism are interrelated aspects mutually supportive of each other and all are essentially based on the modern principle of exchange. The main question is how these exchange processes are generated and in what way individual appreciation becomes a social value producing tokens of exchange (money) which in themselves become valorized. In a second step, these valorized goods influence individual perception, identity and their systems of valorization. Simmel speaks of "Wechselwirkungen" (relations of mutual influences). Erotic, religious or just social drives are the starting point of these relations and motivate people to join struggles for, with or against the coexistence of others. Play, teaching, help, attack and other forms of making these contacts differ, but the underlying intentions are similar. For Simmel, interaction, in its eventual sociological sense, still refers to the whole world of interaction and does not make so much difference between objects and other human beings. Societal desire is the starting point for both, interference and exchange with others and with regard to goods. In his view, the city is a place for individualism as it needs a certain intellectualism based in the individual capacity to reflect on individual desires. The urban intellectual is the most outspoken figure of a modern citizen who undergoes the transformation of his desires by rationalization. It is not only that one needs to calculate cost-effect-relations for social and economic investment, but also the very estimation of values requires a sort of calculation. If money becomes a goal in its own, all other valued objects can be calculated in their monetary distance. Everything becomes more or less – countable in euros and cents – equal important and close or far, because all desirable objects can be measured by money. In contrast to the Marxian observation that this transformation means a kind of alienation, it is rather a melancholic feeling that comes to mind (Rowe, 2005). Many of the contemporary discussions underlining the emotional meaning of the crisis share this point of observation when the greed and avarice of bankers and the rich are addressed. With Simmel, these criticisms can be linked to an understanding of economy where the equalizing effect of the monetization of individual desires is not fully accepted – which Simmel, reading sub alinea, seems to share as well.

Two other important aspects of the monetization of urban life are to be taken into account in contemporary discussions. Firstly, the transformation of desires into money and its "flattening" effect allows a calculated, industrialized and effective way to produce a consumptive answer to those desires. In this way, the societal response to individual needs and wishes allows the construction of the paradox of individual mass society: everybody has different longings, but in this everybody is the same. Acceleration of interactions (Wechselwirkungen) can be ensured by mass organization. As an effect, the massification requires the installation of the individual offer as an illusion. The disillusion becomes sensible as soon as the effects of mass production are becoming obvious. That is the reason for a permanent reproduction of fashion. Intrinsically, mobility, fashion, and speed are the consequence of this upheld theatre of distinctiveness. The individual thereby is captured in the hiatus between the "objective culture" offering infrastructure, means of transport and goods and everything that objectively ensures our lives and his personal "subjective culture" which cannot hold pace with the general production of culture in society. Most obviously, this gap between the objective and the subjective part of modern life expresses itself in the accelerated speed of society. Individuals attempt to cope with the "ups and downs" of the modern and urban rhythms but as the exchanges are realized in an increasingly faster process, the individual suffers greater difficulty to adapt. Individualism therefore is nothing that eo ipso is a beneficial achievement. It puts new challenges in front of society and burdens the individual with a fight against the predominance of objective culture and the ever faster speed of exchange caused by the monetization of individual desires.

2. Learning from Simmel?

In sum, reading the city from Georg Simmel's classical texts, the concern about the mental health and well-being of the individual person becomes evident. As some readers suggest, Simmel offers an additional point of view to the prevalent theorization in critical urban studies which takes much from Marx' theory of exchange as a starting point (Cantó Milà, 2003). Simmel has put an "underground" in the Marxian theory on value creation that allows the capture of phenomena of modern society into a theoretical understanding of money. Significantly, the appearance of an urban life style based not only on the idea of distinction – as in the classical concepts of class society up to studies on the "small differences" – offers a view on the effect of objectivation of spatial organization, the individualism of urban dwellers, the rise of a fashion type of industry and life style. It is the feeling of being separated, overwhelmed, fragmented, and the longing for others and beautiful objects rather than the facts of expropriation, class distinctiveness and alienation from production that are the concern of Simmel's reflection on the city, the monetization of life and the challenged individualism. With his alternative reading of the "mental life in the metropolis", the German philosopher emphasizes aspects of a crisis that derive from modernity and the modern city itself. While Marx would support the crisis nature of capitalism, with Simmel the focus lies on the intrinsic generation of crisis because of the psychological and social construction of life in the modern metropolis.

Already the Chicago School did not follow the melancholic notion of the monetization and its encapsulating effects on urban life. For Robert Park, the city was pushed by the processes of exchange and mobility to a large extent but these forces did not dominate as they did for Georg Simmel and even more so for the Marxists. "The city", as Park wrote, is a place "in which more than elsewhere human relations are likely to be impersonal and rational, defined in terms of interest and in terms of cash." But despite the strong effects of capitalism, the city remains a place of "collective behavior." (Park, Burgess and McKenzie, 1925/1997, 22).

Conceptually, the city is not identical with society and the collective behavior of its inhabitants is worthy of study as an objective in its own:

"The city shows the good and evil in human nature in excess. It is this fact, perhaps, more than any other, which justifies the view that would make of the city a laboratory or clinic in which human nature and social processes may be conveniently and profitably studied." (46)

Social processes in this sense are also separated from a psychological starting point, as Simmel has argued for. In the Chicago School's empirical work, especially with the introduction of first hand material, original wording, photographs, maps, and biographical reports, the individual is given a prominent place in their sociological studies. Nevertheless, it is not individualism and the individual suffering from the predominance of the objective culture that is the interest here. The focus lies rather on those "little worlds" of which the city is composed and which make life exciting but also dangerous. In a more general comparison, the empirically open view on the city and society does not presume an automatic downward spiral of the individual because of speed, objectification and mass society. In a sense, the famous circle model of Burgess aiming at an explanation of urban development can be regarded as an optimistic perspective where people can potentially progress into a more liberal society where their feelings, memories and values are shared. Assimilation as a kind of final merger of cultures and people from different backgrounds has been therefore foreseen in Parks "race relation cycle". Indeed, the Chicago School can be seen as a kind of liberal criticism of capitalism as it leaves open whether "the good and evil in human nature" are getting to the foreground in history (Smith, 1988).

Placing the city into an historical dimension, however, remained a weakness in the sociological analysis of Simmel and the Chicago School alike. The conceptualization of modernity remained in loose contact with the historical narratives. In contrast, Max Weber has been the major thinker of the late 19th and early 20th century who saw the particularities of the European city. He worked out his intellectual position on the basis of the then available sources and contextualized the rise of European modernism as a result of a long lasting historical development overrunning other civilizations' leading positions. As a core idea, the autonomy of the European city was for Weber a nucleus of development of a society where consensus and self-regulation could be achieved. His major concept was, as with Simmel, based on a small-scale construct of society. His focus on the "conjurations" however emphasizes the building of local society rather than the pressure that the individual feels in Simmel's "modern metropolis". In Weber's view, the meeting of strangers and their livingalongside each other is the key element for the development of the European civilization and its advantages comparable to others, especially Asian societies. Today, we know that Weber's perception on the sharp differences between European and other cities does not hold ground and must be blamed on the generally little knowledge about Asia at that time (cp. Bruhns and Nippel, 2000). More critically reviewed, Weber has limited himself to the raising of a partly romantic idea of the Middle Age city in Europe where conflicts, discrimination, segregation, political and religious persecution and other aspects of the "ugly side" of urban life were not appropriately considered. Even more problematic is the neglect of the effects of the industrial revolution on the concept of the "European" city. Though Weber probably saw the technological progress that industrial society embodies as a result of European history, he seems to have closed his eyes to its character as a crisis driven society.

3. The European city

Considerations on the "European city" nevertheless remain in current discussion and are politically powerful constructs of imagination. In many intellectual and political discourses the very understanding of Europe being made up locally and the local as a backbone for democratic politics is simply unquestionable (Le Galés, 2011; Siebel, 2010). However, the debate on the European city is at least partially a normative one and fulfills a socio-psychological need as a quasi authentic place of democracy is identified in which freedom and economic progress are seen as intertwined. In the contemporary readings of the European city, the heritage of the welfare state, political accessibility and social integration are embedded. To some extent this recalls Weber's idealization of the European Middle Aged city and the generation of a rational way of life (Domingues, 2000). While the return to the concept of the European city can be regarded as a counter position to the neoliberal city, its analytical strength remains highly questionable (cp. Kemper, 2012). In the context of the current discussion of crisis, the most critical failure is the lacking notion of crisis at all. This is in particular true for the violent 20th century which Weber could not foresee but which has brought the experience of totalitarianism and fascism with the most painful result that large parts of the historically "grown" European cities have been erased and destroyed.

To explain these historical phenomena would require obviously more space than available. However, it is clear that there is not a convincing argument for the treatment of local and national levels of society in a dual and simplistic way, meaning that the cities have been the victims of nation-wide, non-local structures and processes. On the contrary, local conflicts and crises can evolve and erupt from "local societies" in the Weberian sense and become a global disaster. In the post-totalitarian age, the lesson should not be forgotten that it all started small and local. A simple return to the notion of the historical European city will not explain how this kind of very fundamental crisis of European civilization has happened. If one wants to keep upright the idea of a more democratic society based on the "local", then the potential for crisis needs to be acknowledged and theoretically conceptualized.

From a selective point of view, different accounts can be referenced as the working-out of a historical perspective on crisis that might help to re-conceptualize the European city as a legitimate description. Beyond the most prominent analysis in urban studies referring to regulation theory or neo-Marxist positions, a different approach can be outlined following the key idea of the historian Reinhard Kosellek (cp. Olsen, 2012). His major insight stems from various historical analyses but mainly from his research on the situation in France before 1789. Koselleck wanted to find out at what moment the French Revolution really started. Correctly, he linked the upcoming changes back to changes of thought in the first place. From a structuralist point of view, the social stratification did not change much in advance of the French Revolution. One can say that the consistency of the social inequalities did not have any direct influence on the events happening. Many acts of the revolution, like the storm of the Bastille, did not have a "real" link to a changed society or any other direct political intention. This symbolic layer of the revolution, according to Koselleck, is a consequence of the changes brought about by the long foregoing critique on the absolutist state. In other words, the changes in attitude towards the role of politics and the state are the starting point of a profound crisis of society. It is a critique that is deeply rooted in crisis and vice versa. The impact of critique is ensured by its moral position to question the architecture and the governance of the state. Modernity in this sense has changed the role of the Hobbesian state that needed to ensure peace between citizens but had not to fulfil any of the moral obligations that the Enlightment expected. In his further analysis, Koselleck explains the rise of terror and totalitarian rule as a reaction to the permanent tension that enlightened perspectives are putting on political leaders.

In the light of the analysis of Koselleck, the idea of a crisis needs to be seen as an intrinsic moment of the culture of modernity. As it is correct to point at the role of critique, the term of "critique" should not be confused with a notion of "critical theory" that is often intruding on urban studies. Critique means here an intellectual challenge of politics in its by-then current state of mind. It challenges established ways of perception and self-description. These challenges are not purely academic exercises but are placed in an arena of political decision-making and preparation. As critique is interrupting the management of society, the urge to limit and overcome the questioning of the existing modus vivendi is high. Critique creates a loss of trust, insecurity, moral pressure and time gaps between decision-making and reflection. All this leads to the creation of essential moments where time pressure forces quick (alternative) decisions. If a crisis is understood this way, there is no way back to any kind of "normality". Crisis is then not just a period between two phases of normal life. Rather, modernity can be regarded as a permanent flow of faster or slower crises. Whether changes appear to us as "crisis" or not depends on the speed of these transformations. Critique however is the main source of provoking these crises as they produce permanent irritations. Critique fulfills this societal function not only in its classical manner like the philosophers in the 18th century or the investigative journalists in the 20th century. Irritation of the normality of society derives from everyday life and actors (in the broadest sense) who act differently – the alternative milieu keeping old paper for recycling instead of putting it into the garbage, refugees crossing national borders or critical consumers. The existing socio-political order can integrate this critique by changing political frameworks or with terror. Critique can create dangerous and risky situations for the society and for particular social groups and individuals. Saying that in modernity crisis is normal sounds like neglecting the damaging aspect of crisis. Losing a house, your family, your health or your job or all these together can be the most serious threat in one's life. However, what seems to matter is the speed of events in the first place and the interpretation of the "critique" that goes together with these crises with regard to self-understanding and valorization. Already Émile Durkheim (cp. Girola Molina, 2005) had pronounced that the sudden appearance of collapse creates a situation of losing orientation and an individual or collective status of anomy. As irritations can have different scopes and can concern more or fewer parts of society, the evoked crisis can include different layers of society, affecting socially different groups and impacting society at different scales. A general crisis, as "revolutions" might be counted for, distracts from the fact that the modern crisis has to be thought of on a scale of speed and depth from where it is correlating, impacting and causing other crises in society. If critique initiates crisis, the variety of critique – from small-scale "Manöverkritik" (critique de maneuver, debriefing) to the critique of the grand narrative – needs to be taken into account.

Understanding the interference between crisis, modernity and critique in this way means that history itself can no longer be thought as a simple line of events or the producer of artefacts and achievements. The European city as a picture of a certain form of urban order, social tolerance and architecture therefore is a simplification of the "many histories" (Koselleck) running through at different speeds and on various layers. It has to be discussed what kind of critique this is and what are the reasons for the creation and proclamation of such a picture. Taking it as critique, the "European city" appears in times of a deep crisis but it does not question those forces promoting another way of thinking in Europe. This can be made clear by the example of the so-called "Leipzig Charta" which was launched by the European Union to acclaim the "Renaissance of the European City" in the early years of the 21th century (Eltges and Nickel, 2007). The text itself included not one single coherent new way of thinking but aimed at harmonizing the prevalent rebellion of neo-liberalism and its emphasis on economic competitiveness with the aggravated philosophy of social cohesion derived from the lasting intellectual social-democratic hegemony in Europe. The criticism of the current intellectual basis of our societies by using the stereotype and kitsch version of the "European city" shows only that new ideas that would irritate the current self-descriptions of Europe and the routines of political crisis management are not deriving from a reorientation that once contested the predominance of the modern city.

It remains thus to be critically discussed what kind of critique is produced, if formative and guiding thoughts are still related to the "city" (cp. Bourdin, 2010). The obvious danger is the illusion that local actions can provide an irritation that can challenge the installed narratives of austerity and competitiveness. Will it be possible to think of a critique that allows the creation of another intellectual attack on the omnipresent self-descriptions in the European societies while still talking about the city and referring to politics of nearness and planability? The replacing of the self-descriptors, the "urban" and the "locale", – outside of the neo-liberal attitude to the city as a purely economic entity to be steered and governed as an enterprise – already takes place, but the intellectual powers working in this direction do not irritate the social order in a way that classical left criticism intended. The contemporary re-orientation to the city has nothing to do with a form of societal provocation of existing hierarchies of values and social positions. It is all too well known that gentrification, NIMBY-politics and the panoptical control of the city do not intend to break up existing orders of social perception and interpretation. On the contrary, we can observe more rigid interpretations of norms in the public, a less tolerant attitude to socially deprived persons and an increasingly invisibility of the "unsuccessful". Academic discourses have produced overwhelming evidence and have placed the "just city" at the top of urban research.

4. Critique of the City

Apparently, attempts to cope with the crisis are related to the establishments of new practices or at least reactions and adaptations on the local level. At the end of the day, the crisis always manifests itself into something material and tangible, something than can be felt and that exists in some way or the other in the symbolic order of individual life. This is the description of the crisis that is nevertheless hard to represent. It is assumed to be "visible" and able to be told in a story of before and after-situations with actors which "act" and victims. The relevance of this crisis narrative is related to the communicative situation it is anchored in, that is a mostly multi-media setting combining a real and a textual and metaphorical picture. The logic of the creation of a crisis and the representation of a crisis do not fall together. It can be stated with more accuracy that these two aspects of the crisis are de-coupled and the representation of the crisis is either part of the irritation ongoing or it is bound to be reclaiming the old social order. In this sense, the linkage of crisis to a local representation needs to be reflected as a form of critique that, to a very limited extent and in a particular way, represents the current multiple crises of Europe. If a particular point of the contemporary situation is characterized by financial markets which are "out of control" and are so because they are no longer linked to the "real economy" then how could this feature of the present economic crisis be reflected in representations of the so-called local impact or the urban dimension? The logical argument would derive from a chain of presumed causalities that leads from quasi-bankrupt states to localities without financial space to maneuver, so that the social aspect of the crashes of the job and housing market cannot be counterbalanced. Obviously, the attempt to tell a "local" story of the crisis requires a certain narrative that leaves out many complex layers of society and selects the events, actors and policies.

This crisis narrative reestablishes the city as a place of public drama. In a time where the local has been virtualized in an extensive way and democracy became exhausted, the narrowing of perspectives on something visible, local and which can be represented in a public space is an understandable attempt to revitalize the idea of the city. In the nation state, the public space had an established function for expressing demands and critique and it was part of an opposition to a well-defined government. It is however questionable today whether this kind of "city politics" has the same role. In a globalized world the role of the urban has taken on a different meaning and in this political framework is serving another function. As sympathetic as the newly emerging social movements are to the local story, especially the "Right to the City"-groups everywhere, it needs to be recognized that the idea of a city and the political and societal significance of the "locale" have been transformed in the last thirty years. It is not only that the regime of capitalist accumulation has been changed from a fordist to a post-fordist logic, more important might be that this foregone structural change has been prepared and legitimized by a fundamental critique that wanted to overcome the narrowness of the local and the cemented order of social networks in the welfare state.

"Think global, act local" was the slogan of an internationally oriented ecological movement, but it could have also been the motto of the neoliberal reforms. Thinking local in times of global interferences means something profoundly different when the world market is opened up completely, mobility of goods and people seems to be unlimited, global flow of images and ideas and the speed of technological innovations transform the most private and personal affairs (cp. Bourdin, Eckardt and Wood, 2014). What the city has become or still is remains an open question. Competing ideas are circulating. In the nineties, attempts for new descriptions wanted to irritate the existing concepts by pointing at its fragmentary, dispersed, splintering, regional, virtual, aestheticized, emotionalized and networked character. The coining of another term has not been successful and those that have been proposed remained alive only for the time of an academic fashion (Metapolis, Zwischenstadt, Global City, Postmetropolis etc.). Intentionally understood, these formulations wanted to create a space to recognize the crisis of the city already happening. In its darkest colors, Mike Davis and his "City of Quartz" gained some prominence but a general interruption of the blinded view on the disappearance of the city "as we know it" was not achieved by this noir urbanism. Looking back on these writings of urban scholars, the return to a terminology of the city appears as a capitulation of the critique on the idea of the city. It is obvious that most intellectual responses on the current situation refer back to theoretical discussions before the appearance of the mentioned reformulations of the significance of the "urban". We are "excavating Lefebvre" (Purcell, 2002) with his claim for more accessibility to the city in general and to the street, as it was important for the May 68-movement. In this way, we return to a terminology of "rebellion" like David Harvey which reminds of that same kind of spirit.

It is not clear what kind of effects the rebirth of the idea of the city will have It might be a mighty weapon for some local movements and actions to make their point and to influence certain areas of politics. Conceptually spoken, their terminology of the city differs not from the one that is installed by their ideological enemies, as it reassures the importance of the locale and denies the complexity of global embedding which produces global-local places, so called "glocal" societies. These glocal societies drive on networking thoughts and pictures about "place" which are disturbing, transforming, interrupting, expelling, destroying and recreating local communities and making them losing the power of defining the local. The multiplication of the crises starts, as Koselleck would formulate, with a change of thought – think globally. Yes, we do and we do in all regards. Can we really still act locally when everybody is consuming, producing, travelling, communicating, dreaming and marrying globally? Insisting on the remaining meaning of the city and consequently looking for rebellion – which is a typically local phenomenon – does not give us the necessary answers on this question. Once a powerful critique against the failures of the nation state, globalism has abolished the idea of the city as a Weberian "local society" and has devalued the importance of urban exchange as in the classical concept of Simmel. Intellectualism is no longer the consequence of too many stimuli on the street and the objective culture is deeply embedded in our imaginations of the local.

5. Returning to urban critique

The resurrection of protest in the cities as reaction to the multiple crises has nowhere led to a change in the main fields of neo-liberal activities. Still, the European banks are regarded as little resistant against the next financial crisis. The budgetary reforms have by far not equilibrated the social costs incurred. The disastrous unemployment, especially among the youth, has not been addressed in a substantial way. Nevertheless, many local initiatives have organized their forces to return to some kind of a more solidary way of living. These activities are criticizing the predominant way of capitalist thinking in a more substantial degree. It remains however clear that they cannot evoke a crisis of neo-liberalism. There are many discussions among activists about their own weakness, about why in these times many people do not trust alternatives and why the desire for "business as usual" seems to be the strongest wish. One could say, the crisis has reached all parts of society but not our thoughts about us.

Understanding this book as a contribution towards challenging existing perceptions of the Southern European cities and the multilayered crisis, it was the foremost intention of the editors and authors to make that step. In different ways, the contributions from urban theory and empirical urban studies intend to find a way out of the most concerning situation with its multiple dimensions of crisis.. Learning from urban theory so far, means that we have to struggle forward to a critique of the city, if we want to overcome the crisis of our cities. Learning from urban theory does not mean that we have to see the crisis through the eyes of one theoretical guide like Weber, Simmel, Lefebvre or whosoever. It is rather the treatment of their thoughts that can us help to cope with the current intellectual blockades. The conceptual contradiction between the existing theoretical approaches warns us about the failing attempt to see the city as the key idea of a potentially progressive critique of society. The disillusion with the "lasting" European City (whatever that was), the vulnerability of the "local society", the dangerous isolation of the individual amidst strangers, the overwhelming principles of competition and ownership form the massive intellectual barricade that an urban critique must run against. It is no longer the city but it is a new form of urbanity that has been established in the recent struggles. Often ridiculed or stigmatized as "Facebook revolution", the power of the idea that individuals can meet, cross borders, join forces and return to the essentials of life has been demonstrated:

"There were first a few, who were joint by hundreds, then networked by thousands, then supported by millions with their voices and their internal quest for hope, as muddled as it was, that cut across ideology and hype, to connect with the real concerns of the real people in the real human experience that had been reclaimed. It began on the internet social networks, as these are spaces of autonomy, largely beyond the control of governments and corporations [...] By sharing the sorrow and hope in the free public space of the Internet, by connecting to each other [...] individuals formed networks [...] They came together." (Castells, 2012, 14)

The new social movements from Brazil to Turkey, from Tahir Square to Wall Street, have produced a new way of social networking, something the conventional location-based public would have never been able to create. Interestingly, however, the streets and squares have not become irrelevant and there has been a revolution not only on Facebook. Highly visible, this is an emotional urbanity that strives via physical presence after the authentic experience in the encounter of the others. Physicality and spatial structure are the targets of these activities. You learn to know about these others not only in the public squares, but you already know – or rather feel, wait and hope – who may come.

Therefore, it is short-sighted, if now a renaissance of public spaces is discussed, as if it would matter that places are provided for demonstrations, as was the case in the modern city. Strikingly, the speeches of the great "leaders" of the rebellions and the Arabic revolutions play no role. This applies especially to the Occupy movement, which deliberately wanted to initiate an alternative speech culture. Artists, musicians, journalists and a few politicians in the modern sense can be seen at these places. The new urban movements are not oppositional in the classical sense. That is why there is no opposition leader who can be either arrested or even identified as a legitimate representative. In the light of modern democratic thought these movements are weak because they produce no organized opposition and provide no alternative personages and programs. Such a requirement is, however, completely misleading, because it is not at all about being an opposition with a unifying narrative that could also be action-oriented. The one-issue movements such as the ecology protest have been thoroughly integrated today into the narrative of the "policy for all", however the digitization of the urban – the number of existing narratives – potentialized to almost infinity. Therefore, the logic of these processes is not based on finding one unifying narrative, but to allow the diversity of existing narratives and thus allows very personal body-reconstructing and emotive interactions that provide for the individual search for experience and meaning thereby reacting to the uncertainty of the multiple crises. The common sense structures are fragile and are based on relatively rudimentary statements, but they are an expression of "mass self-communication" as Castells called them. Their structure is diversity. You will not be able to enforce them to be integrative into further existing authoritarian, uniform and abstract narratives, even if they were temporarily transformed into a single narrative. The cracks and contradictions of the dominant narratives, the wild knowledge and unplanned spatial constructions and reinterpretations of existing places are the breeding ground of diversity that can be sometimes subversive and inclusive, sometimes aggressive and sometimes poetic. For this "city", the descriptive vocabulary is missing, because it is a bulky, irritating, exhilarating, seductive and intensive experience of oneself and of others, which you do not want to tame by any language. Rather, the new urban critique derives more from gestures, looks, acts, mimicry and non-verbal symbols and infinite fictional constructs. As a carpet it lays out pieces of a critique in search of new narratives with challenged perceptions, innovated perspectives, dared actions and reconstruction of social lines beyond the "urban" – the city as we have known it so far.

References

Bourdin, A. (2010) L'urbanisme après crise. Paris: L'Aube.
Bourdin, A.; F. Eckardt; A. Wood (2014) Die ortlose Stadt. Über die Virtualisierung des Urbanen. Bielefeld: transcript
Bruhns, H. and W. Nippel (Hrsg.) (2000) Max Weber und die Stadt im Kulturvergleich. Göttingen: Vandenhoek and Ruprecht
Cantó Milà, N. (2003) Las relaciones intelectuales entre Karl Marx y Georg Simmel : Un diálogo sobre la naturaleza humana y la teoría del valor. In: Acta sociológica, 37/0, 123-149
Castells, M. (2012) Networks of Outrage and Hope: Social Movements in the Internet Age. Cambridge: Polity

Domingues, J. M. (2000) The City, rationalization and freedom in Max Weber. In: Philosophy and social criticism, 26/4, 107-126

Eltges, M. and E. Nickel (2007) Europäische Stadtpolitik: Von Brüssel über Lille nach Leipzig und zurück. In: Informationen zur Raumentwicklung, 7-8, 479-486

Fortuna, C. (2013) Georg Simmel: as cidades, a ruína e as novíssimas metrópoles. In: Philosophica, 42, 107-125

Frisby, D. (2013/1986) Fragments of modernity: theories of modernity in the work of Simmel, Kracauer and Benjamin. Abingdon, Oxon: Routledge

Girola Molina, L. (2005) Anomia e individualismo: del diagnóstico de la modernidad de Durkheim al pensamiento contemporáneo. Rubi: Anthropos

Händler, E.-W. (2014) Geld und Wert. Von Georg Simmel zu den modernen Finanzmärkten. In: Merkur, 68/1, 25-37

Hooker, C. (2013) Georg Simmel and naturalist interactivist epistemology of science. In: Studies in history and philosophy of science, 44, 3, 311-31

Junge, M. (2012) Georg Simmel. In: F. Eckardt (Hrsg.) Handbuch Stadtsoziologie. Wiesbaden: Springer VS, 83-93.

Kemper, J. (2012) Max Weber. In: F. Eckardt (Hrsg.) Handbuch Stadtsoziologie. Wiesbaden: Springer VS, 31-58

Le Galès, P. (2011) Le retour des villes européennes: sociétés urbaines, mondialisation, gouvernement et gouvernance. Paris: Presses de sciences po

Maggioni, M. A. (2012) Back to the future? Georg Simmel and C. S. Lewis revisited. In: Rivista internazionale di scienze sociali, 120/3, 325-340

Mieg, H. A.; A. O. Sundsboe and M. Bieniok (eds) (2012) Georg Simmel und die aktuelle Stadtforschung. Wiesbaden: VS Verlag

Olsen, N. (2012) History in the Plural: An Introduction to the Work of Reinhart Koselleck. New York: Berghahn Books

Park, R., E. Burgess and R. McKenzie (eds.) (1925/1997) The city: suggestions for investigation of human behavior

Purcell, M. (2002) Excavating Lefebvre: The right to the city and its urban politics of the inhabitant. In: Geojournal: an international journal of geography, 58/2, 99-108

Rammstedt, O. (ed) (2003) Georg Simmels Philosophie des Geldes: Aufsätze und Materialien. Frankfurt: Suhrkamp

Reichelt, H. (2010) Realabstraktio : die Objektivität des wirtschaftlichen Werts als latentes Problem der Sozialtheorie und die Philosophie des Geldes von Georg Simmel. In: Hanno Pahl und Lars Meyer (Hrsg.) Gesellschaftstheorie der Geldwirtschaft. Marburg: Metropolis, 271-302

Rowe, D. (2005) Money, Modernity and Melancholia in the Writings of Georg Simmel. In: Critical studies, 25, 27-38

Siebel, W. (Hrsg.) (2010) Die europäische Stadt. Frankfurt: Suhrkamp

Simmel, G. (1995/1903) Die Großstädte und das Geistesleben. In: R. Kramme, A. Rammstedt, O. Rammstedt (Hrsg.) Georg Simmel. Band 1, Frankfurt: Suhrkamp, 116-131.

Smith, D. (1988) The Chicago School: a liberal critique of capitalism. New York: St. Martin's Press

Crisis and the city

Neoliberalism, austerity planning and the production of space

Álvaro Sevilla-Buitrago

The current crisis, with its particularly severe configuration in Southern European countries, provides an opportunity to probe the interrelation of economic crunches and the production of space, and also to imagine potential paths of sociospatial emancipation from the dictates of global markets. This introductory chapter offers a preliminary interpretive framework exploring the fundamental role of urban and territorial restructuring in the formation, management and resolution of capitalist crises and, conversely, periods of crisis as key stages in the history of urbanization. I will begin by contextualizing the 2007-8 economic slump, the subsequent global recession and its uneven impact on states and cities in the *longue durée* of capitalist productions of space, studying the transformation of spatial configurations in previous episodes of economic stagnation. This broader perspective will then be used to analyze currently emerging formations of austerity urbanism, showing how the practices of crisis management incorporate a strategy for economic and institutional restructuring that eventually impacts on urban policy, and indeed in the production of urban space itself.

    I will start this discussion with two basic premises. Firstly, capitalism is a crisis-prone system. Crunches and recessions appear as the aggregated result of a continuous and contradictory process of expansion of value; they are structural aspects of capitalist development, not an aberration in a naturally balanced economic organization (Harvey, 2010). According to this viewpoint, the history of capitalism is staged as an evolution through successive regulatory regimes articulated around the emergence and overcoming of recurring crises of overaccumulation (Aglietta, 2000). The current predicament is therefore not an exception but just another manifestation of a broader developmental pattern that we can compare and contrast with previous conjunctures and political-economic responses. Secondly, the production of space and the regulation thereof are key moments in the dynamics of capitalist accumulation and its reproduction. Spatial configurations work at many levels of a given social formation, either as means or sites of production, as productive forces or social relations, as governmental apparatuses or collective representations, and so forth (Lefebvre, 1991). The circulation of capital under capitalism relies heavily on a relentless reorganization of these configurations at several scales, both to expand the network of production and as a means to absorb surplus value (Harvey, 1975).

What happens when both phenomena overlap in time? How is the logic of capitalist production of space transformed in a time of crisis? The capitalist mobilization of the production of space is especially acute during economic crunches (Gottdiener and Komminos, 1989). In such conditions the very creative destruction of territorial formations turns into a key vehicle for crisis management through the orchestration of successive layers of spatial and economic restructuring. As Lefebvre suggested, '[c]apitalism has found itself able to attenuate (if not resolve) its internal contradictions for a century ... We cannot calculate at what cost, but we do know the means: by occupying space, by producing a space' (Lefebvre, 1976:31). David Harvey (2006a) has elaborated upon this hypothesis in his analysis of short- and medium-term 'spatial fixes' to capitalist crises. Amongst other means, capitalism tends to overcome recessions through inner and outer rearrangements of space that allow the displacement and deferral of contradictions geographically and temporally so that immediate devaluation of capital is avoided. In a recent work Harvey (2014) extends this idea by suggesting that capitalism thrives and resolves its crises through a constant shift of its contradictions from one structural or productive moment to another, from one economic sector to another, from one scale to another, from one region to another, or between these different elements themselves. By circulating local and context-specific conflicts capital manages to reconfigure the limits to accumulation. However, this procedure simply internalizes capitalist contradictions in new temporally and spatially evasive maneuvers. In the long run there is no possible 'absolute fix' for the system and local crises develop into global depressions. As these preliminary propositions suggest, there is a particular dialectic whereby spatial (trans)formations are fundamental to understanding the onset and subsequent evolution of any given crisis and, vice versa, crises management patterns are essential indexes to grasp how the regulation and production of space is constantly recast under capitalism.

Let us consider this dialectic movement in detail with a first glance at the development and spatial mutations of the current conjuncture. As a result of the dotcom bubble at the end of the 1990s and the early 2000s, and the parallel decline of stock-markets, surplus capital changed the target and investment in property and related assets soared worldwide. The pace of urbanization and construction was particularly intense in the US until 2007, when the crisis broke as a compounded result of housing overproduction and speculation in real estate and mortgage markets. From the US, the crisis spread unevenly around the world, impacting on diverse regions depending on their position in the international division of labor and the geopolitical scene. Through these trends the crisis has developed and deepened previous patterns of uneven geographical development, an aspect that is completely obvious in the European case, where the crisis has widened the gap between Southern and Northern Europe. There is, therefore, a *horizontal*, geopolitical distribution (or spatial mutation) of the crisis. It is also important to consider the transformations in the nature and scales of the crisis throughout the years. Starting as a crash at the level of built environment production and the related credit system, the crisis adopted a financial form soon. The collapse of stock-markets turned into a global recession and a sovereign debt crisis when certain governments decided to save their banks from bankruptcy. Finally, the nation-state crunch is becoming a crisis of particular regions and cities as national and supranational agencies push down budgetary pressure to regional and local governments in the form of new austerity policy-regimes. Hence there is also a *vertical*, scalar circulation of the crisis, from one country to the globe, to specific regions and cities —and, even, particular neighborhoods— in other countries.

The synthesis above may oversimplify the actual intricacies of recent economic decline, but it allows us to grasp the crucial role of the production of space as both a cause of the crisis and a strategy to manage and overcome it. Two spatial fixes stand at the temporal extremes of the recession, showing that the absorption of surplus capital at a given point provides just a temporary solution, one that is likely to generate deeper contradictions in a subsequent stage of development. The potential administration of this conflict-ridden process through rational management — such as that provided by the most lucid manifestations of reformist town and regional planning — is always abandoned in the long run. The circulation of capital through built environments demands a systematic, ever-expanding reconfiguration of inherited spatial formations in order to avoid obsolescence and devaluation, and as a material basis for subsequent rounds of investment and accumulation. In that sense, real estate speculation and constant urbanization and re-urbanization are not a deviation, but are essential to the survival of capitalism (Harvey, 2006a:398). As Brenner and Theodore argue:

[C]apital continually renders obsolete the very geographical landscapes it creates and upon which its own reproduction and expansion hinges. Particularly during periods of systemic crisis, inherited frameworks of capitalist territorial organization may be destabilized as capital seeks to transcend sociospatial infrastructures and systems of class relations that no longer provide a secure basis for sustained accumulation. As the effects of devaluation ripple through the space-economy, processes of creative destruction ensue in which the capitalist landscape is thoroughly transformed: the configurations of territorial organization that underpinned the previous round of capitalist expansion are junked and reworked in order to establish a new locational grid for the accumulation process. (Brenner and Theodore, 2002:354-5).

These spatial transformations require and at the same time trigger associated processes of institutional and regulatory change, new modes of urban and regional government, new modes of intervention, and so on. Each stage of capitalism generates specific regulatory arrangements that produce a series of historical regimes of urban and regional policy, including particular assemblages of the state and the private sector, particular articulations between different state levels and jurisdictions, and particular interrelations of planning practices and policy with other moments in the production of space.

1. Space and Crisis in *The Longue Durée* of Capitalism

In this section I will briefly explore several historical episodes in order to illustrate how different assemblages of capital and space generate diverse crisis regimes in the *longue durée* of capitalism. Each historical stage of development privileges certain scales, territories and agencies in the deployment of new waves of spatial creative destruction in times of crisis. Accordingly, cities, urbanization and urban policy take on different roles in the process of spatial and economic restructuring and are in turn reshaped as they become instrumental in the strategies to manage and overcome stagnation. These cycles rework not only the urban fabric, but also the techniques we use to govern it. It is helpful, therefore, to look backwards in order to understand the material conditions for the transformation of urban policy and planning in the past, and to gain some insight about the potential evolution of the field in the future and the possible scenarios we will face.

This cursory review starts with the classic case of mid-nineteenth century Paris, an interesting example for many reasons. First of all is the fact that Haussmann's *grands travaux* in Paris and the broader programs of infrastructural development in the country at large during the Second Empire were devised strategically to absorb capital and labor surpluses after a crisis that had threatened to reactivate revolutionary change (Harvey, 2003). The slump originated abroad; indeed the contradictions of the production of space had a role in the formation of the crisis: by the mid-1840s, the railway mania in Britain had unleashed a spiral of investment and speculation in related assets (Evans, 1848; Berger and Spoerer, 2001). French capital partook in the short-lived feast. The impact on French investors and banks was hard when the bubble burst; the Bank of France, for instance, saw its deposits reduced from 320 million in June 1845 to 57 million in January 1847 (Traugott, 1983:457-8). France was not alone in the repercussions of the British crash. The crisis spread to the entire continental Europe, galvanizing a chain reaction of revolts and riots in France, Germany, Poland, Italy and the Austrian Empire in 1848 — the so-called Springtime of Peoples (Hobsbawm, 1975:21-40). Hence a crash generated as the combined outcome of overproduction of space and associated financial speculation triggered a sequence of economic and political crises that developed unevenly throughout the continent.

In France the change of government after the uprisings and the subsequent *coup d'état* paved the way for a new approach that relied heavily and consciously on urban- and national-scale spatial fixes to exit the crisis.[1] The vast program of public works in Paris included not only the opening of new boulevards carved through the dense city center, but also the widening and extension of existing roads, the creation of new parks and hospitals, schools and colleges, markets, prisons and barracks. New water, drainage and gas systems were adopted as well (Girouard, 1985:288-9). Radiating from Paris, the new national railway system constituted another (ironic) element of Napoleon III's fix to the crisis. In the 1870s, immediately after his mandate, ten railway lines arrived in the capital; three decades before there was only one. France passed from less than 500 km. of railway line in the 1840s to more than 2.300 km in 1880 (Martí-Henneberg, 2013). In brief, a major process of urban and regional restructuring reshaped the economic and social landscape. Together with the reinforcement of its centrality in the country, Paris experienced a complete reconfiguration of the relation between the inner city and the peripheries, with the reorganization of residential areas along class lines and new locational patterns for industrial and retail activities.

These spatial transformations required parallel efforts of institutional and regulatory restructuring. New legal and technical frameworks were developed to implement the interventions. A new urban form of governance emerged, with distinctive relations between the national and the local state, as well as novel alliances between public administration and private enterprise. Indeed, the Second Empire's growth machine hinged as much upon Haussmann's vision and managerial capacity as it did upon his financial creativity and relation with venturesome investors. Only in Paris the public works expenditure between 1853 and 1869 amounted to a previously unseen figure of 2.5 billion francs, which Haussmann would gather from a number of sources including public bonds and loans from new financial agencies such as Crédit Foncier de France and the Société Générale du Crédit Mobilier, both created by the Pereire brothers, who were also directly involved in the creation of railways, gas supply, public transit systems and, of course, residential building (Harvey, 2003:113-120). In short, the rescaling of urbanization and infrastructural development triggered the formation of the modern credit system in France. Both the spatial and the financial fixes of the Second Empire collapsed together in

---

1 | Louis Napoleon Bonaparte had expressed beforehand his support for the active promotion of economic prosperity through investment in public works (Bonaparte, 1840:59).

the late 1860s, when their aggregated contradictions hit again. The crash of risk capital put an end to Haussmann's projects and Napoleon III's mandate. The resulting crisis would incite anew the specters of revolution in the 1871 Commune.

Jumping forward a few decades we meet another key crisis period, the 1930s Great Depression in the US. Despite the huge number of studies on the 1929 crash, few economists have taken note of the previous development of a real estate bubble and subsequent fall in the mid-1920s, starting in Florida and spreading to the whole country. In just a few years land development and housing rose irrationally in Florida, fuelled by a feverish wave of investment that galvanized an emerging middle-class. By 1925 the exchange in land property and associated shares had become a purely speculative dynamic, with scarce relation to actual construction activity: lots could be sold several times in a single day (Frazer and Guthrie Jr., 1995). The bust in the state was just the tip of the iceberg and the whole country experienced a steady decline in real estate development the following year. As White (2009) shows, this contraction marked the starting point of the stock issues boom, with massive doses of surplus capital being transferred to the equity market as an alternative investment. Again, we see the close relation between the conflicts at the level of spatial production, financialization and economic crises.

Roosevelt's New Deal tried to tackle the depression by mobilizing spatial policies in several ways. Firstly, during the intense years under the dominance of the first Brain Trust —including strong supporters of central planning such as Rexford G. Tugwell and Arthur E. Morgan— a program blending civil works in both the city and rural areas and a back-to-the-land vision promoted a substantial restructuring of the social geography of the country. Agencies such as Milburn L. Wilson's Subsistence Homesteads Division, Morgan's Tennessee Valley Authority or Tugwell's Resettlement Administration were attempts at countering the spontaneous deterioration of rural regions under capitalist uneven spatial development, taking the regeneration thereof as an opportunity to foster economic development and pacify urban unrest by moving surplus labor power to the countryside. After 1936, however, a more pragmatic anti-cyclical approach was adopted to stimulate construction activity that would reshape the social landscape of the nation. One the one hand the federal government guaranteed private domestic mortgages for the middle-classes in order to ease credit flow and prevent foreclosure; on the other hand, the administration launched a concerted effort to build public housing for the working-class and the 'deserving' poor. While agencies such as the Public Works Administration and the United States Housing Authority and its state branches focused on building collective housing in inner-city neighborhoods for low-income population groups, the Home Owners' Loan Corporation and later the Federal Housing Administration established redlining practices using class, race, typological and locational criteria, insuring mostly middle-class, white, single-family houses in the suburbs (Jackson, 1985:190-218). Together with the investment in the expansion of the road and highway system, this strategy secured new niches of household consumption, fostering a process of suburbanization and spatial segregation that would pervade the post-war era (Hayden, 2003:128-153).

Thus a new national horizon of economic recovery was established based on a profound reconfiguration of preexisting social divisions of space. The polarization of housing patterns along class and racial lines remained as a contradictory legacy of an alleged progressive period. At all events, the New Deal restructuring was not limited to a reorganization of core-periphery-suburb relations. As was the case with nineteenth-century France, the redesign of the urban fabric required major regulatory and governmental reforms – with the federal and regional administrations assuming an unprecedented role in the management of local activity – and also a strong reorganization of the relations between the state and the financial sector. The 1930s crisis paved the way for an increased presence of the nation scale as the pre-eminent level for accumulation and the regulation of political-economic life (Brenner and Theodore, 2002:358). I have focused here on the US for its central role in the geopolitical context and its ascendancy in this path at that time, but of course similar arguments apply to most of the contemporary Western world and their concurrence in what some have termed the Fordist exception (Neilson and Rossiter, 2008).

The US and, particularly, New York City, led the outbreak of the next episode in this quick overview of the connection of crises to major spatial restructurings, and indeed one that might be read as the inception of our current predicament. Several authors have identified the management of New York City's fiscal crisis in the 1970s as the blueprint for subsequent nation-wide neoliberalization agendas in the US and abroad, inaugurating a trend of austerity measures in social welfare, incentives to business, and intervention in local affairs by supra-municipal agencies, corporate interests and unelected institutions (Harvey, 2005:48; Tabb, 1982:9; Zevin, 1977).[2] In the late 1960s the decline of manufacture and suburban flight eroded the local revenues; the city was more and more dependent on federal funds. In view of the growing deficit, however, the Nixon administration changed its approach and began to diminish federal aid in 1972. 'The urban crisis', declared the president, should be refashioned as an 'urban opportunity' (Nixon, 1972). The Manhattanite financial elite understood the gist behind the message: urban restructuring could become not only a chance to exit the crisis but also a bridge to restore upper-class power and capital preeminence after a long period of state-rule oriented to maintain welfare programs.

For a couple of years the banks covered the gap left by federal retrenchment but in 1975, amidst a global recession, they finally decided to stop rolling the debt over (Tabb, 1982:21-2). New York City faced technical bankruptcy. In lieu of direct subsidies, the (Republican) state government and financial institutions put the city under the control of a bailout agency, the Municipal Assistance Corporation, followed by the Emergency Financial Control Board, incorporating representatives from the financial and corporate spheres. The new agenda should be as innovative as exemplary. According to Secretary of the Treasury William Simon, the program had to be 'so punitive, the overall experience so painful, that no city, no political subdivision would ever be tempted to go down the same road'.[3] And so it was. In little more than a year the city fired almost 50,000 employees and cut down welfare departments' budget by 25 percent; additional rollback would ensue after the initial shock treatment (Tabb, 1982:30). The new agenda also included a transition to entrepreneurial approaches to urban governance, whereby the local administration should not only strive to create a good business climate through all manner of incentives, but also to brand the city itself as a major cultural hub and, of course, as a succulent niche for real estate investment (Greenberg, 2008). Together with finance and ancillary activities, the restructuring of the urban fabric through successive rounds of gentrification reshaped

---

2 | Of course, more violent, merciless versions of a new experimental neoliberalization were imposed on a national scale in contemporary Chile and other Latin American countries afterwards.

3 | Quoted in Harvey (2005:46).

the local economy (Harvey, 2005:47). In these processes new alliances of public and private actors fostering corporate profit opened a path of institutional change that would spread later to other scales and regions.

The neoliberal agenda imposed by Reagan in the US, Thatcher in Britain, and in Europe and other countries afterwards, had of course a national and global horizon, but its impact was especially severe in cities. May large metropolises bore the brunt of budgetary austerity and became the major victims of rollback policies. Indeed, as Brenner and Theodore (2002) suggest, in the following years they became a crucial arena for economic and regulatory restructuring, a pivotal point to displace and manage the crisis. Certain cities and city-regions transformed into nodes of a new planetary division of labor that would widen the gap between global centers and global peripheries. They worked as the engines of a new round of uneven spatial development and as key sites for regulatory experimentation, with state institutions being constantly recast at the local scale as protean galvanizers of transnational surplus capital. This blend of intense governmental restructuring, inflexible austerity and entrepreneurial urbanism is at the root of today's round deepened urban neoliberalization.

2. THE AGE OF AUSTERITY AND THE ALTERNATIVES FOR PLANNING

> [E]conomic recovery was never the point; the drive for austerity was about using the crisis, not solving it. (Krugman, 2012:n.p.)

The crisis today presents strong structural similarities with the cases above. Again, following conditions of capital overaccumulation, a massive switch of surplus wealth from the primary (production of standard commodities) to the secondary (production of space and the built environment) circuit of capital triggered property market speculation and securitization, which in turn led to the collapse of the financial system and a global recession. Far from inciting institutional change oriented towards a progressive reform of the system, the outcome in terms of policy is a redoubled effort to extend the neoliberal agenda further (Hall et al, 2013). In fact the 1970s recession and subsequent transformations in urban governance are especially relevant in the context of the current conjuncture for several reasons. Given that Western governmental agencies and international economic institutions are pushing to 'exit' that model's crisis through a development of its main tenets, many authors suggest that we are undergoing a stage of deepened neoliberalization (e.g. see Callinicos, 2012; Peck et al, 2012). Of course, the austerity recipe and the strategic use thereof are not new. A common mantra since the early 1980s, 'austerity' is the perfect euphemism for fiscal retrenchment and the dismantling of the welfare state. Left aside of the severe rollback as a necessary evil, the veritable cause for the sovereign debt crisis — the trillions spent in the public bailout of private banks and other financial institutions — becomes an opportunity to further downsize the public sector. As Harvey (2006b:154-5) contends, crisis management is in fact one of the fundamental modes of neoliberal accumulation by dispossession — that is, of accumulation through direct extraction of profit out of public or common forms of collective wealth.

But the distribution of this agenda is spatially variegated, socially unequal, and it deepens earlier paths of policy rescaling and restructuring: the impact is most severely felt by certain population groups living in vulnerable areas in cities located in already weak regions and countries. As was the case during previous crises, the outcome of the recession intensifies preceding trends of uneven geographical development according with specific patterns of path-dependency in terms of economic restructuring, social change and policy innovation (Brenner et al, 2010). In the US, the epicenter of the crisis, there are around 300 municipalities nationwide in default on their debt (Peck, 2012:633). But the origins and the solutions for their problems are very different and vary depending on the recent history of these places. In Rustbelt cities subprime lending was especially intense in deprived African American neighborhoods, but minor in comparison to the Sunbelt real estate boom, more focused on middle-class buyers and speculative investment, which made 'the housing bubble ... bigger and more likely to bust' in the South (Aalbers, 2012:7). However, it is precisely those states already under structural weaknesses that face harder times now. For instance, in view of the fiscal emergency at the local level, the state of Michigan made a controversial move and bailed out cities through external management, which have taken hold of local policies at many different levels, including planning programs (Peck, 2012:635).

The situation is more dramatic in Europe. As Costis Hadjimichalis (2011:255) suggests, the foundations of the sovereign debt crisis are embedded in the patterns of uneven regional development at the heart of the structure of the European Union. In fact, the imposition of extreme austerity measures in the wake of the financial crisis has reactivated regional divergence, doing away with the EU's alleged goals of territorial cohesion and reinforcing the economic and political hegemony of particular regions and certain forms of capital in central European countries. Before the crisis 43 percent of the EU GDP was produced in only 14 percent of its territory; since the euro's introduction Southern Europe had become a main destiny for German exports, exceeding the total dispatches to US, China and Japan together in 2007 and developing a spiraling negative trade balance with Germany (Eurostat, 2009:148-9, 152). Both aspects, uneven production and commercial dependence, are likely to worsen after the imposition of bail out programs which render the South increasingly subordinated to political decisions coming from Northern and central countries.

The spatial unevenness of the reaction to the crisis also incorporates a scalar element. Cities —or, more precisely, particular cities and neighborhoods within them— are likely to become the major victims in the medium and long term for several reasons. Firstly, they experience greater impact from the construction slowdown following credit scarcity (and, in some cases, the collapse of real estate markets) since housing and infrastructural development have a stronger role in their economies, including the collection of public revenues through building taxes; a general state of depressed consumption also hits fundamental sectors of urban economies such as tourism and conspicuous commercial activity. Furthermore, compared to rural areas where family and kin networks are tighter, urban populations are more dependent on formal mechanisms of social reproduction such as those provided by public services, a sector under special pressure in a context of austerity. Of course, it is the disenfranchised population living in large urban areas that bears the brunt of welfare cuts (Matsaganis, 2011; Hall et al, 2013). Finally, in recent years certain countries have developed a trend to push down the management of austerity-derived conflicts to lower levels of government, what Jamie Peck terms 'scalar dumping': '[c]ities are ... where austerity bites ... The projection downward of these pressures establishes a socially regressive form of scalar politics — with cities positioned at the sharp end' (Peck,

2012:629,631,647). Together, these phenomena create the conditions for the emergence of an 'austerity urbanism' — again, Peck's (2012) term — with variegated manifestations across the world but common features related not only with cities' shared structural elements but also with their role as key sites to overcome the depression.

Just as this double movement of conflict condensation and regulatory restructuring in urban areas prolongs the path opened in the 1970s, we can expect emerging forms of urbanism and urban policy to deepen the features of previous rounds of policy innovation and institutional transformation. For the time being we are perhaps witnessing only the 'destructive' moment of this deepened neoliberalization of urban agendas along the line of the earlier dismantling of managerial, Fordist-Keynesian urbanism. Public assets and facilities are at the frontline of this new attack on already meager forms of welfare: public estate and companies are sold, granted or pulled to pieces as part of the downsize program; potentially profitable services and goods such as healthcare, education, security and even public space itself are privatized, submitted to private management, or charged with user fees; the public administration surrenders normative and economic prerogatives to corporate agencies and developers, and so forth.

Though still inchoate, the 'creative' moment of the process is likely to revisit previous aspects of entrepreneurial urbanism starting from the new platform provided by these measures. In a context of limited investment and lending, cities and city-regions will have to reinforce their strategies to attract capital amidst intensified inter-urban competition. This trend will widen the gap between the top and bottom tiers of urban areas, aggravating the predicament of those already under pressure from economic and social conflicts. Megaproject- and megaevent-oriented initiatives are to galvanize the public sector of those cities who can afford such enterprises, and structural developments will probably adopt the public-private partnership formula on a regular basis, with corporate investment leading the initiatives in search of profit and leaving the public sector to assume the risk and unprofitable expenditures. Private interest is likely to embrace previously progressive urbanisms as novel accumulation niches, including environmental management and city greening, as well as urban redevelopment and regeneration of both city centers and historic peripheries. In a context of construction decline soft urbanisms will privilege the reorganization of the city's content —rather than the built environment itself— as a realm of commodification, as is the case with the pervasive initiatives of smart cities and the urban mobilization of big data through new electronic devices and communication services. However, once real estate markets are reactivated we can expect new urban developments to spread that, especially in the case of Southern European countries, could be increasingly targeted at international corporate investment in high-end touristic areas and capital cities. At an everyday level traditional public services will probably undergo a process of segmentation along class lines depending on the users' capacity to afford fees and extra taxes for enhanced assistance and facilities; those lacking economic resources will face the bare support of basic assistance.

In any case, this dismal view on our urban futures presupposes a preliminary achievement that is still to be proven: the capacity of deep neoliberalization to fix the growing contradictions resulting from the crisis and to govern the intensification of uneven development without triggering further social upheaval, armed conflicts, environmental disaster and, of course, new economic collapses. Instead, Brenner et al (2010:339-341) consider the possibility that a dysfunctional 'zombie neoliberalism' is developed as a 'putative [solution] to persistent regulatory dilemmas across scales, territories and contexts'. Given the undesirability of any of these scenarios, it is extremely urgent that we think of potential alternatives to revive the social breath of planning and urban policy. Four levels and scales of engagement should articulate this endeavor:

- Activist urbanism: The crisis has sparked an archipelago of small-scale interventions and public space occupations as a direct response to state retrenchment in fundamental dimensions of sociospatial regulation. Together with traditional forms of urban social movements and ephemeral guerilla urbanisms these new experiences show 'the potential of the temporary and the mobile to refigure the city around spaces that were dormant, disregarded or dead' (Tonkiss, 2013:322), but also and especially the importance of laying claim to public space and producing new regimes of publicity by an active, collective self-management of the city (Harvey, 2012). Both everyday, piecemeal reappropriations of the streets and massive urban protests can be assembled through activist urbanisms to engender novel forms of urban commoning that palliate the crisis of formal social reproduction and create the opportunity for a more human urban life.

- Progressive urbanism: On a more formal basis, we need an alliance for a new progressive alternative to neoliberal planning and urban policy, including civic leaders, planning practitioners, the non-profit sector and scholars on the left. These actors should operate as an advocacy body mediating and aiding the penetration of social movement's demands in governmental agendas, promoting the renovation of urbanism's social function and undoing recent entrepreneurial approaches. At the same time they should develop a convincing discourse to underpin such new forms of urbanism, appealing to social justice and democratization to counter the devastating effect of 'common-sense' neoliberal ideologies.
- Urban-regional solidarity: The efforts on a local level should be paralleled with the creation of a network of inter-urban solidarity across regions and nations so that the harmful effects of spatial competition are lowered. Such networks ought to exchange experiences in regulatory experimentation, establish common political agendas and elaborate protocols to resist and support each other in case they undergo fiscal problems or face attacks from corporate capital or institutions. Within Europe this network should include not only cities across the South, but also those suffering from endemic structural conflicts and social vulnerability in depressed regions in the North and the East.
- Rescaled social struggle: The city is not enough. Current patterns of intensified uneven geographical development show the urgent need for a realignment of national and supranational levels of government pursuing to rebalance social and territorial inequalities. Certain aspects of the regulation of contemporary social formations cannot find an appropriate solution through urban and regional strategies alone, but need to be orchestrated from higher agencies. In Southern European countries the main lines of austerity agendas are imposed by bodies including representatives from national governments, EU institutions and international financial agencies, while the detailed distribution of budgetary retrenchment is pushed down to lower levels of administration — a clear evidence of the need to rescale social struggle to target power centers beyond the urban scale.

Taken together, these moves gesture towards a collective reappropriation of planning at several scales, including both those in which the state stands as the fundamental agency and those currently undergoing a transition to a growing presence of forms of commoning and self-management. Of course, the state is still the fundamental actor in terms of economic and regulatory innovation; but it is also —as it always was— the main promoter of advances in the field of planning and the orchestration of spatial production. In my opinion, the point —at least from a possibilist perspective departing from the reality of our cities and not from a timeless, placeless ideal— is to take the state and put them to work for the collective interest. This does not mean that we have to focus on taking formal, institutional power and forget about the commons for a while, rather the reverse. We need to mobilize the energies of commoning to define what the common good should be, to reorient the state in the right direction. At the same time, the re-socialization of the state must be implemented in such a way that, by creating a new public, the state no longer erodes the commons but, on the contrary, it concentrates efforts to become a formal infrastructure from which new forms of commons can blossom. Both projects, the commoning of urban space and everyday life and the constituent reconfiguration of the state should strive to palliate the current crisis of socioenvironmental reproduction, pursuing a new notion of good living based on the achievement of real sustainability —realized through the transformation of our lifestyles, not through the proliferation of new marketable technologies— a project of care and mutual aid —capable of combining formal and informal networks of social reproduction— and a commitment to radical democracy.

References

Aalbers, M. (2012) Subprime cities and the twin crises. In: M. Aalbers, M. (ed.) Subprime Cities. The Political Economy of Mortgage Markets. Chichester, West Sussex: Wiley-Blackwell, 3-22

Aglietta, M. (2000) A theory of capitalist regulation: the US experience. London: Verso

Berger, H. and M. Spoerer (2001) Economic crises and the European revolutions of 1848. In: The Journal of Economic History 61: 293-326

Bonaparte, N.L. (1840) Des Idées Napoléoniennes. On the Opinions and Policy of Napoleon. London: Henry Bolburn.

Brenner, N. and N. Theodore (2002) Cities and the geographies of "actually existing neoliberalism". In: Antipode, 34, 349-379.

Brenner, N., J. Peck, J., and N. Theodore (2010) After neoliberalization? In: Globalizations, 7, 327-345.

Callinicos, A. (2012) Contradictions of austerity. In: Cambridge Journal of Economics, 36, 65-77.

Eurostat (2009) External and Intra-EU Trade – A Statistical Yearbook. Data 1958-2008. 2009 Edition. Luxembourg: Office for Official Publications of the European Communities. Available at: http://epp.eurostat.ec.europa.eu/cache/ITY_OFFPUB/KS-GI-10-001/EN/KS-GI-10-001-EN.PDF (accesed 31 July 2014).

Evans, M. (1848) The Commercial Crisis. 1847-1848. London: Letts, Son, and Steer

Frazer, W. and J. J. Guthrie Jr. (1995) The Florida Land Boom. Speculation, Money and the Banks. Westport: Quorum

Girouard, M. (1985) Cities and People. A Social and Architectural History. New Haven: Yale University Press

Gottdiener, M., and N. Komminos (1989) Capitalist Development and Crisis Theory: Accumulation, Regulation and Spatial Restructuring. New York: St. Martin's Press

Greenberg, M. (2003) The limits of branding: the World Trade Center, fiscal crisis and the marketing of recovery. In: International Journal of Urban and Regional Research, 27, 386-416.

Hadjimichalis, C. (2011) Uneven geographical development and socio-spatial justice and solidarity: European regions after the 2009 financial crisis. In: European Urban and Regional Studies, 18, 254-274.

Hall, S., D. Massey and M. Rustin (2013) After neoliberalism: analysing the present. In Soundings: A Journal of Politics and Culture, 53, 8-22

Harvey, D. (1975) The geography of capitalist accumulation. A reconstruction of the Marxian theory. In: Antipode, 7, 9-21

Harvey, D. (2003) Paris, Capital of Modernity. New York: Routledge

Harvey, D. (2005) A Brief History of Neoliberalism. New York: Oxford University Press

Harvey, D. (2006a) The Limits to Capital. New York: Verso

Harvey, D. (2006b) Neo-liberalism as creative destruction. In: Geografiska Annaler: Series B, Human Geography, 88, 145–158

Harvey, D. (2010) The Enigma of Capital and the Crises of Capitalism. London: Profile Books

Harvey, D. (2012) Rebel Cities: From the Right to the City to the Urban Revolution. London: Verso

Harvey, D. (2014) Seventeen Contradictions and the End of Capitalism, London: Profile Books

Hayden, D. (2003) Building Suburbia. Green Fields and Urban Growth, 1820-2000. New York: Pantheon

Hobsbawm, E. (1975) The Age of Capital. 1848-1875. London: Abacus

Jackson, K.T. (1985) Crabgrass Frontier. The Suburbanization of the United States. New York: Oxford University Press

Krugman, P. (2012) The austerity agenda, The New York Times, May 31. Available at: http://www.nytimes.com/2012/06/01/opinion/krugman-the-austerity-agenda.html (accesed 31 July 2014)

Lefebvre, H. (1976) The Survival of Capitalism. St. Martin's Press, New York

Lefebvre, H. (1991) The Production of Space, Oxford: Blackwell

Martí-Henneberg, J. (2013) European integration and national models for railway networks (1840–2010). In: Journal of Transport Geography, 26,126-138

Matsaganis, M. (2011) The welfare state and the crisis: the case of Greece. In: Journal of European Social Policy, 21, 501-512

Neilson, B. and Rossiter, N. (2008) Precarity as a political concept, or, Fordism as exception. In: Theory, Culture and Society, 25, 51-72

Nixon, R. (1972) Radio Address on Urban Affairs, November 1, 1972. In: The American Presidency Project. Available at: http://www.presidency.ucsb.edu/ws/?pid=3681 (accesed 31 July 2014)

Peck, J. (2012) Austerity urbanism: American cities under extreme economy. In: City, 16, 626-655

Peck, J., N. Theodore and N. Brenner (2012) Neoliberalism resurgent? Market rule after the Great Recession. In: South Atlantic Quarterly, 111, 265-288

Tabb, W. (1982) The Long Default. New York City and the Urban Fiscal Crisis. New York: Monthly Review

Tonkiss. F. (2013) Austerity urbanism and the makeshift city. In: City: analysis of urban trends, culture, theory, policy, action 17,312-324

Traugott, M. (1983) The mid-nineteenth-century crisis in France and England. In: Theory and Society, 12, 455-468

White, E.N. (2009) Lessons from the Great American Real Estate Boom and Bust of the 1920s, National Bureau of Economic Research Working Paper No. 15573. Available at: http://www.nber.org/papers/w15573 (accesed 31 July 2014)

Zevin, R. (1977) New York City Crisis: First Act in a New Age of Reaction. In: R.E. Alcaly and D. Mermelstein (eds.) The Fiscal Crisis of American Cities. Essays on the Political Economy of Urban America with Special Reference to New York. New York: Vintage Books, 11-29

Spain

Madrid

A tale of an ambitious city that failed to fulfil its global vision*

José Miguel Fernández-Güell

Acknowledgements: The author thanks Enrique Martínez-Vidal and Ambrosio Aguado for providing access to the photo collection of the Madrid Municipality.

A brief overview of the recent development, present situation and future prospectus of a metropolis like Madrid -which is physically large, socially heterogeneous and economically diverse- is not an easy endeavour. Nevertheless, the case of Madrid can be intriguing to a foreign observer because its immediate past has been full of excesses, its present is dominated by a deep recession, and its future is faced with major challenges and uncertainties.

Under these premises and from a personal perspective based on several years of consulting practice with Madrid-related projects, this essay sets out the ambitions, troubles and expectations of the Spanish capital in the last twenty years. The sequence of events is organized into three periods. Firstly, the golden years of high economic growth and an unparalleled building spree are analyzed and assessed. Secondly, the economic recession and its aftermath are frankly exposed. Finally, future prospects for the metropolis are explored and some suggestions for policy makers are given.

Before starting the analysis, some clues of the nature, limitations and general context of Madrid should be given. First of all, the city is the

---

* "Madrid" by José Miguel Fernández-Güell, published in disP – The Planning Review, Vol50:1, pp6-15(2014) is reprinted by permission of Taylor & Francis Ltd, www.tandfonline.com<http://www.tandfonline.com/> on behalf of ETH – Eidgenössische Technische Hochschule Zurich.

political capital of the nation, but at the same time it is also the capital of an autonomous region with comprehensive political powers. The 8.028 km² Madrid Region is in the centre of the Iberian Peninsula with a population of 6.49 million inhabitants. Although the region only occupies 1.6% of the national territory, it accounts for 13.8% of the Spanish population and generates 19.6% of the gross national product (Comunidad de Madrid, 2013).

Within the region, the Municipality of Madrid occupies 604.3 km², holds 3.23 million inhabitants and generates 11.7% of the gross national product (Ayuntamiento de Madrid, 2013). At the European level, Madrid is the third biggest urban agglomeration after Ile de France and Greater London. Despite its vigorous growth since the late 1990s, the city has managed to preserve, within its limits, large natural areas and urban parks thanks to the maintenance of a highly compact dense urban fabric (Figure 1).

Fig. 1: Municipality of Madrid

Source: Ayuntamiento de Madrid, 2012a

To proper understand the city's spatial and socio-economic transformations, we must look beyond its political boundaries. In fact, Madrid is the centre of a functional urban region that extends into cities such as Guadalajara and Toledo, located outside the limits of the Madrid Region. Regional, metropolitan and municipal statistics are therefore used indistinctly to explain the evolution of the city.

Madrid lacks the strong, distinctive socio-cultural identity that other Spanish cities such as Barcelona and Bilbao can project to outsiders. This feature can be valued as both a weaknesses and an asset. On the one hand, a strong identity reinforces social capital and tends to pull citizens together in search of a common goal, which is missing in Madrid. On the other hand, this missing attribute opens up the city to foreigners and increases its cosmopolitan atmosphere, which occurs in Madrid.

Lastly, Madrid has to attend two major roles, which are sometimes contradictory. On the one side, as a capital city it must provide a whole range of services to a country with very distinctive regional features, while on the other, it must lead development in a relatively small region that competes at the national and international level.

1. A CITY IN SEARCH OF A GLOBAL POSITION

Since the 1990s, Madrid's politicians and economic agents were transfixed with the idea of placing the city at the top of the global urban hierarchy. This obsession may well have started in 1989 when the famous French study on 165 European agglomerations was published and widely distributed on the continent (Brunet, 1989). This study had a considerable media impact as it was the first display of the continent's city hierarchy in a comprehensible manner. It also identified the European development backbone, popularly known as the "Blue Banana", where most decisions were taken and productive forces were concentrated (Faludi, 2010).

The French analysis placed London and Paris in the first category, Milano in the second category, and Madrid in the third group together with Munich, Frankfurt, Rome, Brussels, Barcelona and Amsterdam. Madrid was also in a peripheral position with regard to the European backbone. This study caught the attention of Madrid's stakeholders, who felt that the city should climb up the European urban hierarchy. This belief was reflected in several planning documents in the coming years.

During the early 1990s, Madrid drafted a Strategic Plan (PROMADRID, 1993) which pursued a consensus amongst public officials and socio-economic stakeholders on the vision that should guide the city's future development. Although the Plan was never implemented as originally intended, many of its strategies prevailed in the coming years in the minds and agendas of politicians and economic agents. A brief account of that strategic vision follows.

First and foremost, Madrid wished to enter the prime league of global cities by becoming a financial, advanced services and decision making hub for Southern Europe. The undeclared goal of the Spanish capital was first to get even with and later surpass cities like Barcelona, Lisbon, Rome and Milano. Once its position was consolidated in the Mediterranean Arch, Madrid would then try to get closer to the top rank enjoyed by London and Paris.

In order to fulfil this ambitious objective, among other things Madrid needed to become an airport hub for flights coming to Europe from Latin America and Africa. Obviously, a powerful airport hub would be a prerequisite to transform Madrid into a first rate logistics centre, which in turn would attract additional economic activities. High-frequency air connections would also stimulate tourism and help to increase the city's cosmopolitan character.

At the national level, Madrid wanted to become the integrating link between Spain's urban system and the European Union. This goal was to be achieved by a high-speed railway system. Madrid would be converted into the hub of a radio-concentric system that would provide high-speed connections to most Spanish cities. Even major Portuguese cities were to be integrated into this system. Thanks to this network, anyone living in a coastal city could travel to the capital in just three hours and on to Barajas airport, with its wide choice of international flights.

Besides providing an excellent level of transport accessibility, Madrid needed to build large facilities to become a scientific and technological pole, an attractive cultural and tourist destination, a city known for its quality of life and a cosmopolitan metropolis receptive to new trends and ideas. These goals meant large public investments to develop technological facilities, build sophisticated museums, increase office space and improve public zones.

To implement these objectives, the city needed to satisfy three key conditions: a favourable economic context, a friendly planning framework for urban development, and a managerial political style to push complex projects forward. The first condition was met from 1997 onwards, when Spain enjoyed an unprecedented economic bonanza thanks to its entry to the Eurozone and the provision of very cheap financing. During this period, the country was the recipient of large amounts of international capital seeking for high returns from a booming economy.

The second condition was also met when a new City Plan was approved in 1997. Under Spanish legislation, a City Plan is the central instrument for guiding urban development and assigning building rights. The objectives of the new Plan were well aligned with the ambitious strategic vision pursued by the city (Ayuntamiento de Madrid, 1997): facilitate urban growth in order to minimize real estate speculation; release new land for business activities; regenerate the historical district; build emblematic projects to reinforce Madrid's capital role; and develop an infrastructures programme to support the transformation process.

The third condition was met under the political leadership of Ruiz-Gallardón, Premier of the Madrid Regional Government from 1996 till 2002 and Mayor of Madrid from 2003 until 2011. Gallardón was clearly determined to build large, complex urban projects before the end of his political terms in order to ensure his re-election and project himself onto the national political arena. This strategy required resolute power brokers and competent technical teams capable of executing very large and complex projects in record times. By the same token, these costly projects also required large financial resources which were happily met by the Spanish financial system.

Consequently, all the enabling factors were set for propelling a development spree in the city.

2. Reliance on infrastructures and megaprojects

The transformation strategy followed by Madrid during the 1997-2007 period was heavily based on building large transport infrastructures and urban megaprojects. The city strove to overcome its peripheral position in the European Union and emerge as an international reference point in urban culture by upgrading its external accessibility and modernizing its urban fabric. In turn, Madrid was expected to gain critical mass by attracting more residents and economic activity to its urban realm. The following initiatives are illustrative examples of this strategy.

Extension of the metropolitan highway system. In the last 25 years, Madrid has built an extensive radio concentric highway network that provides greater accessibility and mobility to the entire metropolitan area (Figure 2). Four ring roads (M-30, M-40, M-45 and M-50) are intersected by twelve radial highways which connect Madrid to the rest of the country. This expensive and environmentally intrusive road infrastructure, nevertheless provides reasonably good mobility to a highly complex urban region.

Fig. 2: Madrid highway network

Source: Ayuntamiento de Madrid, 2012a

Enlargement of Barajas Airport. In 2006, Terminal 4, a huge building designed by Richard Rogers and Lamela Architects (Figure 3), was completed and two new runways were added to the existing Barajas Airport. With this new infrastructure, Madrid airport can now handle up to 70 million passengers a year. Although the airport enlargement has created acoustic impacts on some nearby residential areas, this infrastructure is considered to be a big asset for the city because of its large capacity and its convenient railway and metro connections to the business district.

Growth of the high-speed rail system. The high-speed strategy followed in Spain has definitely benefited Madrid. Nearly 3,000 kilometres of high-speed tracks are organized in a radial pattern, whose central hub is Madrid. Recently, criticism has emerged because of the large public investments dedicated to the high-speed network in detriment of other transport infrastructures. Despite the economic and political debate, high speed trains are highly popular among travellers and have become a fearful competitor to air transport on the Peninsula.

Fig. 3: Terminal 4 of Barajas Airport

Source: Ayuntamiento de Madrid, photo collection

Improvement of the public transport system. In the last 20 years, Madrid has made a significant effort to upgrade its public transport system. Presently, Madrid has 10 regional railway lines with 100 stations which annually transport more than 180 million passengers (Renfe, 2013), while the metro system has 300 stations and 293 kilometres of lines which moved nearly 602 million passengers in 2012 (Metro de Madrid, 2013). The combination of the regional railway and metro system is an acceptable car substitute for hundreds of thousands of daily commuters.

Madrid-Rio project. By far the most expensive and ambitious project recently undertaken by the city is Madrid-Río (Figure 4). During 2003-2007, nearly 25 kilometres of the M-30 along the river Manzanares were buried and large spaces were freed from highway traffic. As a result, a large linear park was created and the riverfront area was reclaimed for the citizens. Madrid-Río was finished in 2011 and was almost immediately a great success among the residents of the nearby congested neighbourhoods, who eagerly enjoyed the new recreational facilities. On the other hand, the city will be heavily indebted for many years to come because of this expensive project.

Fig. 4: Madrid-Rio

Source: Ayuntamiento de Madrid, photo collection

Construction of a new business centre. By 2009, four imposing 58 storey skyscrapers were completed and stood ready in the extension of Castellana Avenue to house Madrid's new business centre (Figure 5). Their location seemed just right because of their close proximity to Chamartin's railway station and its excellent connection with Barajas airport. Nevertheless, the towers, finished when the "bonanza" was coming to an end, now wait for a new growth cycle, with many vacant offices.

Fig. 5: New business centre

Source: Ayuntamiento de Madrid, photo collection

Urban renewal. A significant effort has been made to undertake an integral rehabilitation of historical districts and run-down neighbourhoods. Not only 17th and 18th century quarters have been renovated (Figure 6), but also the early 20th century Gran Vía district has been restored and brought back as one of Madrid most popular entertainment areas (Figure 7). Likewise, vast spaces in central areas have been reclaimed from the automobile for pedestrians in order to revitalize shopping and leisure activities. Renewal has indeed contributed to improve the quality of life in the heart of the bustling metropolis, but it has also ignited a gentrification process yet to be assessed.

Fig. 6: Historical district rehabilitation

Source: Ayuntamiento de Madrid, photo collection

This short-list of urban and regional projects gives an overall idea of the scope and magnitude of public and private investments during the 1997-2007 period aimed at pushing up Madrid in the global hierarchy. In fact, just before the onset of the economic crisis, there were several signals indicating that somehow these gargantuan investments were paying off. Some global city rankings were placing Madrid in the top categories as an Alpha city (GaWC, 2008), and an updated French study of European agglomerations ranked the Spanish capital alongside Milano and Amsterdam (DATAR, 2003). In the Iberian context, by the beginning of the 21st century Madrid enjoyed an undisputed dominance over the Spanish and Portuguese urban systems.

Fig. 7: Gran Via rehabilitation

Source: Ayuntamiento de Madrid, photo collection

Official statistics also showed Madrid's rising fortunes. The building spree and frenzied economic activity was accompanied by a slight increase in Madrid's population, fed by immigration flows which reversed the declining trend of previous decades (Figure 8). Madrid's per capita income also rose to the top of Spanish cities and came closer to the ranks of the most prosperous European metropolis. Lastly, the real estate sector joined the party by building more than 500,000 dwellings in the Madrid Region between 2001 and 2011 (Del Río, 2013). Definitively, by 2007 Madrid was the centre of media attention because of its economic momentum and urban megaprojects. However, the metropolis was set on weak foundations.

Fig. 8: Madrid population evolution (2002-2013)

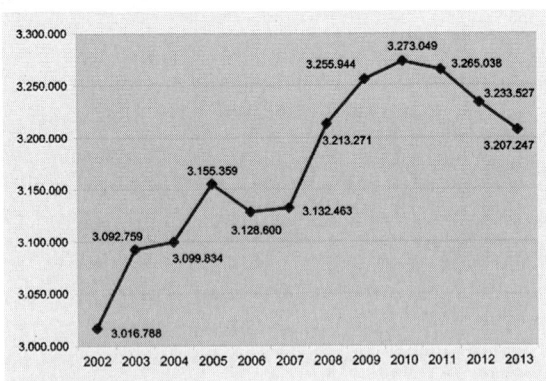

Source: INE, 2014a

3. Exposure of a Fragile and Questionable Urban Model

In the summer of 2007, after the collapse of the subprime market, nobody in Madrid's municipal government anticipated that the coming crisis was going to have such a long, vicious and powerful impact on the city's development ambitions. By the end of 2008, after the Lehmans Brothers bankruptcy, Madrid became fully aware that both its national and local economies were facing serious problems due to structural weaknesses that had been ignored during the previous growth years.

Since then, the trends in economic indicators have been devastating. Madrid Region's per capita income has declined from 30,944 Euros in 2008 to 28.915 in 2013 (Figure 9) and its unemployment rate has skyrocketed from 6% in 2007 to almost 20% in 2013 (Figure 10). The city's fiscal debt has risen from 1,033 million Euros in 2001 to 7,074 million Euros in 2013 (Figure 11). As a matter of fact, Madrid has become the most indebted Spanish city in both absolute and per capita terms. Airport traffic in Barajas has decreased nearly 24% since 2007, leaving the brand new Terminal 4 worryingly underused (Figure 12). Lastly, real estate value for residential uses has decreased by 30% on average since 2007 (INE, 2013).

Fig. 9: Madrid Region's income per capita in Euros (2005-2013)

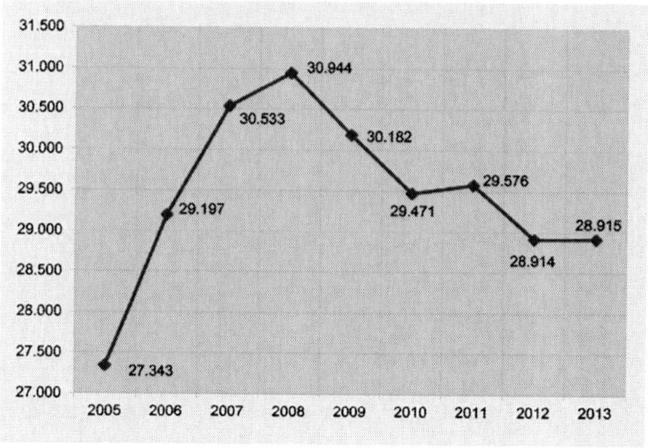

Source: INE, 2014b

Fig. 10: Madrid Region's unemployment rate (2005-2013)

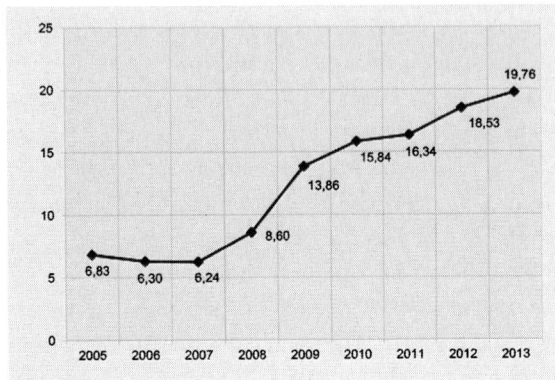

Source: INE, 2014c

Fig. 11: Madrid municipal fiscal debt in millions of Euros (2000-2013)

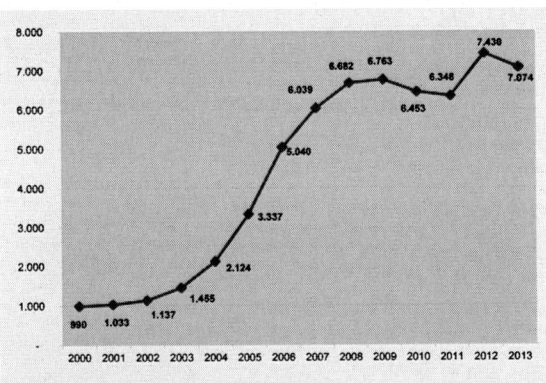

Source: Ayuntamiento de Madrid, 2014

As a result of the enduring crisis, the city has many visible scars in its urban fabric. Large urbanized areas remain empty because there is no demand for real estate products, unfinished building structures can be seen in several spots of the metropolitan area, brand new toll highways carry much less traffic than planned, and several urban megaprojects such as Operación Chamartín and Operación Campamento have been put on hold because of the real estate meltdown.

Fig. 12: Passengers traffic at Barajas Airport (2000-2013)

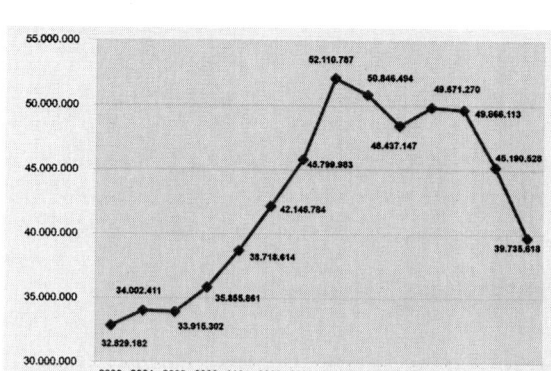

Source: AENA, 2014

From the environmental point of view, Madrid's region has followed an aggressive urbanization model characterized by the over-construction of infrastructures, housing and business facilities. Despite trying to preserve a compact city model, rapid growth in the metropolitan area has inevitably increased urban sprawl, the duration of commuter trips, the demand for motorized mobility, suburban shopping and leisure centres, and environmental impacts generated by an intrusive network of heavy transport infrastructures.

The crisis is not only visible from strictly economic and spatial perspectives, but has also shown a relevant social dimension. The popularly known "15-M Movement" emerged in Madrid on May 15 in 2011 at a public demonstration against the adverse effects of the economic crisis. For 28 consecutive days, citizens camped in "Puerta del Sol" square, the very heart of Madrid, to protest against the crisis and the recovery policies imposed on people by the Spanish Government, the European Union and multilateral organizations. Citizens were disenchanted, indignant and resentful with the political and economic class. The pacific 15-M Movement demanded a more participative democratic system to prevent public corruption and political mal-practices.

In brief, it can be said that in Madrid "the streets were not paved with gold", a reminiscence of Ken Auletta's book about New York's decline in the 1970s (Auletta, 1980). A fragile questionable urban model was exposed in the aftermath of the crisis. In economic terms, the city was excessively dependent on construction and on service sectors focused on the local market, while it lacked a stronger focus on high-tech sectors oriented towards the global markets. The crisis thus unravelled a vicious circle: the real estate market crashed, the financial sector became entrapped, the construction sector collapsed, industrial output decreased, unemployment went up, consumption went down, fiscal revenues diminished, social needs augmented, fiscal debt skyrocketed, and so on. To make matters worse in September 2013 Madrid failed in its bid to host the Olympic Games for a third time in a row, another sign of the city's declining image.

4. Hope and Future Challenges after the Building Hangover

Confronted with such a gloomy picture, it is timely to ask whether there is hope for Madrid in the near future. At the time this article was written, Madrid had yet to achieve financial stability and economic activities had not recovered from the recession. It is thus difficult to predict whether the exit from the crisis will take place in the shorter or longer term. Nevertheless, several reasons give grounds for hope.

Firstly, Madrid has invested heavily in large infrastructures and buildings which are either idle or have a low occupancy rate. Thus, the Spanish capital has an oversupply of brand new physical assets that provide a competitive edge over other European metropolis with limited capacity for urban growth.

Secondly, Madrid has a diversified industrial fabric, a large concentration of advanced services as well as a broad range of technological spaces. In fact, the city has developed an emerging network of clusters in the aero-space, ICTs, automobile, biology, renewable energy, health sciences, logistics and financial services industries (Madrid Network, 2013). With the right stimulus, a new generation of entrepreneurs and scientists may be able to lead the transformation of the city's economy into a vibrant set of innovative industrial and service activities.

Thirdly, the Madrid Municipality has recently drawn up two strategic documents which are clearly concerned with the city's future. The first one "Futuro Ciudad Madrid 2020" acknowledges the adverse effects of the economic crisis on the city and proposes a new development model (Ayuntamiento de Madrid, 2011). The second one is a strategic plan for the international positioning of the city, which aims to attract more investments, events and tourists (Ayuntamiento de Madrid, 2012b). To a large extent, the successful implementation of these initiatives depends on the support of politicians and the involvement of economic stakeholders.

Finally, the Madrid Municipality has a new City Plan underway that will guide future urban development. Fully aware of past urban excesses and wrong policies, the new Plan aims to give Madrid better economic opportunities and make it more sustainable, more socially cohesive, and improve its quality of life (Infanzón, 2013). If these general objectives are properly developed and implemented, they may become the starting point for a change in urban policies.

Despite these assets and initiatives, there are still many uncertainties about the foreseeable future of the Spanish capital. Assuming the best possible scenario for the city, a number of suggestions can be made for Madrid to take full advantage of the emerging opportunities and therefore make an effective resurgence.

a. *Ignore the global race.* For the time being, a more humble and pragmatic vision is needed. Madrid should not strive to become an Alpha Global City like London, New York or Tokyo. In the first place, Madrid will never get to challenge these cities, and secondly, the economic gains of becoming a global city will not compensate for social, environmental and governance losses.

b. *Turn from megaprojects to human talent.* Instead of investing in huge infrastructures and urban megaprojects, the city should pay more attention to promoting and incubating talent. Madrid needs to attract the best and most creative people worldwide to work in advanced industrial and services sectors. These people obviously respond to financial incentives, but they also expect a high quality of life in the form of cultural activities (Florida, 2005).

c. *Promote innovative economic activities.* From the economic point of view, a two-fold strategy should be implemented. On the one hand, existing clusters such as financial and consulting services, aeronautical industries

and logistics industries should be made more competitive. On the other, support should be given to innovative sectors such as biotechnology, nanotechnology, hybrid technologies or advanced materials.
d. *Decentralize urban growth.* The capital city should be generous and share its prosperity with neighbouring urban centres. An intelligent economic decentralization policy should be pursued based on the high-speed railway network built in recent years. To avoid increasing congestion and environmental deterioration, Madrid should form a well-articulated urban system in a 100 kilometre radius that can accommodate homes and economic activities.
e. *Recharge underused assets.* More sustainable development should be pursued in the city and its hinterland. Underused infrastructures and facilities should be filled with new activities or recycled in order to avoid consuming more land and natural resources. Urban regeneration should be given top priority versus new developments.
f. *Shift from emblematic architecture to small-scale urban operations.* Austerity and sustainability get along better with small-scale operations than with fancy architectural projects. Instead of promoting expensive iconic buildings, the municipality should focus on improving public spaces, public transport and public housing.
g. *Innovate in planning.* Contemporary cities are plagued with complexity and uncertainty. To operate successfully in this context, cities should roll out innovative planning approaches based on future studies, strategic thinking, integrated planning (social, economic, environmental and spatial) and flexible implementation mechanisms. Madrid should overcome administrative and political barriers in order to push forward planning innovation.
h. *Develop an advanced governance system.* Politicians should not be allowed to impose grandiose, unfeasible projects without being accountable to a wide spectrum of stakeholders and citizens. Moreover, efficiency should not be used as the flagship argument to justify the lack of consultation processes. Critical urban decisions should therefore be taken in a more transparent, collaborative and participative mode.

The fulfilment of these requisites is by no means an easy endeavour. However, strong guidelines have to be provided if past mistakes are not to be repeated. As in any contemporary city, Madrid faces challenges and optional strategies that have to be resolved in a tricky equation: exploit economic opportunities + increase quality of life + guarantee a sustainable environment + improve urban governance. The way these sometimes contradictory objectives are combined and balanced will be the key to a promising or disappointing future.

REFERENCES

AENA (2014) Evolución del tráfico de pasajeros en el Aeropuerto Madrid-Barajas. URL http://www.aena-aeropuertos.es Accessed 28.10.14

Auletta, K. (1980) The streets were paved with gold. New York: Vintage Books

Ayuntamiento de Madrid (2014) Endeudamiento consolidado del sector público municipal. URL http://www.madrid.es Accessed 28.10.14

Ayuntamiento de Madrid (2013) Madrid Economía 2013 – Análisis Socioeconómico. URL http://www.madrid.es Accessed 28.12.13

Ayuntamiento de Madrid (2012a) Revisión del Plan General – Pre avance – Propuestas de ordenación urbanística. Madrid: Ayuntamiento de Madrid, Área de Gobierno de Urbanismo y Vivienda

Ayuntamiento de Madrid (2012b) Plan Estratégico de Posicionamiento Internacional de la Ciudad de Madrid (2012-2015). Madrid: Ayuntamiento de Madrid, Área de Gobierno de Vicealcaldía

Ayuntamiento de Madrid (2011) Futuro Ciudad Madrid 2020 – Proceso de reflexión estratégica. Madrid: Área de Gobierno de Economía, Empleo y Participación Ciudadana

Ayuntamiento de Madrid (1997) Plan General de Ordenación Urbana de Madrid. Madrid: Oficina del Plan

Brunet, R. et al. (1989) Les Villes Européennes. Paris: La Documentation Française

Comunidad de Madrid (2013) The Region of Madrid in figures. URL http://www.madrid.org Accessed 28.12.13

Del Río, I. (2013) El Plan General de Ordenación Urbana de Madrid de 1997. El último clásico. In: J. Vinuesa et al. (eds): Reflexiones a propósito de la revisión del Plan General de Madrid. Madrid: Grupo TRyS

Délégation à l'Aménagement du Territoire et à l'Action Régionale (DATAR) (2003) Les Villes Européennes – Éléments de comparaison. Paris: La Documentation Française

Faludi, A. (2010) Cohesion, Coherence, Cooperation: European Spatial Planning Coming of Age. London: Routledge

Florida, R. (2005) Cities and the creative class. London: Routledge

GaWC Research Network (2008) The World According to GaWC 2008. URL http://www.lboro.ac.uk Accessed 28.12.13

Infanzón, J.L. (2013) Fortalezas y debilidades del planeamiento general. In: J. Vinuesa et al. (eds): Reflexiones a propósito de la revisión del Plan General de Madrid. Madrid: Grupo TRyS

Instituto Nacional de Estadística (INE) (2014a) Padrón Municipal. URL http://www.ine.es Accessed 28.10.14

Instituto Nacional de Estadística (INE) (2014b) Contabilidad Regional de España- Base 2008. URL http://www.ine.es Accessed 28.10.14

Instituto Nacional de Estadística (INE) (2014c) Encuesta de Población Activa – Metodología 2005. URL http://www.ine.es Accessed 28.10.14

Instituto Nacional de Estadística (INE) (2013) Índice de Precios de Vivienda – Base 2007. URL http://www.ine.es Accessed 28.12.13

Madrid Network (2013) Network Clusters. URL http://www.madridnetwork.org Accessed 28.12.13

Metro de Madrid (2013) Metro de Madrid in Figures. URL http://www.metromadrid.es Accessed 28.12.13

PROMADRID (1993) Madrid Futuro – Plan Estratégico de Madrid. Madrid: PROMADRID

Renfe (2013) Cercanías Madrid. URL http://www.renfe.com Accessed 28.12.13

Contest Discourses of Austerity in the Urban Margins (A Vision from Barcelona)

Nuria Benach

> "...the contradictions of capitalism may be witnessed more clearly at the margins" (Katz 1996:172)

> "Sin trabajo, sin casa, sin pensión, sin miedo"
> ("No job, no house, no pension, no fear",
> street protests of the youth in Spain, 2011)

The global crisis has been the perfect excuse for the deployment of neo-liberal policies that have had their most visible effect in the severe cutbacks of social rights and the growing concentration of both public and private investments in certain privileged issues and spaces. As a result, there has been an accentuated social and spatial polarisation at all levels, from the global to the urban. These policies have been accompanied by the existence of a tremendous gap between a hegemonic neo-liberal discourse that evaluates the present crisis in very abstract terms (such as foreign debt, markets weakness, risk premium, investors' confidence and so on) and the terrible effects of such policies in the spaces of people's daily lives. In these spaces, the so-called economic crisis is by no means an abstraction but a very material and tangible situation that has appalling effects on the weakest population: foreclosures, lack of social assistance, increasing waiting times, environmental degradation, urban stress. Very often, the worst side of this so-called economic crisis is not the crisis itself but the effects of the unfair policies that have been deployed. For this reason, in recent times the global crisis appears to have awakened the social unrest that seemed to have been dormant in a welfare state that once was perceived as everlasting. Today, the very same cities that keep their discourse as motors of economic growth and as strategic nodes of capital concentration have increasingly become the centres of protest and resistance as the many urban mobilizations all over the world demonstrate during 2011 and 2012. The aim of this chapter is therefore to explore this urban discontent by analysing the potential of urban spaces as sites of generation of alternatives to the social and political crisis. To do this, I will base my argument on the many contributions from the critical urban theory that have recently reworked some of Henri Lefebvre's ideas on the urban process, urban centrality and the right to the city.

1. The right to the (imagined) city

Let us start with the evidence of how neo-liberal policies generate growing social and spatial inequalities. Any analyses of the evolution of a variety of social indicators in the last ten years in most western cities would show that the gap between the richest and the poorest has widened. For the less privileged it can be an extreme economic situation without the minimum means necessary to guarantee their basic needs. For the middle classes, who during the years of economic growth lived a "golden age" of high consumption – and also of high indebtedness –, it has meant a progressive impoverishment and a drastic reduction of their consumption levels, which is assumed to be both a symptom and a cause of the recession.

Austerity is indeed a very aggressive way of doing politics, the last facade that neo-liberal politics uses to undermine the basis of a welfare state that was created to save the system but that in the end turned out to be too expensive and inefficient for capital's interests. Capitalism has already shown many times its capacity to restructure and to survive even at the cost of the use of violence and of unbearable human suffering. But unjust, violent and intolerable as it is, alternatives to capitalism have become less and less imaginable, especially for the left. It was Neil Smith who stated that "the tragedy is less the political onslaught by the right than the political non-response of the left" (Smith, 2009:51). A couple of examples can evoke the state of mind of some leftist intellectuals. It was Fredric Jameson who echoed the idea that it was easier to imagine the end of the world than the end of capitalism (Jameson, 2003:76). Moreover, in any case, one may wonder how a non-capitalist world would be? And it was Donna Haraway who openly complained about having almost lost her capacity to imagine such a different world (quoted in Smith 2009:51).

Such a collective incapacity could leave us in a difficult situation for thinking about alternatives. A possible hint takes us back to the urban ground. Back in 1968, Henri Lefebvre wrote that capitalism could not be understood nor resisted without understanding and re-imagining the city (Lefebvre, 1974). This was a bold statement made by someone who firmly believed that the city was nothing but an abridged model of society as a whole. There is no question that studying cities from a critical perspective means to contextualize the process of urbanization in the present form of capitalism. And similarly, following Lefebvre's train of thought, the urban must be a key element to understanding the contradictions of capitalism. Thus, fighting for a new city (for the right to the city as Lefebvre would say) inevitably means fighting for a new society. But we need to be able to at least think of it, to be able to imagine it. Hence, we urgently need to use the right to imagine the city, another city, another society.

Our first step to inspire such imagination could be then to unmask the neo-liberal ideology, to look for the creation of some rupture in this hegemonic neo-liberal discourse. Thatcher's famous (or infamous) "there is no alternative" narrative, like it or not, went directly against our imagination since it is difficult to counter any discourse based on the same logic that supports it. The necessary rupture can only be created from other values and logic than the ones that support the neo-liberal discourse, that is, from the values and logic of the materially lived-in space and not from economic abstractions.

Let us discuss now for a moment the common hegemonic discourses on cities. The usual aims pursued by city governments have been the adjustment of urban space to their potential demands, transforming some areas in a frantic and sometimes ephemeral way, and converting them into a commodity ready to be sold. Urban politics and urban planning have been rapidly adapted to these new priorities and selling the city has become a normal item on the agenda since the 1980s. But besides producing the commodity (adapting spaces), urban marketing experts would say one needs to sell them, find potential consumers, position the merchandise in the market, and compete with other possible alternatives. This is about promoting and expanding urban qualities, availabilities, comparative advantages and about finding ways to do it (Harvey, 1989). But when citizens realize that their needs lie outside such commercial logics, then the only thing that can be sold to them in order to maintain the necessary social harmony is ideology: to persuade them that the decisions are beneficial to everybody, that they serve the principle of the common good. The weight of urban discourses has thus inevitably become heavier: what is said that it is done, what is said that it is, what is said that is wanted, are all part and parcel of "what is done" to occupy a better position in this international context and at the same time a way to try to convince everyone that this is the correct and only path to be followed. For many years, this hegemonic discourse on the city succeeded in stopping the emergence of alternatives, transgressions and resistances to that "imposed point of view" as Sharon Zukin once put it (Zukin, 1995:23-24). Thus the right to the city must also be about having a "different point of view", about envisioning the city as a space for living, as having use value and not only as exchange value. The right to the city must start with the right to the (imagined) city.

2. QUESTIONING THE HEGEMONIC COMMON SENSE

It is nothing new to say that power uses every possible means to reach its goals. And language, if properly used and amplified, can be very powerful in creating "truths" and make any other different explanation look unreasonable and even ridiculous. The main strategy used by the hegemonic neo-liberal discourse is to describe the situation as being so far away from any personal experience we may have that it is actually very difficult, almost impossible to counter. Moreover, when said discourse, often unintelligible and therefore practically unquestionable, seems not to be enough, it is immediately added that, anyway, "there are no alternatives". With the never-ending echo of the media and the complicity of intellectuals, neo-liberal ideology creates in this way a hegemonic "common sense" that naturalises all kind of decisions as unavoidable and undermines all possibilities of resistance to that extremely critical situation.

Nevertheless, on the other hand, it can be said that those strategies, when looked at closely, are not very sophisticated after all. They consist of blaming people (guilty for being too indebted, guilty for having lived beyond their means, guilty for having a job so they don't have the right to protest, guilty for not having a job and being a burden on the entire society, guilty for being ill, guilty for demanding care for kids and old people instead of personally taking care of them...), in being confused (a situation too complicated to be explained to ordinary people, use of lies or euphemisms like "healing or recapitalizing or injecting liquidity standing for giving public money to private banks), or creating a state of collective fear by threats or even repression if needed (Valverde, 2013).

However, despite an unemployment rate that seem out of control[1] and growing levels of poverty, there is an increasing perception among people that the no- alternatives discourse is actually hiding a reality of public resources spent in benefit of financial capital and the already very rich (Peet, 2012). This growing perception cannot be said to be a counter-discourse since it is not so well organised but it does indeed open an important fracture in this incapacity to respond to this direct alliance between economic and political power. Looking to open fractures to this common sense was the objective of Doreen Massey's 2011 paper called precisely "Ideology and Economics at the present moment". In that paper we were urged to think of the relations between economy and ideology in some other way if we were to fight the neo-liberal space. Massey was of course talking from and for London but lots of things she talked about are perfectly applicable to other contexts (paradoxically, the magic of theorizing from the ground up that has always characterized Massey's thought). For Massey a real space seemed to exist for an effective answer and to produce any breaks to that hegemonic ideological common sense considering three areas of potential engagement. These areas are: 1) considering the economy with a completely different prioritisation of values (one that stresses the cooperation needed in social reproduction instead of the exchange in markets), 2) putting equality back on the agenda and into the discourse (as opposed to the neo-liberal stress on liberty), and 3) reinforcing the collective self-organization of people in relation to growing individualism.

With these three possibilities in mind, we move from the abstract and ideological to the personal and political, where we address the effects of the crisis in the urban spaces where the abstract explanations of the

---

1 | The unemployment rate in Spain is over 25%, in Barcelona it's "only" over 15% although the rate in the worst neighbourhood can often double that in the best one, not to mention the scandalous rates of youth unemployment all over the country that are currently over 50%.

neo-liberal discourse have now a material and real form: people at risk of losing their house, people who cannot satisfy their basic needs, people who are tired of growing waiting times, people who get demoralized with their progressive worsening of the conditions of their life. Put another way, what it is hidden by global neo-liberal ideology is indeed shown in space.

3. From Global Discourse to Everyday Life: The Scales of the Urban

Merrifield has sensibly pointed out how easily we identify the dominant role of financial capitalism in the global neo-liberalism and at the same time how easily we accept the idea that "the urban" is the natural place to contest the neo-liberal project, as the wide-ranging and relevant social movements at the present time show (Merrifield, 2013). For decades, we had witnessed with some puzzlement at first, then with much avidity to understand, a systematic oblivion of the "urban scale" in the claims of social movements. In the so-called new social movements, there has been a change in the goals and ways of organising but also a change in the scale of the issues they are concerned by. Complaints move very naturally from the smaller local (my house, my street) to the global (third world debt, environmental crisis, super exploitation of labour etc.) skipping that urban scale than once was so characteristic of social movements (as described, for example, in Castells, 1983). Notwithstanding this change of priorities, the city has forcefully remained as the place for the expression of complaints and protests. Andy Merrifield again gives a possible answer: "It is too vast, because the scale of the city is out of reach for most people living at street level; yet it is too narrow as well, because when people do protest and take to the streets *en masse*, they frequently reach out beyond the scale of the city. What is required is something closer to home— something one can touch and smell and feel—*and* something larger than life, something world-historical: a praxis that can somehow conjoin both realms at once" (Merrifield, 2011:108).

Again Lefebvre provides a framework of how to conceptualise the question in his notion of social totality, this is, society as formed by three levels of socio-spatial reality: the global, the urban, and the quotidian (Lefebvre, 1983). For him, revolution should be based on the possibility that the quotidian acts over the urban and the urban over the global although they should not be seen as separated scales but simultaneous ones. The big episodes of social fights against capitalism have not only been political events but revolutions of the urban space and of daily life; changing the world has meant changing the way that every day we live our daily life (Goonewardena, 2012). And although not comparable to Lefebvre's big cases such as May 68 in Paris or the Commune in Paris in 1871, the occupy movement fits very well into this new definition of social movement and also in Lefebvre's idea of taking urban space and the will to change the way we live our daily life. However, even though these are exciting and in some way "new" movements, our former question still remains: whatever happened to the urban scale as the target of protest at the moment when it seems that urban inequalities are growing even faster? The distinction between "the city" and "the urban" that Lefebvre so decisively stated and that has been retaken so convincingly by the urban critical theory is a key issue to answer (Brenner and Schmid, 2011; Merrifield, 2013). Despite its "tenacity", the city concept has been superseded by a changing reality to the point that it has become practically useless in many senses. A good strategy here is the idea to approach the city not as a category of analysis but as a category of practice, not as a place but as a process (Wachsmuth, 2014).

4. THE RIGHT TO (CENTRALITY AT) THE MARGINS

One of the key aspects of Lefebvre's thought is the notion of "implosion-explosion" that has also been redeployed to analyse the re-scaling of neo-capitalist forms of urbanization. (Brenner, 2000:369). The capitalist process of urbanization constantly destroys and creates urban centres to create generate new forms of urban centrality and peripheries (what I call here margins to escape from a geometrical determinism). This is a crucial point. It means that centres created by capital by definition generate new peripheries or margins left without necessary urban qualities such as accessibility, connectivity, quality of the spaces of encounter, a good urban image... Thus, in creating such new centralities, spatial inequalities are also created. The state always works in favour of mobilizing space as a productive force (planning, investment, infrastructures) and, under particular conditions, it becomes the mediator of such inequalities, regulating the worst effects of socio-spatial polarization and preserving social cohesion (Brenner, 2000). However, in the present neo-liberal context, public intervention focuses exclusively on the forms of capitalist centrality, leaving aside its mediating role (thus leading to the austerity discourse for the poor). Abandoned spaces are those with less capacity to generate profit. David Harvey, basing himself on Rosa Luxembourg's theories on imperialism, stated in his well-known thesis on "accumulation by dispossession" that capitalism needs to exploit non-capitalist territories to survive or, in other words, that capitalism perpetually needs something " outside itself" to survive as a system" (Harvey 2003:137). Harvey applies this idea, this time following Marx directly, to the notion of the creation a reserve army of labour (capitalism would expel workers outside the system to be able to use them later). The same logic can be applied to urban spaces: central spaces –this is, spaces of capital accumulation – need non central spaces as reserve spaces for future needs of expansion (Tello, 2005). Around the centres, Lefebvre would say, there are only subjugated, exploited and dependent spaces. These reserve urban spaces are in many senses "colonized spaces" with their own symbolic codes, their diverse forms of resistance, all of which is rendered invisible and dismissed (and if needed, repressed) for the sake of the colonizer, this is, the capital. In other words, centres and peripheries are immanent to accumulation of capital, immanent to the secondary circuit of capital. The more profitable locations are squeezed while the rest are of disinvestment (Merrifield 2011).

Capitalist urban dynamics always creates by definition social and spatial inequalities, in moments of expansion and creation of new central areas (with episodes of serious urban violence against individual and collective spaces of existing residents, as Neil Smith so positively theorized (Smith 1996) but also during times of crisis (with disinvestment in non-central areas, this is, without regulating the extreme effects of the polarization that is inherent to the functioning of the system). In the last decade, we have witnessed these two extreme situations and in both cases, there has been one single ideology although with different discourses. Until the outbreak of the crisis in 2007-08, the voracity of capital was obvious in massive urban transformations where the profit expectations were high. It involved the destruction of collective spaces and often involved the rendering invisible and criminalization of entire neighbourhoods while owners were responsible for vicious episodes of mobbing. The general discourse was nevertheless of extreme optimism: it was about opportunities for economic growth that benefited "the city" and that would eventually trickle down positive effects for everybody. After 2008, optimism has been replaced by the growing pessimism of inaction both in the private and in the public sector because of the lack of expectations or the lack of money to invest. However, the political action continues attached to the discourses of urban competitiveness (paving the way for private investment to levels that would have been considered unacceptable, at least on paper, until recently) and renewed urban discourses of growth that respond to the same ideology (urban regeneration, creative cities, smart cities).

In those areas, which we have called "urban margins", one can see more clearly the social effects of rising social inequalities and also where disinvestment and being rendered invisible points to a growing spatial injustice. In many ways, all complaints made from the margins are but a cry to become central, not with those centrality features that feed capital accumulation, but at the service of an improved urban collective life: "You cannot forge an urban reality (...) without the existence of a centre (...) without the actual or possible encounter of all 'objects' and 'subjects'" (Lefebvre 1976:18-19 quoted in Marcuse, 2011:19).

Centrality is therefore the essential feature of the urban and thus, it is necessary to redefine it in order to formulate alternatives. In "The Urban Revolution" Lefebvre argues that if the dialectic explosion/implosion characterizes the various manifestations of centrality that are created and destroyed, overcoming the process of creative destruction of late capitalism will involve the emergence of a "higher form of centrality" until the reaching of a radically new "space of encounter" (Goonewardena, 2011). In other words, the right to the city of Henri Lefebvre would not be anything but a "right to centrality" (Merrifield 2012).

5. Another Barcelona urban lab

"Barcelona Urban Lab" is the name of one of the projects of the 22@ Barcelona municipal company designed to consolidate Barcelona's role as an innovative city through which "companies with innovative projects can test their infrastructures and services for the future in a real environment"[2]. However, perhaps we can also think of some other ways to use the city as "an urban laboratory". We would like to think of it as a place to check the creation of centralities and as a space of resistance where experiments of counter-neoliberalisation are produced and can be assessed. At first sight, it may be somewhat shocking trying to look for growing urban polarization in an apparently successful case of urban management such as Barcelona. At the beginning of the 1980s, Barcelona was not even on the map, as proudly stated by current political leaders to highlight the international recognition achieved since then. In 30 years, the city has indeed experimented a profound urban transformation that had been widely acclaimed by politicians, journalists and not least by academics. The hegemonic discourse was one of an urban model that had presumably found the magic formula of being simultaneously capable of satisfying investors and citizens, foreigners and local people, a recipe that was able to combine economic promotion with social cohesion (Benach and Albet, 2005; Benach, 1993, 2004). The brand "Barcelona model" was used to legitimate the diverse interests involved in this process of urban transformation and at the same time to promote the city internationally but that, in the end became a taken for granted myth that did not need to prove its very existence. During the 1990s only a few realized what was going on (Benach, 1993; Lopez, 1993; Tello, 1993) and the bulk of critical visions did not appear until much later, when the problems generated by such transformations became rather obvious (Capel, 2005; Delgado, 2007; Unio Temporal d'Escribes, 2004). It can be said that such a model started showing its limitations precisely from the very moment it worked according to their objectives, and contradictions rapidly arose. In the process of stimulating the entry of capital and people (tourist), tensions, conflicts and inequalities were more and more visible (i.e. high rocketing housing prices, limited maintenance of public spaces, urban pressure on popular neighbourhoods, loss of memory and social spaces...) while the public sector was diminishing its mediating role to compensate for inequalities and polarization. The glossy city of the tourist guides had definitely another more complex and not always so bright side. After 2008, the social situation has become more dramatic with rising levels of unemployment, with many people overly indebted (with immoral figures of evictions) and visible poverty in many parts of the city.

---

2 | http://www.22barcelona.com/content/view/698/897/lang,en/

What we have been able to see in the last 30 years of urban regeneration is that renewed areas (new centralities) have always created new margins around them as reserved spaces waiting for a new round of investments. These areas are being left aside on purpose, stigmatised or rendered invisible as if nothing had ever existed there (Benach and Tello, 2013). The economic crisis suddenly stopped most real estate investments but also public expenditure was dramatically blocked, and these areas, with no economic expectations and no urban visibility, became more and more irrelevant. At a time of crisis, these reserve spaces have become "anomalous spaces", they are not central nor they have any expectation to become so, they have plenty of problems and needs but there is no public money to invest, they are outside the system. However, residents in those areas have shown enormous capacity of resistance, organization and creation of new ways to face urban pressures in the past and in the present "nothingness", they have been able to read unusually well the global roots of daily situations.

In the last few years, we have seen at least three different kinds of responses. First, the progressive creation of a global counter-discourse that started affirming the possibility of alternatives with the slogan of "another world is possible" (and it is at least somewhat curious that because the proposed alternative does not please the powerful, it has been accused of not providing an alternative). This is the example of an urban movement with complaints that are able to clearly relate local, even personal, issues with global trends. Secondly, there has been a variety of openly spatial claims such as the defence of spaces of social interaction (for example, regaining public spaces from privatization projects with self-management forms of organization), the appropriation and production of space with collective aims (from community gardens to precarious occupations by the most excluded). And, finally, the important movements related with the needs of social reproduction in defence of basic rights have to be mentioned such as housing, education or public health care (in Spain these have been called "human tides" that identify themselves for the colour they wear in mass demonstrations).[3]

What is most interesting is that, in all three cases, this resistance show how the feasibility of the triple possibility stated by Massey, in which

---

3 | A good account of these movements can be read in English in Méndez de Andés (2014).

cooperation, equality and self-organization show how to move, in a good lefebvrian sense, from the everyday space to the urban and to the global.

6. Conclusion: THE RIGHT TO RETHINK THE RIGHT TO THE CITY

There is something interesting regarding these small-scale spatial initiatives that are often analysed with undoubted sympathy but as isolated cases with no real relevance. With some good sense they have been labelled as limited "experiments of counter-neoliberalization" (Brenner, Peck, and Theodore, 2011) that are insufficient to resist the tremendous attack to the rights of people (Harvey, 2012). There are, clearly, many dangers: to have no other consequences beyond themselves, to be repressed or destroyed, to be tamed or co-opted. Many authors have called to look farther, to work in another scale, to relate what goes one in the daily sphere with global processes for which we urgently need explanatory theories. However, others have asked for caution, to avoid building theories in the air for what happens on the ground. Merrifield has widely reflected on the difficulties and huge possibilities of bridging theory and daily life practices: "Theory can guide the latter [the action]: that is its acid test. But it can only do so if it articulates within it a discourse of daily life." (1997:419) And he goes further by putting the question on how to build such an articulation elaborating from Gramsci: "knowledge and feeling should and can mutually interlock and dialectically fuel each other" (1997:427)

He has forcefully argued that nobody mobilizes for a theory, and it could thus happen that a good theory could be hardly useful. This is the case, for Merrifield, of the almost unquestionable idea of "the right to the city" that is no longer working according to its initial objective. Even before it was made banal and depoliticised as Mark Purcell has shown so well (Purcell, 2013), it was probably too abstract an idea. Merrifield has almost proposed to abandon the idea of the right to the city, seeing the city as being too vast and at the same too narrow an idea to fit the scale of people's needs and expectations. And he has found some alternative in the same works of Lefebvre, in his notion of "spaces of encounter" which, if I understand him correctly, refers exactly to that notion of the new forms of centrality (Merrifield 2013). When the city has no defined shape nor limits, nor even a clear identity in a completely urbanized planet, and when the forms of communication are increasingly virtual ones (Diaz Parra and Candon Mena, 2014) and facilitate new encounters, we should look at the emergence of new forms of encounters and new forms of spaces. Here is where rethinking the geographical scales as socially produced is most important, where spaces are crossed, the personal becomes collective, the daily life spaces become global and where these new forms of centrality can question the whole functioning of the capitalist process of urbanization.

References

Benach, N. (1993) Producción de imagen en la Barcelona del 92. In: Estudios Geográficos, LIV(212), 483-505

Benach, N. (2004) Public spaces in Barcelona 1980-2000. In T. Marshall (ed.) Transforming Barcelona. London: Routledge,151–160

Benach, N. and A. Albet (2005) Barcelona 1979-2004, entre el modelo y el espectáculo. In C. Minca (ed.) Lo spettacolo della città. Padova: CEDAM, 1-34

Benach, N. and R. Tello (2013) Les transformations du centre historique de Barcelone. Des espaces-réserve versus des espaces de résistance? (avec la collaboration de Andoni Egia et Elisabeth Rosa). In: N. Semmoud, B. Florin, O. Legros, and F. Troin (eds.) Marges urbaines à l'épreuve du néolibéralisme. Regards croisés sur les villes méditerranéennes. Tours: PUFR, Presses de l'Unversité François-Rabelais de Tours, 41-55

Brenner, N. (2000) The Urban Question as a Scale Question: Reflections on Henri Lefebvre, Urban Theory and the Politics of Scale. In: International Journal of Urban and Regional Research, 24/2, 361–378

Brenner, N., J. Peck, and N. Theodore (2011) ¿Y después de la neoliberalización? Estrategias metodológicas para la investigación de las transformaciones regulatorias contemporáneas. In: Urban, (NS01), 21–40

Brenner, N and C. Schmid (2011) Planetary urbanisation. In: M. Gandy (ed.) Urban Constellations, 20–13

Capel, H. (2005) El modelo Barcelona: un examen crítico. Barcelona: Ediciones del Serbal

Castells, M. (1983) The City and the Grassroots. Berkeley and Los Angeles: University of California Press

Delgado, M. (2007) La ciudad mentirosa. Barcelona: La Catarata

Díaz Parra, I. and J. Candon Mena (2014) Espacio geográfico y ciberespacio en el movimiento 15M. Scripta Nova. Revista Electrónica de Geografía Y Ciencias Sociales, XVIII(470). Retrieved from http://www.ub.es/geocrit/sn/sn-470.htm

Goonewardena, K. (2011) Henri Lefebvre y la revolución de la vida cotidiana. In: Urban, (NS202), 25–39

Goonewardena, K. (2012) Space and revolution in theory and practice: eight theses. In N. Brenner, P. Marcuse and M. Mayer (eds.) Cities for people, not for profit. Criticar Urban Theory and the right to the city. New York: Routledge, 86–101

Harvey, D. (1989) From managerialism to entrepreneuralism: The tranformation in urban governance in late capitalism. In: Geografiska Annaler, 71B(1), 3–17

Harvey, D. (2012) Rebel cities. From the right to the city to the urban revolution. London: Verso

Jameson, F. (2003) Future City. In: New Left Review, 21, 65–79

Katz, C. (1996) The Expeditions of Conjurers: Ethnography, Power and Pretense. In: D. L. Wolf (ed.) Feminist Dilemmas in Fieldword. Westview Press,170–184

Lefebvre, H. (1974) El derecho a la ciudad. Barcelona: Península

Lefebvre, H. (1983). La revolución urbana. Madrid: Alianza

Lopez, P. (1993) Barcelona 1992. La requisa de una metrópoli. Villes et Territoires, 217–236

Marcuse, P. (2011) ¿Qué derecho para qué ciudad en Lefebvre? Urban, (NS202), 17–21

Massey, D. (2011) Ideology and economics in the present moment. Soundings, 48(29-39).

Méndez de Andés, A. (2014) Spain's radical tide. Red Pepper, 195, Apr-May, 17–19

Merrifield, A. (1997) Between process and individuation: translating metaphors and narratives of urban space. In: Antipode, 29/4, 417–436

Merrifield, A. (2011) Crowd Politics. Or, "Here Comes Everybuddy." In: New Left Review, 71, 103–114

Merrifield, A. (2013) The Politics of the Encounter. Urban Theory and protest under planetary urbanization . Athens and London: The University of Georgia Press

Peet, R. (2012) Crisis financiera y catástrofe ambiental. In N. Benach (ed.) Richard Peet. Geografía contra el neoliberalismo. Barcelona: Icaria editorial, 265–285

Purcell, M. (2013). The right to the city: the struggle for democracy in the urban public realm. In: Policy and Politics, 43(3), 311–327

Smith, N. (1996) The new Urban Frontier. Gentrification and the revanchist city. London and New York: Routledge

Smith, N. (2009) The Revolutionary Imperative. Antipode, 41(S1), 50–65

Tello, R. (1993) Barcelona post-olímpica: de ciudad industrial a escenario de consumo. In: Estudios Geográficos.

Tello, R. (2005) Areas metropolitanas: espacios colonizados. In A. F. Carlos and C. Carreras (eds.) Urbanizaçao e mundializaçao: estudos sobre a metrópoli. Sao Paulo: Editora Contexto

Unió Temporal d'Escribes (2004) Barcelona, marca registrada. Un model per desarmar. Barcelona: Virus

Valverde, C. (2013) No nos lo creemos. Una lectura crítica del lenguaje neoliberal. Barcelona: Icaria editorial

Wachsmuth, D. (2014) City as ideology: reconciling the explosion of the city form with the tenacity of the city concept. In: Environment and Planning D: Society and Space, 32/1, 75–90

Zukin S. (1995) The Cultures of Cities. Oxford: Blackwell Publishers

Italy

Urban crisis or urban decay?
Italian cities facing the effects of a long wave towards privatization of urban policies and planning

Maria Cristina Gibelli

Considering the urban crisis and the spatial planning crisis affecting cities in advanced countries, the Italian case presents some peculiarities closely linked to reforms in spatial planning implemented in the past two to three decades. Owing to these peculiarities, exit from the crisis seems rather uncertain and difficult. Italian urban policies have been characterized by a continuous and pervasive deregulation process that has led to generalized disregard for common goods and a reduction of urban quality and livability, though not everywhere with the same intensity. What has happened is a sort of bifurcation of planning culture and planning practice, with some instances of innovative and rejuvenated planning in a few regions and middle-size cities, but a radical back-to-the-market approach in spatial planning in many others – especially large cities like Rome, Milan and Naples (Baioni, Boniburini, Salzano, 2012).

Today, the list of unsolved problems and emerging new ones is lengthy: high levels of old and new urban poverties impeding exercise of the right to the city; ceaseless agricultural and open space land consumption due to uncontrolled sprawl; poor safeguarding (or outright abandonment to degradation) of an immense cultural heritage; inertia in activating preventive strategies in a country affected in large part by seismic and hydrogeological risk, growing infiltration by organized crime in building, construction and large-scale projects, not only in southern regions but also in northern ones, particularly in Lombardy (Legambiente, 2013).

These problems combine with, and are exacerbated by, the uneven distribution of power between rent interests (landowners/finance) and public administration due to the weakness of regulation in the field of urban transformation. Instead of a tough but fair confrontation between the private and the public spheres, this condition has generated what has been called a "monstrous brotherhood" (De Gaspari, 2013), hampering the chances of exiting the crisis through advanced and forward-looking regeneration projects, improved livability and social cohesion, and advanced economic development schemes. These are the main causes of an urban crisis that I interpret as a true and unrelenting process of 'urban decay'.

Section 2 presents evidence of urban decay in Italian cities and their underlying causes. Section 3 conducts more in-depth analysis of Milan and its urban region, which still represents the economic capital of Italy, but no longer its 'moral capital', at present losing competitiveness in the European context. The peculiar kind of spatial planning adopted by the municipality will be analyzed, because it is considered to be one of the major causes of Milan's decay. Section 4 draws some conclusions.

1. A COUNTRY THAT SEEMS TO HAVE FORGOTTEN ITS PAST URBAN EXCELLENCE.

Italy is a 'country of cities', where the urban hierarchy has evolved in close and harmonious relationship with the countryside. As Carlo Cattaneo wrote[1] in the mid-19th century, in the age of "free municipalities" dating back to the medieval era, cities in the Northern and part of Central Italy became powerful hubs of political control, production of sophisticated goods, supralocal trade, financial innovation, sublime art and culture. Cattaneo maintained that their "intimate union" with the agricultural hinterland, especially in North and Central Italy, was the main reason for the formidable competitive advantage with respect to other European countries that Italian cities achieved in the long term.

This competitive advantage was very evident at the beginning of the industrial revolution, especially in Lombardy, an "industrious and

---

1 | In particular, in his essay of 1858 on "La *Città considerata come principio ideale delle istorie italiane*" (Castelnuovo Frigessi, 1972).

civilized" region (Cattaneo, 1975). Here, as in many other European regions, industrialization began in rural areas – in the dry piedmont areas – where capital deriving from primitive accumulation in a highly modernized agricultural region located south of the River Po was first invested. But a more important and generalized competitive advantage, which concerned the entire national city system, was the cultural heritage and beautiful landscape accumulated across the centuries which made Italy and its cities the destination of the *grand tour* by European intellectual élites, and which still survive despite constant assaults (Bevilacqua, 2005).

Moving to contemporary times, it looks rather paradoxical that, in a country so rich in urban history as the *"Belpaese"* (a term dating back to Dante and Petrarca), spatial planning and cultural heritage conservation have received such little attention from public opinion and large part of cultural and technical debate, especially since the 1980s. From the reconstruction period after World War II until the 1980s, urban policies, and the relative urbanization processes, generated rather controversial outcomes ranging between two extremes: from pillage of big and beautiful cities like Palermo, Naples and Rome assailed by building speculation, to some significant conquests in the fields of general interest and safeguarding the cultural heritage (the latter constantly put at risk by private-interest oriented interpretations of the Constitutional Law (De Lucia, 2006 and 2013). But a radical attitude in favor of delegitimizing urban planning and its comprehensive and regulatory approach has appeared only in the past twenty years, with the approval by Regions of many 'second generation' spatial planning laws[2] of diversified nature and deeply influenced by the political majorities ruling the individual regional governments.

In parallel, during the 1990s the country saw the political success of a radical back-to-the market, neo-liberal approach to planning policies and tools clearly influenced by the centre-right majority ruling the central

---

2 | In Italy, legislative power on spatial planning has pertained to regional governments since 1972: the first generation of laws on spatial planning (lasting for two decades) was reformed in the 1990s, giving way to legislative apparatuses, which differ, greatly across regions.

government, but which was also legitimized by strong cultural and technical support.[3]

The Italian case therefore presents significant specificities in the international context because, in the past twenty years, it has undergone one of the most radical processes of urban planning de-regulation and privatization of urban policies ever experienced in advanced Europe (Salzano, 2011)[4]. The main outcomes have been that Italy has not invested sufficiently in improving the public city, guaranteeing social cohesion, safeguarding the commons, or upgrading economic and transportation infrastructures. This is because the spatial transformation process has been mainly assigned to market mechanisms, thus weakening the essential role of the state as the regulator, and not just the facilitator, of private interests (Calafati, 2009).

It is for these reasons that, with regard to Italian cities, it seems more appropriate to use the term 'decay', rather than 'crisis' to portray and interpret what has happened: a long-lasting trend of destruction of common goods, involving above all the major urban poles but also the country as a whole, and which has relentlessly consumed open and agricultural periurban spaces around cities, irreversibly degraded wonderful landscapes and cultural heritage, and cementified coastal areas in both the densely and sparsely populated regions (Settis, 2012a). The negative effects of this decay are very evident: a constant loss of quality for both cities and countryside exacerbated by recurrent natural and human disasters[5]. This long-lasting process of urban decay has accelerated and intensified in recent years with the global crisis affecting advanced

---

3 | One of the favorite catchphrases of erstwhile Prime Minister Berlusconi was "everyone is master in their own house" (Gibelli, 2006).

4 | Somewhat comparable to urban policies under the Thatcher government, but implemented in a different phase of urban development: a phase in which qualified development had already become the main challenge for cities and their regions; not a phase of decline and deindustrialization as it was in the UK when the Inner City Policy was implemented.

5 | Italy has a fragile territory, largely artificial, second only to the Netherlands with regard to hydrogeological risk, struck by earthquakes every five years, which require constant prevention and care. Guaranteed over the centuries, this has been entirely neglected in recent decades (Guidoboni, Valensise, 2013). The failed reconstruction of L'Aquila after the earthquake, with the correlated episodes of

countries, and it has impacted on spatial planning in two ways. First, resources for the provision of public infrastructures and public goods have diminished further. Second, in very recent years, a major crisis has hit the building and construction sectors after the 'golden period' 1996-2007 when transactions and private surplus values skyrocketed.

The crisis, or better the decay, should have been countered by relaunching national spatial guidances and rules, supported by critical reflection on the negative effects of the privatization of urban policies and planning. In parallel, required at local level were new visions and strategies for cities based on a renewed attention to sustainability and livability. This did not happen; and responsible was also the considerable part of planning culture fascinated by the discourse on 'streamlining the city'. Some quantitative empirical evidence can be cited in this regard. From 1990 to 2005, the surface of cultivated agricultural land abandoned or urbanised amounted to 3,663,000 ha (more than the surface area of two Italian regions – Lazio and Abruzzo).

The loss of agricultural land was accompanied by heavy land consumption for urbanization due to the constant urban sprawl allowed by the 'flexibilization'(in fact, the delegitimization) of planning rules and tools, and the simplification of implementation procedures. However, despite the economic downturn, land consumption and soil sealing continued to grow in 2012, doing so at a pace of 70 ha/day. Northern Italy leads the phenomenon because the Lombardy and Veneto regions have permanently sealed 10% of their territory. At municipal level, Milan was top of the list in 2012, having consumed 61.7% of its open space resources, immediately followed by three middle-size cities of Northern Lombardy (Monza: 48.6%, Bergamo: 46.4%, Brescia: 44.5%) (ISPRA, 2014). Moreover, all these data are underestimated because they do not include illegal building (probably 9% in 2006; 16.9% in 2013) and 'ghost' building.

Whilst at the turn of the century, sprawl containment became an important issue on the EU's environmental agenda (EEA, 2006) and in many national policies and local plans, in Italy, despite the alarming evidence of growing public and social costs (Camagni, Gibelli and Rigamonti, 2002), no national or regional guidance to halt urban sprawl

---

corruption, the frequent collapses in Pompeii are only recent examples – reported also by the international press – of a constant assault on common goods.

was approved or implemented (with some rare exceptions in certain regional and municipal contexts) (Gibelli and Salzano, 2006).[6] Thanks to national and regional laws aimed at dismantling previous urban planning rules and operational tools through simplification of building permits procedures – by allowing cubage bonuses and even, as in the case of Lombardy, by abolishing functional land use zoning, and thanks to *condono edilizio* (legalization of illegal building upon payment of a fine[7]) – from 1995 to 2009 in Italy, at a time of demographic stagnation, 4 million houses were built: mainly second homes or buildings which did not remedy the huge housing shortage for lower income groups; or constructed without building permits[8].

Moreover, one should add the generalized weak commitment to transparency, accountability and citizen involvement and, most of all, the widespread corruption and the persisting uneven distribution of powers which favors rent interests (landowners/finance) rather than safeguarding the commons.

However, the so-called "monstrous brotherhood" is probably the main factor responsible for urban decay in Italy. With this phrase, which I borrow from De Gaspari (De Gaspari, 2012), I refer to the alliance among landowners, developers, banks and local administrations that has created a sort of parallel currency, the "cubic meter", thanks to flexible land-use plans, piecemeal public/private negotiations and extended use of TDRs. The "cubes", i.e. the building permits issued by the local administration, represent in fact a guarantee of future earnings, an asset on companies' balance sheets, and a guarantee to banks for super-loans to developers. In addition, this alliance has certainly hugely amplified the ongoing building crisis (Tocci, 2009).

With regard to the real estate sector and the burst of the bubble, we can identify another anomaly of the Italian case compared with other

---

6 | A bill on curbing land consumption has recently been presented in parliament, but it is unlikely to be approved soon.

7 | The *condono edilizio* has been approved three times by national governments: in 1985, when Bettino Craxi was prime minister in a center-left coalition; in 1994 and in 2003 under the government of Silvio Berlusconi.

8 | Between 1995 and 2006 local governments issued building permits for almost 723,509,845 square meters (60%: retail, offices, industrial spaces; 40%: marketable housing) (Bellicini, 2013).

EU advanced countries. Between 1997 and 2006, Italy's building sector registered a boom phase, with an increase in the average price of realties, in real terms, of 35% overall and 55.6% in big cities, and an increase in total transactions of 57.0%.[9] All these factors generated skyrocketing real estate prices and skyrocketing profits for developers, banks, loan brokers, real estate agents and sellers, lenders and builders.

Thereafter, starting in 2007, the crisis began. With respect to the peak of 2005, investments in the building sector decreased by 30% in 2012 (in new housing by 51%, in new nonresidential building by 39%), while housing transactions collapsed (-47%). Strangely, housing prices decreased much less (-28%), and only in the last two years. In the early phases of the crisis, whilst in other countries severely hit by the bubble burst, like Ireland, Spain and France, prices were abundantly reduced, allowing faster realization of unsold properties and an easier relaunch of the building sector, in Italy they remained substantially stable until 2010 (Figure 1).

The reasons reside in the low interest rates keeping the cost of unsold estate low; in the interest of banking institutions, because decreasing prices would reduce guarantees on their loans (the banks kept refinancing large debtors, some of whom were later investigated by the judiciary and convicted or still on trial); in the huge surplus values made in the preceding 'golden decade', thanks also to the very light taxation on real estate rents.[10]

The paradox is that, at present, 350,000 unsold residential units of poor quality and unsuited to demand are on the market, while no affordable housing has been built for a long time, while 650,000 households are still

---

9 | The record of annual transactions was reached in 2006: 1,000,000.

10 | Share of public obligations on the market value of transformations (housing):
Munich: 30-32%
Milan: 5-8%
Rome: 4-4.5%
In Rome, a recent study on important new housing schemes realized through negotiation with the public administration in the years 2000 found that the share of land rent in the market value of buildings reached 34-36%, and that the total share of land rent + profit of the financier, net of the profit of the builder and developer, reached 54-57%. (Camagni, 2008; Camagni and Modigliani, 2013).

in search of a house (whilst the Italian Constitution stipulates the right to own a dwelling: Art. 47) (Bellicini, 2013).

Another serious problem concerns the huge wastage of public money and the skyrocketing corruption associated with the so-called "great public projects" and "great events". Apparent here is another anomaly of the Italian 'governance' system: with the purported aim of accelerating decision-making, but in reality in order to avoid controls, for decades emergency procedures have been privileged. This happened, for instance, in the cases of the World Football and World Swimming Championships, the Jubilee in 2.000, and many large-scale infrastructure projects. The story is always the same: many years devoted to preliminary debates on the projects; then headlong acceleration accompanied by exemptions, direct award of contracts without competition or through rigged bidding, extraordinary powers attributed to a commissioner, spiralling costs compared to those budgeted through cost/price revisions, costly 24-hour construction sites, relaxed controls on subcontracting firms and, last but not least, growing risks of mafia infiltration.

Fig. 1: Average prices of residential units in a selected group of EU countries. (Average variations with respect to the same period of the preceding year)

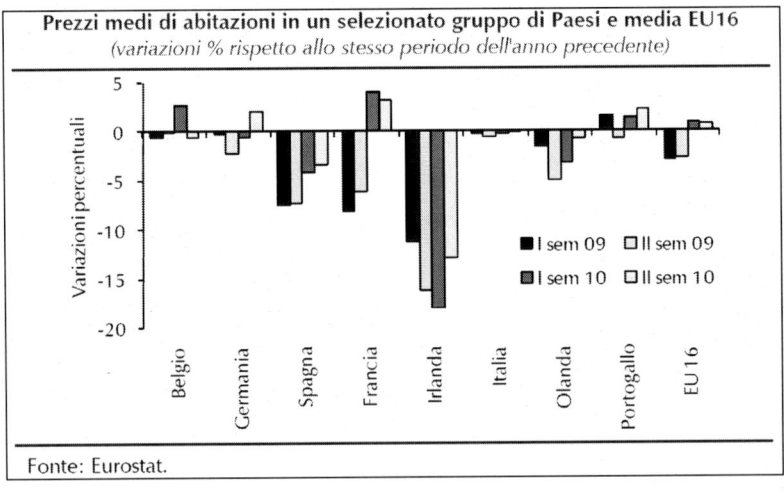

Source: Nomisma, 2012.

The more recent and striking case erupted in May 2014. It involves more than thirty persons arrested and many more investigated for corruption concerning the "Progetto Mose": the construction of underwater mobile barriers to protect the historic center of Venice from flooding when *"acqua alta"* occurs. Although criticized by many experts[11], the Mose construction work began in 2003. At present, it is one of the most expensive public projects in Italy and probably the most grievous case of corruption in the history of the country. The investigating authorities seem to have proof of huge corruption practices and of an immense flow of money for bribes: a flow deriving from the consortium of construction companies, "Consorzio Venezia Nuova", and distributed to institutions, which should have performed functions of supervision and control (local administrators, excise officers, the water magistracy, the state audit board...). If the trial will confirm the results of the investigation, this will demonstrate that since "Clean Hands" of the first '90s corruption has not stopped, but has evolved into a much more structured, costly and entrenched system[12].

Some risks are also apparent in the field of national urban and territorial planning reforms. The present government headed by Matteo Renzi seems determined to proceed towards a more simplified and market-oriented planning system. The present minister of Transport and Infrastructure, Maurizio Lupi, who will be cited below because he was the strategic initiator of the Milanese model of deregulation in urban planning in the late 1990s, recently again submitted[13] a draft bill on national principles for urban and territorial planning which is an accumulation

---

11 | The increasingly frequent episodes of *"acqua alta"* cannot be attributed to climate change alone because, in order to enable big ships, and especially cruise liners, to enter the lagoon, the access channels have been dredged and deepened, while routine maintenance work has been neglected (Mantovani, 2014).

12 | The increasingly frequent episodes of *"acqua alta"* cannot be attributed to climate change alone because, in order to enable big ships, and especially cruise liners, to enter the lagoon, the access channels have been dredged and deepened, while routine maintenance work has been neglected (Mantovani, 2014) .

13 | Maurizio Lupi had already presented a similar draft bill during a Berlusconi government in 2005. Approved by the Chamber of Deputies, the bill was not approved by the Senate because of strong cultural opposition – of which *eddyburg. it* was a protagonist – and, above all, due to expiry of the government's mandate (Gibelli, 2005).

of provisions with a specific beneficiary: the real estate sector (Ministero delle Infrastrutture e Trasporti, 2014).

Without going into details, in Article 1 (Object and purpose of the law) at Paragraph 4, the draft bill assigns to private owners the right to participate in planning in order "to guarantee the value of their property". This is the Milanese model that it is extended to the entire national territory, but, most of all, it is a reversal of a principle of the Italian Constitution which imposes constraints and obligations on private property in the name of collective utility and which states the principle of the "social function" of property (Baioni, 2014).

2. Milan and the crisis

Let us now turn to Milan's urban crisis and its spatial planning crisis. In 2012, the population of the municipality of Milan was 1,262,101, which was one-third of the total population of the province (the Milan conurbation) encompassing 134 municipalities in only 6.6% of the territory of the Lombardy region, but 30% of the population and 31% of the housing stock.

The Milan urban region extends far beyond the province and has between 4.5 and 6 million inhabitants. Land consumption for urbanization is very intense in the province: according to DUSAF[14], the anthropized areas in the province of Milan represent 39.76% of its total area (62,620 ha) and, considering the new expansions made possible by recently approved municipal plans, they reach 42.3%. With its extremely high density (1,983 inhabitants/sq.km), the city of Milan had an average annual per capita income of 31,980 euros in 2009 (the highest in Italy after Bologna).

Assuming the EUROSTAT definition, the urban region ranks 4th in Europe in terms of economic and demographic size, after Paris, London and Düsseldorf-Ruhrgebiet. Its medium-term annual average growth rate from 1995 to 2009 (GDP at current prices) was 0.4%. This was indubitably substantial?, but it was mostly determined by its past splendor, rather than by its more recent performance, which has been among the weakest of the EU, together with that of the country as a whole.

---

14 | DUSAF is the database of the Lombardy Region that since 2001 monitors the Use of Agricultural and Forest Land.

Compared with the other Italian big cities, Milan excels in living standards and certain public services (like public transport), but not in urban quality (exceeded by Bologna and Florence). Milan's most critical weaknesses –which have worsened in the past twenty years due to the local administration's urban planning policies – are over-density coupled with congestion, spatial segregation, low quality of recently-built fabric, and the irrational location of large functions in relation to transportation infrastructure. However, other major weaknesses of Milan have been highlighted by recent international comparative analyses based on quantitative indicators and the perceptions of international city-users. Urban ranking exercises refer to Milan as the capital city of fashion, design and publishing; an engine of vitality at the core of the Lombardy region; one of the richest and most advanced areas in Europe; and a modern and international metropolis. But the same analyses also underline that in recent decades the city has been unable to build a long-term vision; that it appears no longer credible in the role of national leader (the label of 'moral capital' is no longer applicable after the 'Clean Hands' investigation[15]); unable to counter the assaults of real estate and building speculation, with heavy symptoms of mafia infiltration; and burdened by worsening environmental quality and livability (OECD, 2006; Meglio Milano, 2013 and various years).

According to recent studies on competitive positioning, Milan now ranks fifth among the ten best European cities from a strictly economic point of view (number and quality of firms, advanced services, finance and congress sectors), but it is well below tenth place in regard to other aspects (science, politics, culture, international transports) (BBSR, 2011). CushmanandWakefield's annual Report on 2010 performances, based on a survey of 500 major European firms, lists Milan as twelfth, behind London, Paris, Frankfurt, Berlin, but also Amsterdam, Barcelona, Madrid, Zurich, Geneva and others[16] (Cushman and Wakefield, 2011).

---

15 | The expression 'Clean Hands' (*Mani Pulite*) denotes the investigations initially conducted from 1992 by the public prosecutor's office of Milan against exponents of the political, economic and institutional system of both Milan and Italy. The investigations uncovered a web of corruption, bribery, and unlawful party financing at the highest political, financial, and administrative levels.
16 | In particular, Milan ranks 32nd for environmental quality; 22nd for quality of life; 27th in value for money for office space.

Gone are the days when studies on Europe's urban hierarchy assigned to Milan the role of "economic capital of Southern Europe" (Camagni and Pio, 1988) and of "unique brilliant princess", ranking second after the queens: London and Paris (RECLUS/DATAR, 1989).

In sum, Milan today maintains its role as the international gateway to the large North Italian market, the main international headquarter city and the principal financial marketplace in the country, but it has deteriorated in terms of physical, urban and metropolitan structure and design, and of environmental quality, owing to the peculiar model of city planning and management pursued by the regional and municipal governments since the late 1990s mainly dedicated to 'privatizing and streamlining the city'. Milan has forged and pioneered this model in the country.

Since the late 1990s, urban planning in Milan has been based on two main principles:

- private initiative must have the main role in shaping the metropolis, without merely building upon the basic framework and rules of a well-defined public planning policy;
- public interest can ensue from private choices, and more specifically from the results of public-private partnerships (Bottini, Gibelli, 2012).

On these principles, a negotiated process of planning took place without clear rules and procedures, and without adequate transparency, growing haphazard for years. It was often unbalanced due to the relative strength and management competencies of private actors, with a communication flow that was mostly market-oriented instead of being characterized by public responsibility and accountability. The process was mainly managed by the private sector for private purposes, and it resulted in questionable renewal plans and projects devised without citizens' involvement.

Clear signals of this market-oriented planning perspective emerged in the late 1990s with the Lombardy Regional Law 9/1999 establishing the *Programmi Integrati di Intervento* whereby individual developers were expected to propose complete urban regeneration projects derogating from the existing land-use plan; and new simplified procedures of approval were established, allowing virtually any proposal to pass quite rapidly from the drawing desk to the building stage.[17] This planning model eluded fundamental principles of spatial and social solidarity and of sustainability, leaving all problems without proper solution and placing excessive trust in the invisible hand of the market.

The Lombardy Region waited for a long time before approving a second-generation general planning law, passing through various stages of progressive deregulation whose explicit aims were: simplification, acceleration, flexibilization, and debureaucratization. All these laws and rules generally tended to legitimate the experiments conducted on the living body of the city of Milan.

These general aims seemed to be inspired by the contemporary European discussion (on sustainability, urban densification against suburban sprawl, affordable and social housing, subsidiarity, strategic assessment, and monitoring of projects and plans). But the real aim, and the result, was in fact a radical simplification coupled with a downgrading of the public role in strategic choices. All assessments were confined to academic debates, without any real impact on the final decision; all the laws and rules weakened the protection of green belts or agricultural areas, even in classified regional parks; and no fixed percentage of affordable and social housing was imposed, unlike in other advanced regions and cities (for example, Emilia-Romagna).

The contribution of the planning culture was crucial: many steps in the deregulation process were strongly supported by the Milanese professional and academic milieu disillusioned with comprehensive planning. Nevertheless, a critique somehow justified by past errors and failures strongly pushed for the dismantling of the entire planning system (Palermo, 2001; Mazza, 2004; Moroni, 2007). With the enthusiastic support of all categories of owners and interest groups, the foundations were laid for a new market-oriented planning model with blind belief that public benefit would derive automatically from private initiatives, with no real checks and balances; a model quite unprecedented even in the liberal economic tradition.

---

17 | As Maurizio Lupi, now minister in Renzi's government and at that time urban planning councilor in the local government, declared: "Now investors are free to propose, and if their proposal is accepted, specific design rules are drawn ad hoc, and not superimposed" (Comune di Milano, 2001: p. V).

In Lombardy, the new regional Urban Planning Law (*Legge per il governo del territorio*: n. 12/2005) was approved in 2005: an act entirely consistent with the former free-market oriented laws approved since 1999. And the pillars of the new General Plan of Milan which resulted from the Law (*Piano di Governo del Territorio/PGT*)[18], approved by the right-wing municipal government in 2010 and adopted by the subsequent left-wing government with minor revisions in 2012, are rather questionable. Aside from a substantial reduction of the absurd development rights admitted in the 2010 version, it seems burdened by the same weaknesses and risks.

Simplified procedures for approval of regeneration projects are still in place; true subsidized rental housing is residual: only 0.05sq.m./sq.m. and only within projects of at least 10,000 sq.m. of land area, and anyway always monetizable; the "free functional mix" has been generalized to the entire urban fabric with no restraints; 182,873 new inhabitants (14% of the present total population) in an already hyperdense city are predicted[19] (Gibelli, 2012a).

Even more questionable and worrying is the use of the TDR (Transfer of Development Rights) tool in a new, generalized and 'extended' way so that development rights assigned to some properties (even in a peripheral location) are transferable anywhere in the city where development is admitted (and therefore, also in the city center) (Gibelli, 2012b)). This mechanism, present with no change in both versions of the Plan, represents in reality an undue premium to real-estate speculation[20]. The Plan does not seem to tackle either the true economic problems of the economic capital of Italy or the social and environmental emergencies. In particular, recent reports on land consumption show that in Milan urbanization grew between 1999 and 2007 by 10.5%, and that not just the municipality, but the entire northern part of the province of Milan is reaching total saturation (over 90% of urbanized land) (CRCS, 2012).

---

18 | A synthesis of the Plan, made by the technical scientific committee consisting of university researchers appointed by the municipal government is online (AA.VV., 2013).

19 | However, a much larger estimation of more than 500,000 inhabitants has been made by some critical commentators of the Plan (Boatti, 2012).

20 | See the criticisms by planners (Gibelli, Goggi), jurists (Roccella) and urban economists (Camagni) collected in a special issue of the journal "Scienze Regionali-Italian Journal of Regional Science" (Camagni, Micelli and Moroni, 2014).

Overbuilding is already high, and will be even more so in the future due to new development rights guaranteed by the master plan, with an already enormous supply of vacant office space of low quality and irrationally located.[21] The imbalance in the housing supply is a problem, with a huge availability of luxury or expensive apartments, and a severe lack of affordable and subsidized housing.

The option in favor of the free functional mix has generated through gated communities even in central areas, within large regeneration projects that could represent an outstanding opportunity for Milan to create new public spaces, better facilities, and a renewed urbanity. This is the case, for instance, of the "Citylife" regeneration project for the re-use of the old trade fair site. Designed by international archistars, this is now transformed into a luxurious residential neighborhood (over-)filled with condos and towers and accessible for pedestrians only through a patrolled gate.

The future realization of CERBA (Centro Ricerche Biomediche Avanzate) in Parco Agricolo Sud Milano – the largest agricultural park in Europe, situated in Milan's southern urban fringe and the only large 'green lung' in the city – also seems risky, as a 'Trojan horse' for wide residential developments. Also still uncertain is the future of EXPO 2015 project, located in the northern periphery of Milan: an event that since the outset had been mainly supported by rent-seeking real estate interests but presented by the public administrators as an important opportunity to relaunch Milan and the entire country. Due to long delays and the subsequent adoption of the above-mentioned emergency procedures for "great events", EXPO 2015 is now in the midst of a storm and, for the time being, stands out as an example of bad practice: with bipartisan corruption, investigations, arrests, and dramatic uncertainty about accomplishment of the project in due time[22]. Everywhere in Milan and its hinterland, what has happened in recent years is the mere adding of cubic meters, with

---

21 | At present, there are 1,500,000 sq.m. of empty offices, of which 150,000 sq.m.built in 2012 and 76,000 sq.m. in 2013. The vacancy rate is 12.6% (source: PNB Paribas Real Estate, City News Milano, 2013).

22 | Already arrested have been the general director of Infrastrutture Lombarde, the operational arm in public projects of the Lombardy Region, the general director of EXPO, the owner of a large construction company who received important contracts through bribes, and the collectors of bribes for the political parties.

almost no attention paid to new qualitative functions that could be hosted and usefully developed.

In sum, considering the planning negotiation introduced in Milan and in other cities of Lombardy, we can itemize the following weaknesses:

- a generalized lack of vision concerning Milan's economic role and the new functions that could be developed in a public-private partnership;
- lack of a comprehensive structural plan for the urban region;
- locational randomness of single projects submitted to the administration and approved in an incremental way;
- weak public control over duties assigned to private parties in planning negotiation, especially with regard to infrastructure building and provision of public spaces and facilities, not to mention the generalized low local taxation on building permits and developments;
- no transparency in the private/public sharing of surplus values and costs;
- a scandalous premium to real-estate speculation inbuilt in the new extended procedures of tradable development rights and the lack of control on urban transformation;
- densification without intensification, considering the poor and free functional mix allowed;
- overbuilding coupled with increasingly empty buildings, which boosts vacant built-up spaces;
- risk of unsustainable greenfield building amid the present severe shortage of green spaces;
- increasing qualitative mismatch in housing demand and supply and, in particular, an extreme shortage of affordable housing.

3. Some concluding remarks

In Italy, the effects of the present urban crisis have been amplified by the long-lasting and uneven distribution of powers which has favored rent interests (landowners/finance) rather than safeguarding the commons and, for at least two decades, by deregulation in urban and regional planning. These features are very evident in big cities like Milan, Rome and Naples, but they are widespread throughout the country.

Although crucially required to overcome the present crisis, strategies for a new pattern of livable and sustainable urban policies are hardly visible: local public administrations seem powerless and shortsighted, while proposals by the entrepreneurial milieu continue to be rather conventional in that they ask for incentives, tax reductions, increased development rights, and building opportunities. On the public side, one notes renewed attention to the opportunities offered by the new programming period of UE Structural Funds, but not yet a true project capability, while opportunities may arise from the recent constitution of an Inter-ministerial Committee for Urban Policies and from the recently-enacted law (Law n. 56/2014) establishing "Metropolitan Cities" (Gibelli, 2014). Nevertheless, many issues remain unresolved.

The need to rethink national and regional laws and rules in order to remedy the disastrous effects of deregulation wave is not felt to be crucial and no longer postponable, with the exception of some regional governments like those of Tuscany, Emilia-Romagna and Puglia. Likewise, building new spatial visions and relative planning agreements in order to face the crisis with new and shared rules and tools does not appear on big cities' agendas, with the (partial) exception of Bologna. Given the unbalanced powers of the public and the private sphere, low transparency and skyrocketing corruption in planning agreements, urban decay in Italy seems bound to last for many years to come.

Some signs of possible change, however, are apparent in a new consciousness arising from below (Settis, 2012b; Maddalena, 2014), the process being supported and disseminated by cultural associations and websites like "eddyburg.it". A new grass roots activism, nurtured by social networks and citizens' associations, is emerging with issues like sustainable and inclusionary urban regeneration, renewed urbanity, halt on land consumption and soil sealing, defence of the commons against privatization: for advocating, in sum, the right to the city.

REFERENCES

AA. VV. (2013) Il Piano Urbanistico di Milano (PGT 2012). The Milan Town Plan (PGT 2012), Milan,TeknoeBook,WoltersKluwer. https://docs.google.com/file/d/0By3pel23h55TRk81LXlhMFZORik/edit

Baioni M., I. Boniburini and E. Salzano (2012) La città non è solo un affare, Bologna, Aemilia University Press

Baioni M. (2014) Una proposta preoccupante, eddyburg.it, may 28.

BBSR (Bundesamt für Bauwesen und Raumordnung) (2010) Metropolitan Areas in Europe, Bonn

Bellicini L. (2013) Immobiliare, debito, città: considerazioni sui primi dieci anni del XXI secolo, paper presented at the Conference Architetture per i ceti medi nell'Italia del boom. Per una storia sociale dell'abitare a Torino, Milano e Roma, Politecnico di Milano, november 29.

Bevilacqua P. (2005) Sulla impopolarità della storia del territorio in Italia. In: P. Bevilacqua and P. Tino (eds.) Natura e società. Studi in memoria di Augusto Placanica. Meridiana Libri-Donzelli: Rome

Bevilacqua P. (2013) La Città Infernale, In: eddyburg.it, may 2.

Boatti G. (2012) PGT: il piano che non serve a Milano. In: eddyburg.it, december 23.

Bottini F. and M. C. Gibelli M. C. (2012) Milán: la difícil herencia de veinte años de desregulación urbanística.In: urban, n.3

Calafati, A. (2009) Economie in cerca di città, Rome, Donzelli Editore

Camagni, R. (2008) Il finanziamento della città pubblica. In: M. Baioni (ed.) La costruzione della città pubblica. Florence, Alinea

Camagni, R. and A. Pio (1988) Struttura economica e gerarchia metropolitana europea: la posizione di Milano nel sistema dell'Europa centro-meridionale. In: IReR/Istituto regionale di Ricerca della Lombardia (ed.) Progetto Milano. La trasformazione economica della città. Milan: Franco Angeli

Camagni, R.; M. C. Gibelli and P. Rigamonti (2002) Urban mobility and urban form: the social and environmental costs of different patters of urban expansion. In: Ecological Economics, n. 40

Camagni, R. and D. Modigliani(2013) La rendita fondiaria/immobiliare a Roma: 6 studi di caso. In: XXVII Congress of INU-Istituto Nazionale di Urbanistica, Salerno, october, 24-26

Camagni, R.; E. Micelli and S. Moroni (2014) (eds.) Diritti edificatori e governo del territorio: verso una perequazione urbanistica estesa? In: Scienze Regionali, Italian Journal of Regional Science, Special Issue, vol. 13, n. 2.

Castelnuovo Frigessi, D. (1972) (ed.) Carlo Cattaneo. Opere scelte, Vol. IV, Turin, Einaudi

Cattaneo, C. (1975) Sulla densità della popolazione in Lombardia. In: C. Cattaneo (ed) Saggi di economia rurale. Turin: Einaudi (First Edition, 1939, edited by Luigi Einaudi).

Comune di Milano (2001) Ricostruire la Grande Milano, Documento di Inquadramento delle politiche urbanistiche comunali. Milan: Edizioni il Sole 24 ore.

CRCS (Centro di Ricerca sui Consumi di Suolo) (2012) Rapporto 2010 sul consumo di suolo in Lombardia. INU Edizioni: Rome

CushmanandWakefield (2010) European cities monitor 2011, www.europeancitiesmonitor.eu.

De Gaspari, M. (2013) Bolle di mattone, La crisi italiana a partire dalla città. Come il mattone può distruggere un'economia. Milan: Mimesis Edizioni.

De Lucia, V. (2006) Se questa è una città. La condizione urbana nell'Italia contemporanea. Rome: Donzelli.

De Lucia V. (2013) Nella città dolente. Mezzo secolo di scempi, condoni e signori del cemento. Dalla sconfitta di Fiorentino Sullo a Silvio Berlusconi. Rome: Castelvecchi

European Environmental Agency (EEA) (2006) Urban sprawl in Europe – The ignored challenge. EEA Report, n. 10

Gibelli, M. C. (2005) (ed.) La controriforma urbanistica. Critica al disegno di legge "Principi in materia di governo del territorio" (approvato dalla Camera dei Deputati il 28 giugno 2005), Florence: Alinea

Gibelli, M. C. (2006) L'étalement urbain en Italie entre Villettopoli et délégitimation de l'urbanisme. In: A. Berque and C. Ghorra-Gobin (eds.) La ville insoutenable. Paris: Belin

Gibelli, M. C. (2012a) PGT di Milano: manca il coraggio o manca la sinistra? In: eddyburg.it, december 20

Gibelli, M. C. (2012b) Ma Pisapia si sta (pre)occupando dell'urbanistica milanese? In: eddyburg.it, may 6.

Gibelli, M. C. (2014) Milano città metropolitana: al bivio fra deregolazione e nuova progettualità di area vasta. In: Meridiana, (special issue Città metropolitana), n. 80

Gibelli, M. C. and E. Salzano(2006) (eds.) NO SPRAWL. Perché è necessario controllare la dispersione urbana e il consumo di suolo. Florence: Alinea

Guidoboni, E. and G. Valensise (2013) (eds.) L'italia dei disastri. Dati e riflessioni sull'impatto degli eventi naturali.1861-2013. Bologna: Istituto Nazionale di Geofisica e Vulcanologia

ISPRA (Istituto Superiore per la Protezione e la Ricerca Ambientale) Il consumo di suolo in Italia. Edizione 2014, www.isprambiente.gov.it.

Legambiente (2013) Ecomafia 2012 Lombardia. Le storie, i numeri e le inchieste della criminalità ambientale. Lombardia Legambiente Onlus, www.lombardia.legambiente.it.

Maddalena, P. (2014) Il territorio bene comune degli italiani. Rome: Donzelli Editore

Mazza, L. (2004) Prove parziali di riforma urbanistica. Milan: Franco Angeli

Meglio Milano (2013) Osservatorio permanente della qualità della vita, Milan

Ministero delle Infrastrutture e Trasporti (2014) Segreteria tecnica del Ministro, Gruppo di Lavoro "Rinnovo Urbano". Principi in materia di politiche pubbliche e territoriali e trasformazione urbana, Rome

Montanari, M. (2014) Laguna al collasso. Venezia, storia di un suicidio. In: eddyburg.it, june 5.

Moroni, S. (2007) La città del liberalismo attivo. Diritto, piano, mercato. Novara: Città Studi-De Agostini

Nomisma (2012) Osservatorio sul mercato immobiliare, february

OECD (2006) Territorial Reviews, Milan, Italy, Paris

Palermo, P. (2001) Prove di innovazione. Milan: Franco Angeli

RECLUS/DATAR (1989) Les "villes européennes". Paris: La Documentation Française

Salzano, E. (2011) Vent'anni e più di urbanistica contrattata. In: M. P. Guermandi (ed.) La città venduta, Quaderni di Italia Nostra, n. 29, Rome: Gangemi Editore

Settis, S. (2012a) Paesaggio costituzione cemento. La battaglia per l'ambiente contro il degrado civile. Turin: Einaudi

Settis. S. (2012b) Azione popolare. Cittadini per il bene comune, Turin, Einaudi.

Tocci. W. (2009) L'insostenibile ascesa della rendita urbana. In: Democrazia e Diritto, n. 1.

The city and its crises

Francesco Indovina

Since the crisis of the city is above all a crisis of resources, it seems appropriate to start by referring to a text that was very successful when it was published (in 1973 in the U.S.A. and in 1977 in Italy): James O'Connor's "The fiscal crisis of the State". The author maintained that the fiscal crisis of the State, caused by growth in public expenditure without an equivalent rise in revenue, was not the result of some abnormality in the system, or the outcome of bad administration, but constituted a need for "monopoly capitalism". Nowadays we can safely, and with good reason, expand the author's point of view: the reference should no longer be to "monopoly capitalism" but rather to "financial capitalism".

O'Connor's conclusion, which Federico Caffè adopted as his own in the introduction to the edition of 1979 of the essay, was: "To conclude, in the absence of a socialist perspective able to propose alternatives for every aspect of the capitalist society [...], trade union militancy, organisers and activists will continue to proceed in a relative theoretic void. [...] what it is felt is required is a socialist perspective that will make the effort to redefine needs in collective terms. In actual fact, even if the working class were to manage to nationalise the whole share of national income absorbed by profits, the fiscal crisis would reappear in a new form, unless both social investment and social consumption were redefined as well as individual consumption and individualist life models".

Times have changed, conditions have undergone great transformation and the forms of fiscal crisis of the State have taken on new, more dramatic aspects, but both the reference to the "theoretic void" and the need for a socialist perspective fit for the present time still seem to be valid.

1. The economic crisis

If we wish to refer to the economic crisis we must necessarily try to outline its features.

That it is not a question of a, let us say, short-term crisis seems very clear and this has been stated by many, just as it appears equally clear that the "policies" adopted to overcome it seem to be totally inefficient. But this inefficiency cannot be attributed only to the aberrant austerity policies which, imposed by Germany, have characterised the interventions of the group of European Community countries (an indirect confirmation exists of the relation singled out by O'Connor). The instruments proposed fit into "tradition" and do not seem to grasp the novelty of the crisis; this is the reason for their inefficiency. The negative outcome is the result of a refusal to look directly at the nature of the crisis that is afflicting all economies (including those not adopting austerity policies). Just as virgins were offered to the Minotaur to keep it happy, so men, women and entire countries are offered in sacrifice to the crisis, while no Theseus can be seen on the horizon who will be able to kill the beast.

The economic crisis is the offspring of a systemic change in capitalism. It was not the excess of credit that led to the "bubbles" which caused the crisis as they burst; the excess of credit is the effect, not the cause, while the latter was to be found in the new (speculative) way of accumulation of wealth issuing from the production system. Within the logic of the functioning of the social relations of production in capitalism explanations are found for the continuous increment in "capital" to the detriment of "income", and it is in this outcome that the base of the current crisis is to be found, which corresponds to a change in the substance of capitalism. The accumulation of capital appears to continue to occur according to the well-known formula 'money-commodity-money' (M-C-M), but actually the larger part has separated itself from this mechanism to create growth in capital without the production of commodities. Money has become the direct means to produce other money (we could write M-M). The value of World Finance is ten times greater than World GDP.

At the origins of the modern age, merchants, or the richest of them, acted as a "bank" and lent money to kings, princes, emperors, etc. for their adventures (mostly warlike) in exchange for a tax, often exorbitant, or for trade concessions or other advantages. Modern financiers do the same today (including some State financiers, like China); they lend to

States, regions and municipalities, encourage the middle classes to get into debt (house mortgages, consumer good finance schemes, etc.) and cover themselves against certain insolvency (the famous "bubbles") by inventing financial mechanisms (derivatives) to find who they can unload their insolvency on.

It appears obvious that this is a route leading to suicide of the social system itself, which we call capitalism; we are not saying that we are at the end of capitalism, but that the structural conditions are favourable for a change in the social regime (while political subjectivity in this direction is lacking – who, how, what, when – for ideological reasons). Buffer measures can be taken, and are, in a contradictory way, being taken, which do not reverse the tendency underway but may constitute "rest" stations along the route of the crisis train; but the convoy goes on.

For example – and this has to do with the specific theme of the city – not understanding that the crisis is not the offspring of the public finance break-up (sovereign debts), but that this break-up was born of the needs and impositions of finance, which constitutes a power in itself, and has deprived all national dimensions of strength. When national politicians are incapable and corrupt, they let their hand be taken by international finance; when they are capable and not very corrupt, they practically put themselves at its service, laying claim to both the objectivity of processes and the alleged future improvement in the situation of peoples. After colonial occupation the whole world has been colonised by financial capital. The supranational political institutions that should protect peoples against the excessive power of finance, protect the latter against peoples, also because these institutions have techno-structures at their disposal that often come directly from the financial institutions.

Common sense also suggests – and this holds not only for public finance but also for families – that debts paid with other debts cannot be the solution: the debt actually ends up taking on such a size that it will never be possible to settle it. The example of Greece, which, despite having obtained a reduction in their debt, will not manage to pay what is left, and will therefore be punished further with new restrictions, is a demonstration of how the mechanism revolves on itself.

The so-called "chain letter" is not just the expedient of those who want to cheat their clients by paying old clients' interest with new clients' subscriptions (like Bernard Madoff), but a benchmark that has been revived, though in a different form, at all levels of international finance.

Creative "finance" and its specific instruments, which, though resisted, are continually renewed, are used by international finance that has determined a new economic structure in which it adds to "wealth" production by direct exploitation of workers, peoples being shorn to pay debts, and "builds" a world of depression and ever greater inequality. The 'financialisation' of the economy and the speed of technical progress are clenching the world social-economic system in a deadly grip, in which superfluous capital and superfluous labour do not find (and cannot find, the way things are) real employment.

Real economics, in this picture, seems like an appendix to financial economy, at the same time insignificant and useful. Useful for accumulating those resources that the contraction of demand still permits, to then be "withdrawn" by finance; insignificant because it is an increasingly modest share of total "wealth" (which actually does not exist, but whose existence is determined by the decision to "want to settle debts").

Awareness is increasing in many observers that the social pyramid of various countries is undergoing deep tensions and changes. The middle class has become greatly compressed, an outcome that is taking away one of finance's privileged "markets" (this was the class that supplied the various forms of demand for getting into debt: house mortgages, loans for consumer goods, etc.), while the market of the old and new rich does not guarantee general accumulation. The compression of the middle class, moreover, produces a fracture in continuity between the different social strata, often compromising, but also a source of conflict and contrast, of development and organisation of mass struggles.

2. THE CITY IN THE CRISIS

The reverberation, so to speak, of the phenomena mentioned above (though briefly) on the government of the city and territory is one of the dramatic aspects of the current situation, also because the policies that are adopted end up unloading their outcomes precisely on urban organisation.

Local Authorities have always been praised as the political link that more than any other could exercise the promotion of democracy. The "closeness" between political decision and the people should (could), in fact, constitute a virtuous relationship, making politics (the Local

Authorities) more sensitive to the needs of the population and, at the same time, making it possible for the population to pay greater attention to politics and to their electoral choices (voting with their 'feet'). It is well-known, however, that this virtuous relationship did not work anything like as much as hoped for, with both sides being responsible, and especially due to indifference and uneasiness on the political side. The latter, basically, did not like the oppressive control of the population and did not accept that conflict, an expression of the needs of the people, could become a fundamental fact for "good politics". The crisis of democracy is not, in effect, just national, but also local.

The worsening of the situation of cities, as an effect of the economic crisis, has actually made local politics less self-referential in some cases, due both to the obvious privations in the life of many men and women and to the growing pressure of the population and respective organisations (traditional and new, structured and casual) for decisions to be taken that would help alleviate the situations of hardship. But this change in attitude has not, generally speaking, had positive outcomes.

The hardships the population face because of the crisis are added to the structural ones produced by traditional economic mechanisms. In particular, the most important phenomena concern: poverty, unemployment, growing demand for economic support, increased demand for services, the housing issue (its absence and cost), assistance for the elderly and disabled. Fundamentally, the phase in which each one could imagine cancelling out the shortfalls arising at an urban level (dissatisfaction with services, housing situation, quality of the environment, etc.) with his own resources (a sort of privatisation of solutions), seems to be followed by a phase in which the demand for more cities, a better city and an increase in public intervention is strong and significant.

Note that relative poverty in 2013 at a national level was at 12.6% of the population, while the figure for absolute poverty was 7.9%. The data are worse for the south of Italy, and for large families and those with an elderly head of family.

That the crisis is deeper in Southern Italy is confirmed by other data: in this area the number of people in a state of absolute poverty rose by 725,000 in 2013, to reach a level of 3,072,000. The relative poverty figure also has a severe influence in Southern Italy, reaching 26%, compared with 6% in the North and 7.5% in the Centre. The worst situations are seen in families resident in Calabria (32.4%) and Sicily (32.5%), where a third of the sample is relatively poor.

This is not all: monthly expenditure fell by 4.3% between 2012 and 2013, while 65% of families reduced the quality and quantity of their purchases. Credible statistics do not exist for homeless people, forced to live on the street or in makeshift living spaces. Only the Caritas, a Catholic church facility, distributes meals and offers some beds for the night; in its reports the Caritas highlights that immigrants are diminishing in proportion to an increase in Italian citizens, that it is often a case of families and not individuals, that the Italians have a mean age double that of immigrants and are mostly unemployed, and so on. A dramatic picture (if we consider that in Orvieto and Todi, two cities of average size not considered at the epicentre of poverty, last year the Caritas distributed 30,000 meals).

In Milan, the economic capital of the country, average monthly expenditure in 2013 was 2,874 euros, against 3,068 in 2012.

Faced with this situation, Local Authorities have less and less resources at their disposal. Whereas the reduction in State transfers continues to be constant, fiscal revenue (direct or per share of national taxes) is lower due precisely to the economic crisis and, in the economic difficulties of families and businesses, the tendency towards tax evasion is greater. Then a number of Local Authorities are in debt both with banks and suppliers (and while the former are those that impose settlement according to the commitments made, the latter tend to get postponed over time, thus contributing to depressing the economy).

Finally, the stability pact is a burden on regional boards, imposed by the European Community on Member States and passed on to the regional boards by the Italian government, introducing an expenditure ceiling also for those Authorities that had their own resources (the more virtuous local boards end up suffering greater penalisation).

The result is that many municipalities (a couple of hundred) find themselves in difficulty, on the verge of "bankruptcy". We are not just speaking about large municipalities like Naples, Catania, Reggio Calabria, Messina, etc. but also small and medium-sized ones. And if the government intervened to save Rome (with the Rome capital law), for the other municipalities it does little.

In this situation, which will certainly last a long time (each year the end of the crisis is announced but then postponed till the following year), the Authorities are in a cleft stick between limited resources and the growing demands of the population, with no capacity to intervene. "Pressure" on Local Authorities often becomes intimidation against administrators or technical office staff: wrecked cars, threats against people and their families, car tyres slashed, front doors burnt down, etc. In 2013 the ascertained cases of intimidation were almost 300 (nothing being known of those not verified). Being closest to the population, the Local Authorities end up being pinpointed as responsible for the social disasters.

It is useful to give a brief outline of the situation in many Italian cities:

- growing social polarisation and a reduction in the "middle class". This is a condition that tends to disintegrate the "social continuity" which, though it made turning demands into conflicts more complex and less straightforward, guaranteed them a manageable political outlet;
- deterioration of collective services with increasing phenomena of exclusion of the most needy social strata, thus substantially reversing the actual purposes of those services;
- abandoning of any urban maintenance action, with consequent worsening of liveability of the city;
- deterioration of the environment (quality of the air, for example) due to a reduction in controls and to the choice of more outdated technological solutions that cause greater pollution (e.g. means of transport), etc.

Each of these situations could be subdivided into various sub-items able to specify better the condition referred to, but for the purpose of this article the list proposed appears adequate.

At a municipal level, too, the crisis does not hit everyone in the same way, to the extent that social segments can be singled out that have obtained economic advantages, and continue to do so, from the crisis. In this situation it would be advisable to go into detail as regards the hardships, so as to define coherent political action; territorial authorities also have the knowledge to define ranges of realistic hardships.

Segments of population exist, in fact, that for their demographic condition alone prove more at risk than others (the elderly, large families, unmarried mothers, the disabled, etc.). If the grid of economic situations (unemployed, pensioners, temporary workers, etc.) is superimposed on the previous breakdown, then the conditions of hardship are multiplied but their features become clear. The formation of a map of hardship conditions should be a reference point for organising Local Authorities' interventions. But this singling-out operation is not always carried out.

The conditions the local boards work at concern: the universality of collective services (even if weakened by part-payments and the like), progressive nature of taxation (never respected), liability towards creditors (more or less upheld depending on the power of the creditor), administrative transparency (virtually a fantasy), proper administration ('after' spreading corruption), defence of common assets (often neglected and abandoned), democratic nature of decisions (subordinate to the power of strong contracting parties), responsibility for urban quality (best not mentioned). These conditions are expressed and applied in a variety of ways in the different situations and actually contribute to determining the quality of the different cities, also creating their capacity to intervene.

"Good politics" in this situation should suggest to the Local Authorities that they increase their economic availability and aim at reducing their citizens' claims. Neither of which is easy.

Regional Authorities, encouraged by the European Community and the government, as well as being drained by mass media pressure, picked out the sale of their property assets as the first operation to be carried out. The sale of these assets (social housing, abandoned buildings, ex barracks and factories, land and endless other kinds) is truly absurd: it impoverishes the seller (i.e. the community) giving short-lived "relief" that cannot be repeated (a part of these assets, not actually useful at an operative level and insignificant from the cultural and historic point of view, could also be sold with discernment).

But precisely because the seller is "forced" to get rid of some assets, the buyer finds he has a handful of good cards that he uses first of all to undervalue the property and then to place "straightjacket" conditions. The Public Authorities (local and national) are practically forced, in these conditions, to undersell rather than sell. But this is not enough, the buyer's interest, as is obvious, is to transform the acquired property functionally and volumetrically, so the purchase is strictly tied to a change in intended use and an increase in size. Change in future use and volume is not a "crime" in a city that is changing, but it is nevertheless a case of very delicate operations, which change the pressure of population in that specific zone (including traffic), requiring services to be provided that were not envisaged, etc. Altogether, "changes in use" do not respect a "project for the city" but are just an opportunity to make "cash".

With discerning politics Local Authorities' property assets (but also national ones) could partly be reactivated for collective, social and productive purposes without the need to sell, perhaps by proposing self-restoration and self-renovation mechanisms on the part of those who will use them in the future (housing, handicraft production, innovative businesses promoted by young people, etc.).

But the municipalities' assets do not only consist of property, under the greedy eye and claws of finance; there are also many services that the authorities provide for citizens through their own, or participated, companies (water, electricity, refuse collection, etc.).

It was stated in a report submitted by the Deutsche Bank to the European Commission (2011) that Italian municipalities show high potential for privatisation. This bank, as is well-known, is an expert in financial operations that dispossess peoples. Essentially, the European Union suggests this and the national government presses for it; they would like many of the services provided by local companies belonging to the municipality to be privatised, too. A trend all to the advantage of the citizens: services will be managed better, companies will achieve adequate levels of efficiency, citizens will have better services and, perhaps, will pay less for them. Moreover, the possible losses of these private businesses will not weigh on the Local Authorities' budgets (but will end up weighing on family budgets). This efficiency-minded ideology has been contradicted by experience: private companies that took over to achieve the desired levels of remuneration for capital invested have raised tariffs or caused services to decline (contradicting the fact that privatisation is to the advantage of the people).

We cannot fail to acknowledge that management of these services has often constituted centres of waste (and not infrequently of corruption); departing from this situation, however, it would be easy to improve their efficiency and the satisfaction of families. The fiscal crisis of the organisations and the subsequent reduction in the capacity of Local Authorities to create investment in these companies have thus become the justification for boosting privatisation.

It is precisely the lack of resources that tempts Local Authorities to put these companies on the market, with a consequent impoverishment both of the Authority and the citizens forced to cope with rising tariffs. We are basically faced with an attempt to take the companies providing services away from the communities, so as to make money machines of them, with no respect for meeting the needs of the people, especially the weaker strata.

The situation of indebtedness to the banks is different ('rubbish' bonds included) and constitutes another painful issue in their financial circumstances. Reorganisation of the debt should at least be obtained: repayment periods, reduction in rates, etc. But the contractual power of the Authorities is weak also due to the absence of central support from the State. As already said, many are the authorities on the point of collapse.

Expenditure reduction that many municipal authorities are "forced" to take into consideration causes deterioration in services and makes the economic situation worse (less employed, less consumption, more depression). To counter the reduction in expenditure some municipalities are adopting an increase in tariffs (for example at nurseries), thus causing exclusion of strata of population unable to pay possible increases.

Help for needy families is also being reduced: authentic assistance for poor families, rent contributions, "credit" vouchers, home-helps, etc. This phenomenon also tends to affect employment, with cuts in a large number of "auxiliary" staff, even if temporary (ranging, for example, from traffic controllers, refuse collectors, nursery school teachers, etc.).

Moreover, municipalities in difficulty tend to reduce investments in city maintenance (public spaces, public buildings, etc.). This non-intervention trend not only affects the quality of the city but also employment levels.

Confined between the lack of resources and pressure from citizens (electors) and lacking in instruments coded for suitable intervention, the scarcity of resources tends to prevail, namely a "cuts" policy. Consequently, the hardships caused by the critical situation tend not to be counteracted in the work of local government. There is therefore an accumulation of negative situations of the crisis upon individual citizens: unemployment, reduction in available income, etc., to which cuts in Local Authority services are to be added.

Is it possible to follow different paths to meet the needs of the people halfway? We would need to reject the "realism" ideology" (this is the situation and nothing can be done) to face "reality" (a line that some Authorities are trying to follow, albeit with some contradictions). These are the paths that should be followed:

- take resources where they are available;
- temporarily suspend the universal nature of collective services;
- develop and increase democratic mobilisation processes.

Territorial Authorities have very limited tax-raising ability (nowadays on the increase) and are therefore not able, even if they wished, either to follow equalising, forward-looking politics and thus have an influence on growing inequality, or to collect enough resources. Various paths could be followed in this case.

If, for example, one of the factors causing hardship was the housing question (eviction, impossibility of access to the free market, etc.), the Authority could lead some initiatives for agreements with property owners, fixing lower rents, suspending evictions, etc. or, in the absence of collaboration from property owners, proceed to requisition empty houses, assigning them to the "homeless" (at agreed rents). The opening up in this case of a possible dispute should not be feared, also because it might be the opportunity to make it clear that "ownership" does not solve the problem of housing and that the reduction of social hardship in this sector constitutes a priority element in a responsible society. It would, moreover, be a case of an intervention aimed at opposing the unjust inequalities that are criticised in words both from the point of view of "civilisation" and because of their depressive effects on the economy, but which are actually on the increase.

Those measures that momentarily suspend the universal nature of the rights of citizenship assured of collective services should move in the same equalising direction. The new conception of welfare that is trying to find a way into our society envisages that collective services be guaranteed only for the "needy", a decidedly adverse conception of the rights of citizenship which violates the principle of universality, uniformity and accessibility to those rights. What is proposed does not exclude anyone from the use of collective services but should temporarily modulate rates in relation to the economic condition of the family and the individual, especially because of the crisis. Poor transparency of the distribution of wealth creates doubts on the applicability of this principle, but the Local Authority might have direct knowledge of the economic situation of each family and try to define parameters that will be more accurate than tax statements very often are.

Furthermore, the cost of many municipal concessions, such as, for example, stall-renting, could be modulated following an evaluation of the differences in profitability such concessions produce.

These and other similar measures may be deployed based on the wide-ranging group of activities and services provided by the Local Authority. In order that these initiatives do not take on overtones of arbitrariness, however, commitment is needed for considerable development in democracy, which is not to be assumed just as an instrument of "control" over who is governing, but for the positive contributions it can produce in terms of reciprocity of solidarity.

By this term we wish to denote something very different from what the simple term solidarity refers to, i.e. in this case individual members of the community taking on tasks, including management, which guarantee everyone collective continuity and quality of, for example, a service, and direct support of the action of the population following the paths mentioned above.

Mobilisation of the population is meant, aimed at enhancing the democratic tone of a given territorial reality by means of specific instruments and initiatives. Concrete forms of "direct democracy", with a deliberative capacity, can be linked and related to the traditional forms of "delegated democracy", reviving the latter. Just as forms of direct collaboration in the administrative management of services and the different operative functions of a territorial board can enable greater levels of efficiency and efficacy.

Nowadays an aversion to delegated democracy, historically given, is increasingly manifest; I do not believe we can do without this form of democracy but it needs to be revived, linking it with forms of direct democracy (decisional and managerial).

Voluntary experiments that have been carried out over time are well-known, such as the "time bank", and also the good "council" results (think of schools), as long as these had power; just as well-known are the chances to save created voluntarily by the "farmers' markets", or by the autonomous organisation of the GAS (ethical purchasing groups), etc. We have no problem with the capacity of single groups to voluntarily organise themselves and be operative, but a leap in quality and quantity seems necessary, precisely because of the crisis: local Authorities can and must help these initiatives with contributions to organisation. It is not a case of a route out of the crisis or of outlining different social set-ups, but they do undoubtedly contribute and help to alleviate the discomfort.

It is with extended mobilisation engaging the different groups in specific actions and functions at the disposal and for the use of everyone that what we have called reciprocity of solidarity comes into being.

3. Conclusions

If people who find themselves in growing numbers in conditions of discomfort, on the one hand, hope and request global solutions (national and international), they can, on the other, immediately transform their discomfort, so to speak, into demands to the Local Authorities (the close level of government). Local Authorities, however, have been hit by the same fiscal crisis as the State, with a reduction in resources. Growing "demands" and lower "resources" constitute the claws that tend to crush the Local Authorities' capacity to operate.

The latter are the stage upon which the devastating effects of the crisis are more obviously manifest and where, with just as much evidence, the incapacity and impossibility of giving satisfactory answers to the situation are shown. Authorities also tend to follow lines of intervention that are not only ruinous but tend to worsen the present situation (reduction in services, increase in tariffs, exclusion of maintenance, etc.) and the following one (alienation of own assets). National governments have unloaded the growing social contradictions the crisis was producing onto the Local Authorities (politics has an unbearable level of cynicism).

From what has been said, it is clear that the Local Authorities are not able either to combat the crisis, or to tackle the hardships generated by it. Yet some slight possibility of alleviating the discomfort does exist: by rejecting the prevailing pathways, opposing privatisation processes, using one's own property assets appropriately and appealing to the social forces on the grounds of a principle of reciprocity of solidarity, administrators can mitigate the effects of a crisis, the end of which, despite the predictions, is not in view. Some Authorities are trying, but they are few.

Reference

O'Connor, J. (1973) The fiscal crisis of the state. New York: St. Martin's Press

When it rains, it pours

Urban poverty in a metropolitan suburb during the crisis period

Alberto Violante

1. Premise: Crisis and Urban Poverty

Urban poverty, and poverty in general are subjects that are regularly discussed, so rather than getting lost in such a complex issue, this article will concentrate on analysing poverty within the limitations of a theoretical study restricted to changes in an urban setting using a real case study on Rome's 13th District. It is an interesting case because it is a suburb that has shown demographic growth within a metropolis that has witnessed the rapid development of the job market followed by its equally rapid post-crisis decline. This report will cover only those aspects that deal with the effects of the crisis within the limitations described, but a likely hypothesis is that this crisis will have a profound effect on the urban scenario. It is precisely why the crisis is a useful testing ground for the analyses made.

The concept of poverty changed during the 90s in particular, following the previous slump – and resulting poverty – at the end of the 80s, which has already been widely documented and analysed and formed the basis for the way local social services were structured in the noughties. It also meant that poverty was no longer linked solely to the issue of income but also to the effects of being out of work (social exclusion). Later, the *subjectivity* of social risk was emphasised, and poverty, in the true meaning of the word (vulnerability) was seen to encompass a much broader public altogether.

The first question to consider is whether looking at social exclusion and vulnerability is enough to get to grips with the true impact of social disadvantage in the context of a metropolitan suburb facing crisis. The second, dealt with as part of the theoretical discussion, deals with the relationship between urban poverty and the social polarization generated by the job market, specifically that of a service industry such as Rome's. The third and final point looks at whether social neediness has increased in the post-crisis period and how social services have managed such an increase. These three issues together make it possible to evaluate the way social services work, against the background of what has been recreated in the documentation covering the last decade. A brief review of the debate on poverty, specifically urban poverty, is also necessary if these questions are to be answered. After this, changes in the Roman metropolis, where this case study is set, will be analysed and followed by a brief summary of the conclusions drawn.

2. Poverty: FROM FINANCIAL POVERTY TO SOCIAL EXCLUSION AND VULNERABILITY

During the 90s, the concept of poverty was juxtaposed with notions of social exclusion and vulnerability, two categories born of the debate on poverty that can be encapsulated in two theoretical principles: the multi-dimensionality of the properties needed to measure deprivation; and individualization of the problem of inequality, an issue that initially affects one person at a time. These are the factors – according to European literature – that bring about the transition from mere poverty to social exclusion. The concept of social exclusion as compared to that of poverty should, in theory, imply that there is a dichotomous situation amongst that part of the population that can be said to be in difficulty, significant enough to make it evident (Procacci 1997) that this transition marks an abandonment of equality as a category, in favour of paying attention to absolute marginality. Indeed, the origins of the category can be traced to the levels of unemployment across Europe following the restructuring of industry. It is precisely because the concept of social exclusion was born of the theoretical assumption that paid work was irreproducible – and its importance was therefore diminished – that empirical research in Europe has tended to show that social exclusion was not caused exclusively by unemployment (i.e. lack of paid work). Over time, attention shifted to other determinants: the instability of the nuclear family, loneliness and substance abuse are all factors extraneous to income that can have a chronic effect on poverty and prevent the individual from re-entering the job market and transform his situation into one of exclusion. In America, the debate has focused on how some neighbourhoods might contribute to creating this combination of circumstances, particularly with regard to minority groups (Mingione, 1996).

Even though attempts to explain poverty and social pathology were part of the European debate (Wacquant 1992), the aspect explored was that poverty should be seen as an individual process and what needs to be identified is what causes it and the (absence of a) way out. Data – particularly from countries with higher rates of per capita income and universal welfare, indicated that there are a many more people who experience a period of poverty than those who are permanently unemployed (Whelan, Layte and Maitre 2003). That, however, involves two paradoxes: The first is that during the very same period in which this broad vision of social difficulties was predicated, the government was increasingly inclined to limit any expansion of the scope of where welfare could and should intervene. The second is that although unemployment is not the cause of all difficulties, it nevertheless seems to be an extraordinarily credible predicator not just of monetary poverty but also of deprivation as measured in all its various components, including relationships (Gallie, Paugam and Jacobs 2003). This aspect makes it difficult to overcome the centrality of the work arena, which was – as set out above – part of the discussion that led to the concept of social exclusion. That said, a causal sequence that begins with the absence of work to and progresses to the depletion of social capital, which is implicit in any consideration of the greater social exclusion experienced by the unemployed, would only hark back to an economism that would fly in the face of the initial desire for greater complexity. Levitas (2006) even pointed out that it is often the person with a job who stands in the way of relational life.

How was the relationship between poverty and personal biography investigated? Single episodes of poverty effect many more people than "just the poor" in all countries. In southern Europe however, poverty tends to attach itself to the same people and the gateway to poverty is mostly due to an increase in need rather than a reduction in resources (Layte and Whelan 2003). In Italy, these characteristics coalesce with the concentration of indigents in the south. The main feature of poverty in the south is not just that larger families continue to suffer from the "quantity" of work, but that the "quality" of work available – precarious and underpaid – is also an issue, and the only escape would be stable employment. The combination of all these characteristics have been described (Morlicchio, 2012) as the Italian model. Negri and Saraceno (2000, 196) were already referring to "low income individuals and families" in the late 90s, and they noted that "even the slightest change in their needs and their earning capacity plunges them below the poverty line". Poverty in Italy therefore, is more about low income and precarious employment than the absence of a family support network and healthcare problems: even age-induced poverty is the result of discontinued or interrupted contributions. Some studies (Lucchini and Sarti, 2005) show that the factors that affect the more extreme aspects of socio-economic difficulties are the same as those found in the "Italian model" described above. Studies undertaken by the Bank of Italy (Brandolini, 2005) also include social position as a factor on the basis that the risk of sinking into poverty is higher in the families of the employed (i.e. on a pay roll) and less if the breadwinner is an entrepreneur, self-employed or a professional. By virtue of that evidence, Sgritta (2011) observes that the issue of distributive justice (beginning with incomes set by the job market) must be brought back to the centre of the debate, with structural disadvantage as the starting point.

The second characteristic of social exclusion is in fact that it has drawn greater attention to the individual relativity of the degree of difficulty. In the hypothesis put forward by Sen (1984) an innovative approach to economic poverty based on "capability" was based on the idea that poverty is that "the adequacy of the economic means cannot be judged independently of the actual possibilities of "converting" incomes and resources into capability to function. [...] Income adequacy to escape poverty vary parametrically with personal characteristics and circumstances" (111). One of the original academics involved in the debate pointed out that logically, if that thesis was turned on its head, it might infer that

"with regards to the loss of a person's "inclusion status", we would have to consider not only a person's individual situation, but also the extent to which he or she was responsible for it" (Atkinson 1998, 14).

This is fundamentally approaching the concept of vulnerability, which has been a key word in the Italian debate on these issues (Ranci, 2002). This concept, born of the studies on development, is defined by Ranci as a situation in which the capacity of a person for self-determination is precluded from liable inclusion in the system of social resources and material guarantees. Vulnerability is the impossibility of facing risk which Ulrich Beck defines as considering what choices to make rather than sitting passively as a bystander by. Concentrating on the condition of poverty as an individual was something that had already been done in an Italian study (Benassi, 2002). There are two new aspects considering vulnerability: The first of which is more widespread at a horizontal level and incorporates permanent risk (precarious employment) —which threatens an entire lifetime – rather than unpredictable risk – unemployment, which only comes about within situations determined by one's working life. The second occurs more on a vertical plane because, as Ranci says, "the distribution of risk is certainly influenced by the class one belongs to, but not to the extent that one can conclude it is linked to the class structure of our society in any way that is coherent" (2008, 168).

In order to understand vulnerability, the problem of precariousness in the job market is key, just as unemployment lies at the heart of social exclusion. In the mid-90s, a series of reforms[1] introduced in Italy deregulated the job market by raising the quota of atypical work and jobs for women. This process was met with ambivalence and inevitably contributed to the transition of the familiar, single income model: "The diffusion of precarious jobs (or better still, of contracts) amongst adults who are not the head of the household should not be viewed in such a cut-and-dried fashion as a signal of job insecurity, let alone one of disassociation" (Saraceno 2002, xvii). The distribution of job opportunities would therefore be of particular importance to women; even if according to Reyneri and Scherer (2008) female inactivity only decreased in the North and not amongst the youngest. Job insecurity was seen to be only a transitory issue (Cavalca 2010, 383). According to Fullin (2002, 572)

---

1 | The OECD index on the deregularization of the job market rose by 1.6 points in Italy between 1990 and 2003 (OECD 2004) despite the fact that in reality, the reforms simply remodeled the situation regarding job insecurity that already existed.

"the risks that accompany uncertainty about job continuity [...] are often cushioned by the immediate family and do not therefore – or so it would seem – aggravate the symptoms of vulnerability".

This implies that changes to the job market would help avoid the "exclusion trap", especially as far as women were concerned, although the effect would be to make them – and the other "new" kind's workers – more vulnerable. So-called "familialization" – a strategy adopted in Italy to protect people from the risks of being vulnerable – does however, raise the problem of multiplying inequality, given that family resources shared with the vulnerable member of that family vary from one family to the next and that makes them unequal.

3. Urban poverty

The discussion about poverty is summarized in the preceding section of this chapter, but urban "adjectivization" needs to be further explained. Poverty, as a distributive phenomenon is not especially urban in nature – in fact rural areas are usually even poorer – but this particularity has been associated with two ideas: one institutional, that explores how local institutions respond to the ramifications of local poverty and the other economic in nature.

3.1 Urban poverty in an institutional context: local welfare

Urban poverty has been seen as a social process, created at local level by the institutions, since the 90s. Paugam (2000), interpreted this point of view by highlighting how the welfare system had an indirect effect on the social rendering of how a poor person is viewed, drawing a line between those who deserve social support and those who do not. This line creates national models of social stigmatization, based not only on criteria regarding eligibility and / or disqualification, but also by what the poor person in question has to provide (information) as part of the process of seeking assistance.

Italy was more concerned with a substantive interpretation of this decline of urban poverty as an institutional contextualization, so the focus was restored on what happens locally. The threshold for accessing help, and the extent and duration of this help, produces a different model for the exact same path of poverty experienced in different places. The idea is that the process of decentralizing social policies induces local authorities to create their own models for social services designed for the specific urban situation in which they are provided and that, therefore, contributes to the different paths poverty takes in different cities. In this sense, local welfare is part of the local community, connecting a combination of actors and needs produced in a particular urban context, and it provides a more efficient response than could be dispensed on a national basis. (Andreotti, Mingione and Polizzi 2012). In Italy, this issue has become relevant throughout the last decade and following in 2000 the passing of a framework law on social assistance and the creation of Title V of the Constitution. The latter delegates the responsibility for this problem to the Regions, and leaves the task of planning and providing assistance through a local planning instrument to the local areas themselves. Research concentrated on creating these instruments, the capacity to coordinate the various actors – institutional or otherwise – and to promote participatory processes that supported the programming of social services to meet the needs expressed throughout their respective local territories. It is not by chance that research results are always based on the formalization of governance processes rather than the achievement of any objectives. (Paci, 2008). The degree to which local planning instruments have been able to contain levels of local poverty remains to be seen. This is partly necessary, because there is a chronic lack of reliable data at council and sub-council level and there is no definition of what minimum levels of assistance are due. This leads to the provision of services not only extremely variable between one city and another (Kazepov and Barberis, 2013), but is also, depending on the planning processes that have been activated and the availability of resources – reflected in the ever-present difference between councils in the north and those in the south – dangerously discretional.

3.2 Urban poverty as an economic context: social polarization

It has already been mentioned how the economic structure affects poverty by conditioning class structure. In the same years that Europe was talking about social exclusion, an article appeared in America (Mollenkopf and Castells, 1991) saying that advanced services would create one employment structure built around a hub of ultra-qualified professions and another, in the tertiary sector, that was low-paid. They believed that a new division of social work, particular to urban systems, would increase inequality and as a result the number of those susceptible to poverty increased. Other writers have challenged or criticized this view, maintaining that a two-tiered city hides much greater social differences. Hamnett (1994) argued that if London was showing signs of increasing inequality on the issue of salaries, there was none indicating professional polarization. Objections were raised, arguing that there was no duality in the levels of professionals in Europe because on the question of jobs, it was all about who had one and who did not (Burgers, 1996). This dichotomy was extremely dependent on the conditions of benefits offered by the various welfare states and there was no sense, therefore, in imagining that the processes of economic restructuring would be univocal (Hamnett, 1996). These issues are consistent with the one on social exclusion and have brought about the idea that a model European city does exist (Kazepov, 2004) and is characterized by the institutional capacity to smooth over any excessive inequality.

In this case, welfare is also central to the conceptualization of urban poverty. It is not intended to be seen as a local component, but rather an institutional one (at a Nation State level) that is capable of modifying the social make-up and acting on the post-industrial division of labor (Lehto, 2001). The contextualization of poverty in the urban environment is limited to recording poverty's different processes, without looking at the city in which they are produced (Sgritta, 2010). Instead it was debated whether or not the post-industrial Italian model resulted in the creation of a new service proletariat trapped in low-paid work (Paci, 1995) or if limited freedom impeded training (Becchi, 1996). It should be noted that even the American empirical research (Appelbaum, Benhardt and Murnane 2003) demonstrates that it is not necessarily the concentration in third sector's employment markets that brings about a polarization of wages, but rather the absence of strong industrial relations and organizational improvements within the company that feed this segmentation of the employment market.

In general, we have seen indications that the literature has moved on from analyzing poverty by only considering income, to include the relationship, which has an economic dimension and the capacity to be inserted into the employment market. The welfare policies that favor local employability leave the re-insertion of people with multiple problems to

Social Services. The problem raised by the polarization of the debate at an urban level is that post-industrial employment markets can create social polarization, and even this places those in employment in the category of at risk of poverty. However, paradoxically this is understandable when read from a classic prospective on poverty.

4. Researching poverty in Rome

The first data source we used for our empirical study derived from the "Whip Workshop Revelli". This is important data because it has been gathered through random samples from a wide selection of anonymous administrations. Problems relating to non-responses or biases in quantifying income were not experienced. Using this data, we decided to calculate the classic Gini Index. The index breaks down groups into inequality within groups, between groups and a remainder according to the Pyatt's (1976) mathematical methodology.

The second data source we used was a questionnaire from a survey on Social Services conducted by the Social Observatory in April 2009, using a representative sample from urban areas (taking into account the different social compositions within the country.) Questionnaires were sent to 1,846 families with children enrolled in primary schools in the area. The survey was composed of a series of questions, some of which were identical to ISTAT's[2] multi-scope research and included: the number of people considered as friends (to determine levels of exclusion) and the quantity of moments of economic difficult as well as their quality (to determine the level of vulnerability). A further question was asked to quantify monthly expenditure (excluding mortgage and food) with response categories ranging from €250.

Taking into account the fact that the sample did not include nuclear families without at least one child of school age, it excluded the older and younger parts of the population. Considering the imprecision of self-defined expenditure, we preferred to use a poverty threshold of 60% of the average expenditure per-capita, and then apply the Carbonaro equivalence scale to determine their placement either above or below the poverty threshold. This generated a binary variable, which we then used

---

2 | Istituto Centrale di Statistica, the Italian national statistical Institute.

as a dependent variable in a binomial logistic regression model, in which the dependent variable Y, characterised by the Bernoulli distribution, with a probability p o 1-p assuming the values of 0 and 1. The linear regressions chosen to represent the various dimensions that influence the possibility of being in poverty could not be guaranteed to have identical linear relationships if the choice of model with a logistic function that guarantees probability p remains within admissible values (Pisati, 2003). The binomial logistic regression model directly explains the probability in which p varies when the regressor varies. Instead of being expressed in logit terms, the coefficients are expressed in terms of Odd Ratios. These do not explain the direct effect of random factors on the dependent variables, but the relative probability. The Odd Ratios (OR) do however have the advantage of being able to measure the intensity of the phenomenon in terms of percentage probability. Odd Ratios are expressed in the values shown in Table 2. These represent the relative risk that a particular event has generated vulnerability in a poor family, and the same risk in a non-poor family. The OR should be read as a relative probability of (one category) experiencing an event. The OR general has also been added with the relative intervals of 95% confidence, which are represented in a double entry contingency table with the relationships between the possibility that an event will occur, or not, for each category i.e. the likelihood the two categories will experience the event.

The third data source is administrative data on those in receipts of benefits from the municipal offices. We have selected this service because the population that benefits from this does not correspond to the poor population, but to those below a particular ISEE (equivalent financial situation index): the criteria for supply are, however, objective and enable variations within that population to be verified.

5. Before the crisis: The Rome Model (low income)

The city of Rome is one of the most prominent subjects of Italian social scientific enquiry. Classical sociological interpretations merge to form a kind of dual city *avant-la-lettre*, giving rise to two accounts. The first is the result of the marginalization and social isolation produced by a type of development that is distorted, while the second emphasized the antagonism produced by marginalization itself (Berlinguer and Della

Seta, 1970). After a brief period out of the limelight, the last ten years have marked the capital's return to center stage, however it's a return that stands in opposition to the experience of the 70s. According to current analysis, the labor market has overcome its dependency on the public sector and has grown thanks to the development of the advanced tertiary sector, in line with other ex- industrial cities (De Muro, Monni and Tridico 2011). Here, the physical development of the city has followed a polycentric direction, capable of restoring balance to the capital (Ferrarotti and Macioti, 2009). Nonetheless, these points remain *under-acknowledged*. In Rome, the professionalization of the labor market and the highest-level tasks are still connected to the public sector. Available data (Violante, 2008) shows that the growth of the tertiary sector, that allowed a subsequent growth in employment in the 2000s, constitutes a mixture of consumption services that offer unqualified jobs and advanced business services which (as in the case of ITC), are interconnected to the purchase-money of the public administration sector. The absolute number of public administration employees is destined to decrease as a result of fiscal austerity. Nevertheless, what is most important here is the qualitative change within public administration which began in the 90s with the corporatization of many of its units – a development that had many more repercussions on the Roman labor market than the number of public employees. Indeed, the kind of management of contracts and hirings enacted, has led to a reformulation of the borders between central and peripheral segments, similar to the so-called process of *marketization* of the public sector (Doogan, 1997), with a divergence between professionals who are able to access the "market" of professional appointments and consultancies on the one hand, and the contracted workers affected by the compression of costs on the other. In between the two, lie the lower levels of public employment. In addition to this first change, there is a second and more evident change. In view of the Jubilee, the city center underwent a significant urban renewal, which, together with effective cultural policies, achieved the goal of stimulating the tourist industry. In 1993, numbers using hotel facilities reached around 4,700,000. In the latest available data, they appeared to rise collectively, to more than 8,000,000. These numbers are lower than those in the most prominent European capital cities, but are still sufficiently high to affect the nature of the composition of labor in Rome. As noted by Judd and Fainstein (1999), the productivity model of a tourist city is based on a low productivity sector, and thus, in the absence of a strong system of redistribution, entails deep levels of inequality (in line with the profile of urban renewal within global cities, that bases its polarization on other sectors). Moreover, since the productivity model is based on an exogenous demand, it tends to bolster inflation independently of the strength of internal demand. The first factor has an effect on relative poverty, the second on absolute poverty.

If, by virtue of these considerations, we examine inequality in Rome using available data on salaries for employees of Roman companies from 1993 to 2004 (Figure 1), we find that salarial inequality increased long before the crisis, creating many potential poor workers.

Figure 1: Numbers Average income rate for the first and the last distribution deciles

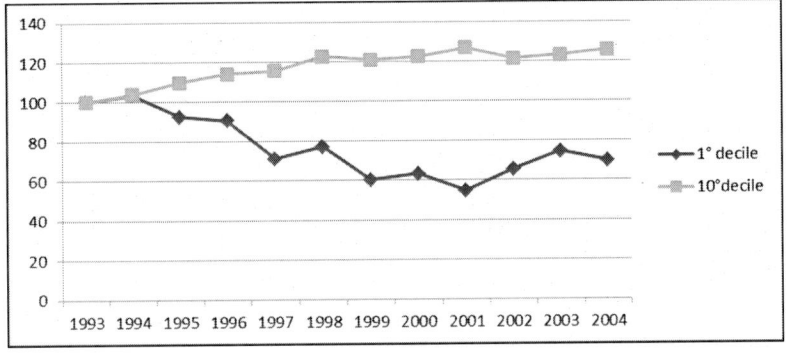

Source: own elaboration on Whip data

Let us take into consideration the annual salary of salaried workers within the private sector, regardless of the number of days worked[3]. The averages for extreme income deciles grow further apart, not due to an increase in the last decile, but rather, due to an absolute decrease in the first decile, that brings it to an annual average that is equivalent to a monthly salary. It is the effect of the incidence of contracts that are shorter than the calendar year, which, even on an equivalent salary, are inadequate. By virtue of the importance of intermittent work, we have therefore evaluated the level of

---

3 | Salarial inequality has to be obviously verified by qualifications and on equal duration of service, but we are interested in the subsistence of workers *as if* earned income was their only livelihood.

inequality among workers by examining three different groups: stable workers, workers who have worked for more than one company during in a single year and workers who have worked for the same company for less than 230 days. A closer look at the Gini Index (figure 2) broken down into individual inequality, as well as into the groups under examination here, shows that it is precisely the inequality that exists between groups that causes the greatest increase in inequality more generally. Together with the inequality quota (overlap) that can be viewed as the overlap of the last individuals of the group of stable workers and the first individuals of the two groups of precarious workers, in which young people and women are the majority. This overlap is one that grows with the increase of inequality within groups themselves.

Figure 2: Gini index of the salaries during a calendar year

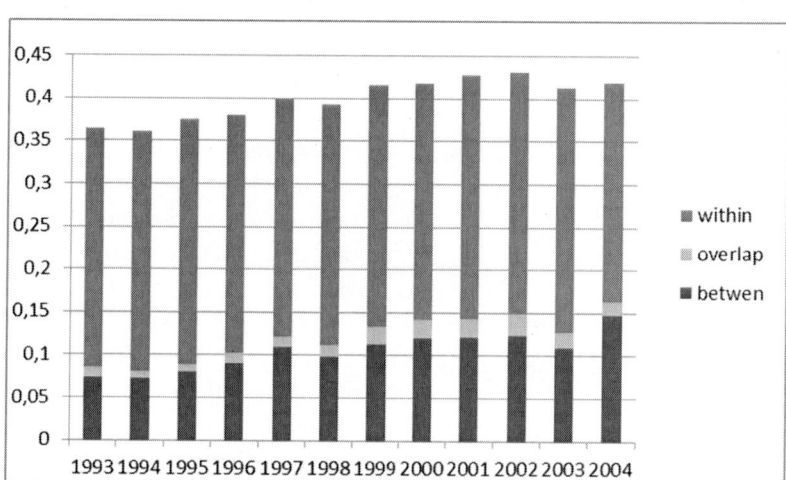

Source: own elaboration of Whip data

Moreover, during the 90s Rome had always had a higher inflation spread than the rest of the country. For families, this had resulted in a 19.3% decrease in spending power, which subsequently continued to increase, causing the progressive expulsion of both Italian and foreign low-income families from central/metropolitan areas. Prior to the crisis, there had been an increase in low-income job opportunities, sustained by the growth of both private and public consumption (which are particularly interconnected in Rome). This model of social polarization differs from the Anglo-Saxon one, both due to the function of income integration played by families, which allows for rates of inactivity, as well as thanks to the very contained increase in the income of workers at the top of the distribution pyramid, but certainly not due to the inexistence of a service proletariat. It is to be expected that spending cuts and the recruitment freeze within the public administration sector will have heavy consequences on this arrangement. The primary source of recruitment into stable employment will be blocked and the casual employment sector will contract, causing a general decrease in income derived from formal work, which, most importantly in the case of casual workers, cannot be replaced by the Italian social safety net.

6. Rome after the crisis

It is in this context of urban renewal that our case study takes place, in contrast to the case of Milan, where the public sector plays a different role (Torri, 2007). Fiscal austerity has not (yet) forced employment cuts in the public sector, although the sector has not been able to play its role of "multiplier of the labor market". After the first phase of the crisis, repercussions were inevitable. In fact, the labor market in Rome underwent significant change, with the most affected being young adults (up to 29 years-old), whose unemployment rate went from 15.8 in 2007 to 23.4 in 2011, even if against an increased rate of inactivity, which created a very wide area of exclusion from the labor market among this group. This group – in the city which has the highest incidence of graduates in the country – is likely to be largely made up of individuals waiting to enter employment, however, its lower segments are composed of unemployed individuals at risk of becoming long-term unemployed and subsequently unemployable. Within this context, data on poverty from the ISTAT shows that in the region of Lazio there do not appear to be effects on the incidence of poverty.

Further increases in the cost of living – a development that is fiscally induced – as well as the lack of income opportunities, will certainly put a strain on the ability of stable workers to support the income of other family members. It is likely that a proportion of the casual work that increased during growth time will be subsumed into the black economy. Besides, it had been foreseen (Becchi, 2007) that labor markets based solely on economies of agglomeration were widely instable development models. Now that we have shown how unemployment became a central problem once again, we will take a look at whether the phenomenon entails cumulative problems, as is implicit in the theory of social exclusion.

7. Urban poverty in the XIII Borough of Rome

The subject of enquiry of this essay will be the 13th Borough, an area on the extreme outskirts of Southern Rome and fully located outside of the city's ring road. It has more than 200.000 inhabitants, making it as big as any district within the city. The borough is made up of 10 urban areas, all quite different from one another. Within the borough, we find the range of different types of Roman urban development: From the luxury buildings of Casal Palocco (a suburb for more affluent classes, located within the city's borders) to the messy growth of the construction industry and accompanying areas of self-construction in Infernetto to the recently built areas surrounding the GRA (The Roman ring road) in the Malafede area; Ex-working-class suburbs built at the time of Fascism that still lack services, such as Acilia and finally, on the coast, we find the urban nucleus of Ostia, with its tourist industry during the summer. Ostia is split into an Eastern side, that possesses a more working-class character and social housing, and a Western side, with a white-collar middle-class workforce. A composite area that initially developed during the Fascist era with the arrival of immigrants from Northern Italy and with the gentrification of the city's historic center. In the 80s, the working-class area of western Ostia underwent a period of stigmatization (Salvati et al. 2012) that is not uncommon in areas with social housing, but one that was worsened by the visible prominence of drug addiction that brought the state healthcare services to open one of the city's first Drug Addiction centres known as SERTs (Servizio Tossicodipendenze, Drug addiction help center) there.

Recently, it has been subject to deep transformations, partially due to the arrival of foreigners in line with broader urban trends[4], as well as due to the growth of the real estate market, which affected the entire city. The

---

4 | The incidence of foreigners registered at the Register Office in this borough rose from 5% in 2001 to 10% in 2011, but it is still under the average in Rome, which was 6,4% in 2001 and reaches 12% in 2011.

center of Ostia and all of the residential areas that surround the suburban railway line connecting the coast to the center of Rome saw an increase in rental income, following the lowering of interest rates at the end of the 1990s. After this initial phase of the real estate cycle that saw values of the 13th borough rise from 25% to 50%, the area surrounding the Roman ring road, similarly to other city quadrants, was subject to a significant increase in private construction, which increased high-end supply.[5] This, in turn, attracted new social groups/populations to the area and worsened the housing crisis. What are the features of poor communities in a context that is undergoing such a significant change?

The proportion of family units living below the poverty threshold is 7.4%. This percentage is below the national level (11%) and in line with the estimates for the Lazio region. The features of our sample, which, from the outset, excludes the lone elderly grouping (among whom poverty levels are high); suggest that the poor population of the borough is much higher than the regional average. In order to describe the situation, the first indicator that must be analyzed is the incidence of poverty in relation to the number of family members. This increases exponentially from the fifth family member onwards (usually a third dependent child). Thus, there exists a typical inverse correlation between the number of children and the level of well-being, although poverty increases less rapidly than in other contexts as the family grows: a 28% increase in the incidence of poverty only occurs with the sixth family member. In only 10.7% of cases, the household breadwinner is unemployed, giving credit to the notion that even the 13th borough, poverty is not dependent upon the quantity of employment[6]. In light of these facts, we can also analyze the intensity of poverty, namely, the other indicator that helps characterize the phenomenon under discussion. When expressed as a percentage of total consumption, it is on average 26% (the national average is 20%). However, if we take into account the number of family members, it

---

5 | Data source is the real estate market overview by the Rome Chamber of Commerce, which shows from 1998 to 2004 an increase from 1500 €/m2 to 2000 €/m2 in Ostia and to 3000 €/m2 in upmarket areas of the borough. These values do not include the tranche paid in advance before the deed. In 1997 1047 out of 3517 construction permits (for works done during the 2000s) were for housing in the 13th borough of Rome (Source: Rome City Council)

6 | However, the real difference is due to female employment. In families above the poverty threshold, there are 11% more housewives and 23% less employed women.

takes a reversed U-shape and, for the reasons mentioned above, its values are much higher than the average, particularly for large family units.

Figure 3: Percentage distance of consumption from poverty threshold number of family members

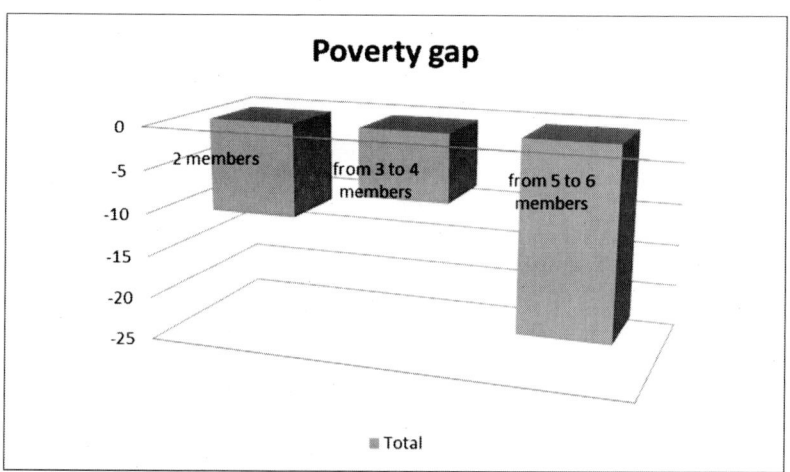

Source: Survey on Minors and Family 13th Borough

The intensity of poverty for families with more than two individuals is higher than for families with 3-4 people. Here, families with two individuals are defined as single parent families and our sample was taken exclusively from families with children of school age. However, when measured against the entire sample, their consumption per head is not the lowest among the different family types.

Let us now examine, with all the areas highlighted in the available literature being equal, whether family types come to bear on the state of being poor. We have estimated a model of logistic regression in order to verify the effect that certain key factors have on the possibility of being under the poverty threshold. We will analyze five dimensions: family type (in order to observe the incidence of atypical family units), nationality (in order to observe the relative disadvantage experienced by non-Italians, employment status (in order to verify the theory of social inclusion), housing status (in order to verify the importance of inequality within the scope of housing) and, the number of individuals who might be considered friends, who are living in the same building (in order to verify social isolation).

Tab. 1 Model of logistic regression on the features of people in poverty

LR χ2 (14)=28.35
Log Likehood= – 398.01166
Prob>χ2= 0.0128

	Odd Ratios	Robust St. Error	z	p>z	[95% Confidence Interval]	
Family type (Marriage)						
Cohabitation	.543693	.2419569	-1.37	0.171	.2272731	1.300647
Single parent	1.62971	.6882688	1.16	0.247	.7122389	3.729021
Couple living with children from a previous relationship	1.04472	.3891443	0.12	0.907	.5034296	2.16801
Citizenship (Italian)						
EU	.5714982	.3607577	-0.89	0.375	.165842	1.969405
Non EU	.9518561	.4954527	-0.09	0.924	.3431709	2.640171
Occupational status (Employed)						
Non standard job	1.251878	.69108	0.41	0.684	.4242964	3.693641
Unemployed	**2.250014	.761232	2.40	0.017	1.159322	4.366832
Inactive	.9781898	.4408875	-0.05	0.961	.4043631	2.366327
Tenure (rent)						
Usufruct/free	.8182038	.319286	-0.51		.3808016	1.758021
Squatted housing	1.83841	1.039168	1.08		.6071525	5.566564
Home ownership	**.5448215	.138929	-2.38		.3305207	.8980695
(family units who have friendship relationships with or more than one family)						
With only one family	.726066	.2274622	-1.02	0.307	.3929266	1.341655
With no family	1.042498	.2280839	0.19	0.849	.6789604	1.600686
There are no families in the building	*2.524578	1.157822	2.02	0.043	1.027569	6.202501

Source: Survey on Minors and Family 13th Borough

Here, there are three statistically significant modes. First and foremost, the fact of being unemployed, which is known to be the most solid predictor of poverty. Individuals who are unemployed have a 125% higher chance of being poor. Secondly, all other things remaining equal, home ownership provides protection from the risk of poverty[7]. In light of these two dimensions, which, in our case, have also proven to be the strongest, nationality does not appear to have a significant effect. Single-parent families have a 62% greater chance of being poor, but it must be noted that this effect is not statistically significant and does not apply when older longer-term residents are taken into account. Thus, there remains no connection between exclusion from labor market and social exclusion, as the number of people classed as friends in the neighborhood does not have an effect, although people who live in single-family households tend to be statistically poorer in a more meaningful and widespread way. This is a spurious effect, which can be explained by examining the territory's urban development: there continues to exist greater inequality among people living in illegal self-built buildings, compared to social housing settings.

Let us now investigate the relationship between deprivation and vulnerability. We do not possess a set of precise questions to be able to objectively measure vulnerability, however, as an indicator, we will use the quantity and type of instances in which families have perceived themselves to be under economic hardship. Here, we will continue to highlight that our interest here is on the state of significant economic hardships and not on indicators of objective states of being. The collation between the number of instances of perceived economic hardship and the state of indigence illustrates how poor communities are set apart from the average population, particularly due to the constant exposure to events that make them vulnerable. Only 18% of poor communities (against 27% of non-poor individuals) consider themselves to have undergone economic difficulties/hardships. It is nevertheless interesting to see that the causes of fragility differ markedly, depending on the profile of indigence. Among the different economic events, those connected to insufficient levels of income and job losses characterize the poor. Among the events that relate to self-employed workers it is clearly more likely that a missed start-up of a personal business venture will involve a poor family. The risk of eviction affects the poor only marginally more than other groups, although this group is much more protected against a failed house purchase, than non-poor groups. Family events only differ when it comes to divorce, which

---

7 | The poverty line does not consider imputed rents.

causes slightly greater difficulties for the poor. These results stand in slight contrast to literature on the subject (Whelan and Maintre, 2005), and require further in-depth analysis of other local contexts. It is clear that the families cover these risks in ways that differ from one another: if we examine the social capital employed during these instances of challenge, the poor do not differ from other groups for having received less support, but are rather set apart by the fact that they have lacked the support that comes from strong familial ties (parents and in-laws).

Tab. 2 Risk coefficients for type of discomfort events

	Poor	Non Poor	General OR	[95% Confidence Interval]	
				Lower	Upper
A period of unemployment	1,557	,958	,615	,395	,958
Insufficient income	1,246	,981	,787	,506	1,223
A disease	,972	1,003	1,032	,484	2,200
Debt of an enterprise	,691	1,028	1,489	,587	3,775
Bankruptcy of an enterprise	1,231	,980	,796	,308	2,059
Start-up of an enterprise	1,921	,921	,480	,219	1,052
Debt at too high interest rates	1,004	1,000	,996	,549	1,807
An Eviction	1,153	,987	,855	,462	1,585
A house purchase	,421	1,059	2,515	1,197	5,287
A divorce	1,171	,985	,841	,495	1,432
The death of a family member	,973	1,002	1,031	,434	2,445
The birth of a child	,901	1,009	1,120	,618	2,027

Source: Survey on Minors and Family 13th Borough

After having outlined these essential traits of social need, let us now analyze what social inequalities look like post-crisis, through the data available from social services in order to ascertain whether the social composition of claimants has changed and whether local institutions were able to adapt to these new conditions.

8. Social assistance in the 13th district since the crisis

In 2008, the 13th district was affected by the crisis that hit the former national airline as its proximity to the town of Fiumicino, the location of Rome's main airport, had made it a popular place for both cabin and ground crew to live. Today, the 13th district is a suburb that continues to experience various social problems including higher unemployment than the average in the city of Rome with those who are unemployed experiencing greater segregation and a crime rate perceived to be greater than it actually is. There is the prospect of further economic and building investments, if the investment project aimed at creating a second tourist hub for Rome on its coast proves to be successful, although paradoxically such investments – quite apart from being difficult to raise due to a lack of capital – are based on a development model that the crisis has already shown to create a degree of job vulnerability.

Within that context, this is an effort to analyse the initial effects of the crisis at local level and to determine if the changes described at market level are causing any repercussions in terms of increased social needs. Our source of reference on this occasion is the data provided by the Social Services' administration department. When Rome's Department of Social Services was reformed at the end of the 90s, it was divided into sections known as Socio-Educational, Cultural and Sporting Units (UOSECS). However, on the eve of the implementation of law no. 328, a decision was made to set aside the idea of providing services according to the categorization of clients (the disabled, minors, foreigners, etc.) and to start by providing primary level services through usual social services channels, and secondary level services by means of integrated actions. During the crisis, the number of people contacting the administrative offices of social services increased steadily and significantly (from 1,918 people in 2007 to 3,638 in 2011). The change in the type of people contacting social services is reflected in that increase as in the final and most intense phase of the crisis, the majority, some 21.1% of the total, were foreigners, even though they only make up 10% of the local population. The particular characteristics of the immigrant population mean that the change of client nationality has also had an obvious effect both on the age and the family composition of those making contact. The 41-61 age group is the largest, followed by those aged 18 to 40 years while the over 65s are in the minority.

As to the type of family making contact, the number of those with at least one dependent minor rose from 21.6% in 2007 to 41.3% in 2011. The change in the social background of social service clients is not a direct indicator of economic difficulty, as the provision of services by local UOSECS is not necessarily connected to lack of income. In Rome, resolution no. 154/1997 provides the regulations if and how benefits are provided to those that seek it. In the 13th District, such requests are not merely considered by the administrative offices but are determined by a points system that takes six different factors into account, namely income, the ownership of any vehicles, housing conditions, health, the type of family unit and enrolment on any educational/vocational courses. Benefits are allocated to three categories of person – the elderly, minors and adults – each of which is assigned a basic score. That said, the number of people assisted ultimately depends on budgetary constraints determined by the district's political bodies.

As requests received by social services can be tracked by their number and according to general socio-demographics, it is possible to analyse and draw up a rough guide to financial hardship in the district. Most subsidies are likely to be categorized as "special payments" in that they exceed the standard €400 provided for. Requests for subsidies have not only increased more than general requests for help, those making them also represent almost half social services clients during the last two years of the crisis. Almost three quarters of those who have contacted social services and are eligible for subsidies are women and between 2008 and 2010, the number of foreigners applying increased by almost 10% (to 26%), the average age of applicants decreased but the overall number of applicants increased (figure 4). New applicants are mostly, therefore, adults with dependent children and not the elderly.

The other financial subsidy, as per resolution 163/1998, is a housing benefit, which covers a specific share of clients' rent (with the evicted having priority) as long as they can obtain a private rental contract. They are therefore those who are at the upper end of the housing emergency in Rome and not those forced to move to residential hotels managed directly by the mayor's office and the Central Department for housing policies. The distribution of these benefits is regulated not only by the number of evictions, but also according to the time social services' existing clients continue to need help – their tenancy agreements are usually for a four year term plus the option to renew for a further four years. The number of applicants peaked in 2008 and 2009 at 125 and 92 respectively and decreased to 73 in 2010. The number of female applicants has steadily increased and now represents 75% of all applicants while the average age, at 46, is lower than it was at the time of the 154/1997 resolution cited above. The overall number of applicants is almost the same as then, but the percentage of foreign applicants has risen significantly from just 4% of the total in 2007 to 24% in 2010. Despite such an extraordinary increase in the number of adults experiencing difficulties who have sought assistance, the district has been able to increase the funds available for both types of benefit[8] and while in 2008 they paid out a total of €540, 856 in 2011 that rose to € 758,298.

Figure 4: Applications for financial subsidies

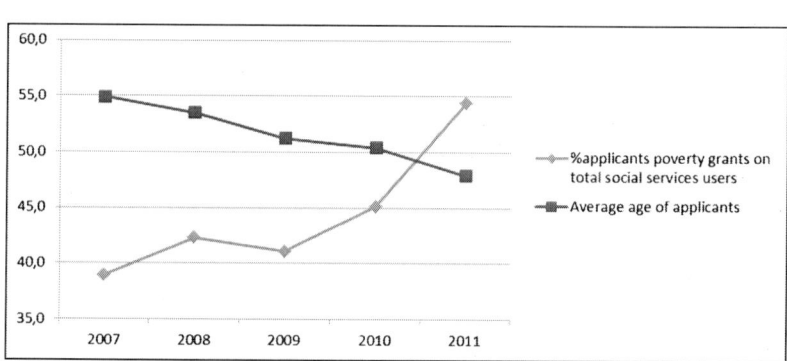

Source: Social Observatory of the 13th district

There has also been a significant change to the categories of people eligible for financial assistance. Initially, by halving what was available for adults, more money was set aside for minors and funding for the elderly remained the same. That shake-up also affected the numbers of those receiving

---

8 | Bearing in mind however that in 2008 that only represented only 2% of the council's total budget (and did slightly increase later). Funds were however divided up in a very different way. In 2011, funds for housing benefits represented almost half of what was available to fight poverty compared with the 11% they represented in 2008.

benefits, the 684 in 2008 rising to 1,596 in 2010, more than half of which were minors. In 2012 however, the number of minors receiving funding came to a standstill, as receipt of funding, once awarded, had been limited to a two-year period. Well aware that the reality of the situation meant that the amount of funding[9] allocated by resolution 154/1997, was not nearly sufficient to fill the poverty gap, the authorities decided to share what was available amongst as many applicants as possible.

Even before the crisis, there had been a significant number of people whose "points" kept them high in the rankings of those eligible for assistance. No less than 49.7%[10] of those eligible in 2007 remained so in 2008, and even since eligibility has been restricted, the number of those who remain eligible remains very high. Comparing 2008 and 2011 for example, 34.9% have remained in the ranking despite being divided into those whose payments had been suspended for a year and those who had not applied for the two preceding years. This proves that it is not at all easy for the poor to move out of the ranks of those who need and are eligible for assistance. It shows furthermore that there are indeed people who are permanently poor (in terms of the "objective" criteria used in the ranking system) and who therefore have an on-going right to assistance, even though this is not enough to raise them out of poverty.

Given the situation described above, more focus and funding was directed towards allocating housing benefits, and the number of recipients increased from 27 in 2007 to 42 in 2012 in order to prevent a significant number of people finding themselves in a housing emergency and consequently falling into extreme poverty. Even so, the effort made is certainly not enough to cope with the potential number of people seeking assistance because of the increasing number of evictions underway caused by the fierce increase in house prices mentioned earlier. If, prior to the new millennium, evictions were a phenomenon that mostly involved the main city of Rome, in recent years, the number of eviction orders issued by the local District 13 section of the Court of Rome has always been in

---

9 | In 2011, the average payment was €544 for the elderly, €1004 for adults (accounted for by special payments to those with HIV – although a great many received much the same as an elderly person) and €1400 for minors.

10 | This number has been calculated following analysis of the relative databases dealing with those receiving benefits and could perhaps be higher given that the list of benefit recipients for 2007 was incomplete.

excess of 200. While the figure is lower than in other districts, it is worth pointing out that evidence of the seriousness of this particular problem in this district is that in contrast to what happens in the rest of the city, people here do not leave their homes on receipt of the eviction order, but wait for the bailiffs to come and evict them.[11]

Conclusions

The first aim of this chapter was to define the characteristics of poverty in a particular urban context by looking at various categories of people. The picture of poverty that emerges from this study is not unlike that associated with poverty in southern Italy and provides a somewhat ambivalent comparison with concepts held in the 90s. On the one hand, looking at the many aspects of neediness confirms, for example, the earlier belief that owning one's own home does provide some protection from poverty.

The housing bubble – houses built before the crisis – has created a new kind of housing related poverty that is linked to employment (or lack of it). What is more, unemployment is also an extraordinarily powerful portent of future poverty. It calls to mind those who have been excluded from society even if that is not linked to either particular demographic groups (nationality, type of family) even in the suburbs, or to the consequences of social isolation in terms of strong relationships. Above all else, suburban families seem to be "normally" helpless when it comes to employment, with poor support from family networks making them particularly vulnerable – especially with regard to job security – and this can lead to a downward slide into poverty.

This consideration leads to the second aspect of this study. Although without any in-depth research on the conditions faced by families in our suburbs, the cross-section of data gathered on income, unemployment

---

11 | To be specific, the number of eviction notices issued in 2007 stood at 244 and at 221 in 2011 of which 195 were due to arrears in the rent and the rest because the rental agreement had expired. Repossessions accounted for 77% of eviction notices in 2007 (although in Rome in general that figure dropped to 44%) and for 80% in 2011. (Source: The records office of the external section of the Tribunal of Rome).

and the increase of requests for help received by social services has to be sufficient here to formulate a theory, even if it is somewhat vague.

The consumer economy of the service sector has created a specific type of social polarization within the labour market, involving an increase in the number of precarious workers, thereby creating a world of opportunities for the poor featured in this report to try and earn some sort of income. It would seem that a metropolitan labor market is unable to identify a development model that will allow it to replace the precarious service sector workers who were responsible for the growth of some cities in the noughties.

The crisis has meant that these income opportunities have disappeared, to be replaced by unemployment and consequently, an increase in poverty, particularly amongst foreign workers who often have more dependent family members than the Italians. The increase of applications to Social Services concerns, above all, young foreign adults, seen in this study to be more at risk even when they are no longer unemployed.

This leads on to the third aspect of this study – how the welfare system has dealt with the crisis. Given the impossibility of a systematic response to the poverty that exists today and continues to grow as a result of the crisis, social services have chosen to concentrate the insufficient resources available to them in trying to prevent new cases involving a housing emergency as that would only lead to even more families finding themselves in extreme difficulty.

It is a strategy of selective assistance that has little in common with the selective universalism identified some years ago (Bifulco and Centemeri, 2007) as it is based on a lack of resources rather than subjectivity. What is more, the current pursuit of equality through downsizing will soon be hit hard by the latest round of austerity measures. In Rome the palpable feeling that the work of the social services department has been ineffective in dealing with the consequences of the first years of the crisis seems to be because of their inability to dealing with the increase of applications, even without having to cope with a cut in resources. This shows their failure to resolve some of the inherent features of poverty that are rooted in the chronic underfunding of the fight against it, before the crisis even began.

REFERENCES

Andreotti A., E. Mingione E. and E. Polizzi (2012) Local Welfare System: A Challenge for Social Cohesion. In: Urban Studies, 49, 9, 1925-40

Appelbaum E., A. Bernhardt and R. Murnane (2003) Low-Wage America: How Employers Are Reshaping Opportunity in the Workplace. New York: Sage

Atkinson A.B. (1998) Social Exclusion, Poverty and Unemployment. In: A. B. Atkinson and J. Hills (eds) Exclusion, Employment and Opportunity. In: CASE Papers of the London School of Economics

Becchi, A. (1996) Un quarto d'idea: In: Archivio di studi urbani e Regionali, 57

Becchi, A. (2007) Le città del consumo oggi. In: Scienze Regionali, 6/3,113

Benassi, D. (2002) Tra benessere e Povertà. Milano: Franco Angeli

Bifulco L. and L. Centemeri (2007) La partecipazione nei Piani sociali di zona:geometrie variabili di governance locale. In: Stato e Mercato, 80

Brandolini, A. (2005) La disuguaglianza di reddito in Italia nell'ultimo decennio. In: Stato e Mercato, 74

Burgers, J. (1996) No polarisation in Dutch cities? Inequality in a corporatist country. In: Urban Studies, 33, 99-105

Cavalca, G. (2010) Transizione post-industriale e cambiamento delle disuguaglianze sociali nelle principali aree urbane d'Italia. In: Rassegna Italiana di Sociologia, 51/3

De Muro, P., S. Monni and P. Tridico (2011): Knowledge-Based Economy and Social Exclusion: Shadow and Light in the Roman Socio-Economic Model. In: International Journal of Urban and Regional Research, 35/6, 1212-38

Ferrarotti F. and I. Macioti I. (2009) Periferie da Problema a Risorsa. Sandro Teti editore, Roma

Fullin G. (2002) Instabilità del lavoro e vulnerabilità: dimensioni, punti di equilibrio ed elementi di fragilità. In: Rassena Italiana di Sociologia vol. 43 n.4

Gallie D., S. Paugam and S Jacobs (2003) Unemployment poverty and social isolation. In: European Societies 5/1, 1-32

Hamnett, C. (1994) Social polarisation in global cities: theory and evidence. In: Urban Studies, 31, 401-424

Hamnett, C. (1996) Social polarization, economic restructuring and welfare state regimes. In: Urban Studies, 33/8,1407-1430

Kazepov, Y. (ed.) (2004) Cities of Europe: Changing Contexts, Local Arrangement and the Challenge to Urban Cohesion. Oxford: Blackwell

Kazepov, Y and E. Barberis (eds) (2013) Il welfare frammentato Le articolazioni regionali delle politiche sociali italiane. Carocci: Roma

Lehto, J. (2001) Le città e il welfare state. In: A. Bagnasco A. and P. Le Galés (eds) Le città nell'Europa contemporanea. Liguori: Napoli

Levitas, R. (2006) The concept and measurement of social exclusion. In: C. Pantazis (eds) Poverty and Social Exclusion in Britain. Bristol: Policy Press

Lucchini M. and S. Sarti (2005) Il benessere e la deprivazione delle famiglie italiane. In: Stato e Mercato, n. 74

Mingione E. (1996) Urban Poverty and the Underclass. Blackwell: Cambridge

Mollenkopf, J. and M. Castells (1991) Dual City: Restructuring New York. New York: Sage.

Morlicchio E. (2012) Sociologia della Povertà. Il Mulino: Bologna

Negri N. and C. Saraceno (2000) Povertà, disoccupazione ed esclusione sociale. In: Stato e Mercato n. 59

Paci, M. (1995) I mutamenti della stratificazione sociale. In: Storia dell'Italia Repubblicana. La trasformazione dell'Italia: sviluppo e squilibri. Einaudi: Torino, 697–776

Paci, M. (ed) (2008) Welfare locale e democrazia partecipativa. Il Mulino: Bologna

Paugam S. (2000) La disqualification sociale. Paris: PUF

Procacci, G. (1997) Studiare la diseguaglianza oggi. In: Rassegna Italiana di Sociologia, 38/1

Pyatt, G. (1976) On the interpretation and disaggregation of Gini coefficients. In: Economic Journal, 246, 243-55

OECD (2004) Chapter 2. In: Employment Outlook, Geneva

Ranci, C. (2002) Le nuove disuguaglianze sociali in Italia. Il Mulino: Bologna

Ranci, C. (2008) Vulnerabilità sociale e nuove disuguaglianze sociali. In: Sociologia del Lavoro, 110

Reyneri E. and S. Scherer (2008) Com'è cresciuta l'occupazione femminile in Italia: fattori strutturali e culturali a confront. In: Stato e Mercato, 83

Rosanvallon, P. and J. P. Fitoussi (1996) Le nouvel âge des inégalités. Paris: Seuil

Salvati L., R. Di Bartolomei, S. Bisi and K. Rontos (2012) Crime and the (Mediterranean) City: Exploring the Geography of (In)security in Rome. In: International Journal of latest trends in Finance and economic sciences, 2/1

Saraceno, C. (2002 Prefazione. In: C. Ranci (ed) Le nuove disuguaglianze sociali in Italia. Il Mulino: Bologna, IX-XXIII

Sen, A. K. (1984) Resources, Values and Development. Cambridge: Harvard University Press.

Torri, R. (2007) Milano tra eccellenze e nuove polarizzazioni. In: C. Ranci C. and R. Torri (eds) Milano tra coesione sociale e sviluppo. Bruno Mondadori: Milano

Violante, A. (2008) La Metropoli Spezzata: sviluppo urbano di una città meditteranea. Franco Angeli: Roma

Wheelan C.T., R. Layte and B. Maitre (2004) Understanding the mismatch between Income poverty and Deprivation: A dynamic comparative analysis. In: European Sociological Review, 20/4, 297-302

Wheelan, C. T. and B. Maitre (2004) Economic Vulnerability, Multidimensional Deprivation and Social Cohesion in an enlarged European Community. In: International Journal of Comparative Sociology 46/3, 215-233

Greece

Greek Spatial Planning and the Crisis

Maria Zifou

Greece's entry into the "Support Mechanism' in 2010, which signaled the 'official' beginning of the crisis, entailed the implementation of a structural adjustment program for the country with the objective to reduce the national deficit and to pay up sovereign debt, which since then, the dominant discourse has equated with the public good. Consistent with its neo-liberal tenet, state retrenchment and privatization are at the core of the restructuring policies 'imposed' by this adjustment program within which the sale of state owned property acquires primary importance as a significant means to pay up the debt. The 'reform' of the spatial planning system has been a core element of this regulatory restructuring process as it has been considered an essential prerequisite for creating 'favorable conditions for economic activity' and entrepreneurship including enhancing of competitiveness. Within this overall framework, and amidst the burgeoning problems faced by major Greek cities due to austerity policies, a substantial number of new laws have been adopted at a very rapid pace transforming in substantive ways the spatial planning system and in more general space production process.

This chapter offers a critical review of the country's regulatory restructuring since 2011 and its effect on the land development process. The objective is to reveal the continuities, ruptures and turns in Greek spatial planning policy. The research makes an appraisal of the legislation that has already been adopted as well as the legislative proposals that have undergone public consultation.

The underlying thesis of this paper is that the debt crisis in Greece has served to legitimize neo-liberalism as "the dominant ideological rationalization" for the state 'reform'(Peck and Tickell, 2002) imposed by the successive Memoranda[1] as part of the 'rescue' program of the country. For the purpose of this paper, neoliberalism is conceptualized as "...one among several tendencies of regulatory change that have been unleashed across the global capitalist system since the 1970s: it prioritizes market oriented or market-disciplinary responses to regulatory problems; it strives to intensify commodification; and it often mobilizes speculative financial instruments to open up new arenas for capitalist profit making" (Peck et al 2012:269). In this sense, along with state downsizing, privatization of commons and flexible labor relations, the 'reform' of the Greek planning system constitutes a core element of the new mode of regulation associated with post-Fordist economic dynamics (Aglietta, 1979; Amin, 1994) that consolidates competition and commodification in all realms of social life including space production, while facilitating the opening up of the Greek economy to global processes of capital accumulation (Harvey, 2005).

1. Greek Spatial Planning before the Crisis

The spatial planning system of the country was in a state of transition right before the outbreak of the economic crisis as illustrated by the effort to implement the spatial planning legislation adopted in the mid-1990s. The preceding planning Act adopted in 1983 (L. 1337/83) – which partially revised the foundational planning law of 1923 – was primarily directed towards the reduction of spatial inequalities in Greek cities by addressing the significant social, functional and environmental problems associated mainly with uncontrolled post-war development (primarily housing construction) and insufficient public investment for service and infrastructure provision. The 1983 Act enabled the central government to prepare physical plans that controlled development only in the built-up / urbanized areas of the country, while it permitted the application of a unified regulatory development framework in areas lying outside the jurisdiction of these plans allowing unplanned and often informal or illegal development to sprawl on peri-urban areas and the countryside.

---

[1] | Refers to the Memoranda of Understanding signed by Greece outlining the conditions for the disbursements of financial assistance to the county by the European Financial Stability Facility.

An essential dimension of the overall Greek planning legislation was its embedding of the social relations underlying the country's post war urban development pattern. A pattern that has been described as 'deviating' from the dominant western European one (Vaiou et al., 2000) and consisting of: (1) small-scale-land property (in terms of the size of property holdings) and small-scale-construction capital both directly related to land fragmentation as well as to the high percentages of home ownership; (2) the increased role of the private sector in space production including the provision of housing often through informal and/or illegal processes; and (3) the promotion of the (small scale) construction sector as the primary vehicle for the economic development of the country. In this framework, the ease of access to home ownership that the planning system afforded to lower and middle class property owners, through formal and informal urban development practices, along with the ability to profit from land rent and surplus values (Mantouvalou, 1980; Mantouvalou and Mavridou, 1993; Vaiou et al, 2000), provided the conditions for a wide social consensus for weak-piecemeal planning and/or for the opportunistic implementation of spatial plans. Implicitly, in this way, Greek planning culture supported the undeclared content of the public interest (Vatavali and Zifou, 2012).

The planning legislation adopted in the mid-1990s (L. 2508/95 and L.2742/97) signaled, at least at a symbolic level, a rupture with this wider consensus and a turn towards the support for increased state intervention in the land development process. This turn was essentially based on a growing demand for a plan-based system posed by two different, seemingly contradictory, trends[2]. The first trend was related with the rapid restructuring of the construction and real estate sectors, both in terms of size and invested capital, a trend directly associated with the development of the 2004 Olympic facilities as well as the construction of large scale infrastructure projects financed by EU structural funds (Mantouvalou and Patrikios, 2008). For these new players, extending the application of statutory land use plans over the country's territory was perceived as a necessary condition to secure the legal certainty required for the approval and subsequent implementation of their investment decisions. The second trend, on the other hand, was directly associated with the need to further

---

2 | Of course EE policies and strategies affecting the development of the European space, such as the European Spatial Development Framework exercised tremendous influence at that time on planning culture and practice in Greece.

integrate environmental concerns in spatial planning derived not only as an obligation to comply with EU environmental policy but also as a claim posed by a rapidly rising environmental movement in the country. In this context, the 90's planning legislation provided for the development of an integrated planning system, consisting of national, regional and local plans, which when fully implemented would extend development control throughout the territory with a (declared) direction towards the promotion of sustainability principles.

In practice, the planning policy exercised by both the socialist and conservative governments that were in power in the 90's and mid 2000's deviated to a large degree from the aim of the legislation. Firstly, there was a gradual introduction of neoliberal policies and practices undermining planning which besides the simplification of permitting procedures for strategic investments, included the wide use of exceptionality measures mainly in conjunction with the construction of the Olympic facilities which were approached as mega-projects that would enhance the competitive advantage and therefore, the strategic role of Athens at the European level. It must be noted though, that the promotion of strategies embedded in wider urban development agendas underlying such notions as 'urban entrepreneurship', the 'creative city' and 'city branding' was very limited and mainly associated with the rhetoric legitimizing the Olympic Games projects. This 'transfer policy delay' was related not only with the then predominant planning culture of the country, but also with the traditionally regulative role of planning as well as the limited development powers and capacities of local governments.

Secondly, even though the preparation and adoption of national spatial plans (in the mid 2000's) was a significant step towards the implementation of the 90's Planning Act, the integration of the planning system never materialized especially in reference to local plans. In fact, it became apparent that these plans – as policy frameworks for the spatial organization of major economic activities promoted at that time, i.e. tourism – were to serve mainly as instruments for overcoming the legal obstacles posed by the Greek Council of State regarding the ad hoc location of these activities in areas not covered by statutory local land use plans. However, the preparation process of national spatial plans contributed in a substantive way towards the establishment of planning as the arena for the resolution of land use conflicts by allowing the articulation of alternative discourses and the redirection, though marginal, of the pro-growth policies of these plans.

2. THE CONDITIONALITY OF REGULATORY RESTRUCTURING

The reform of this planning system – strictly oriented towards development control – is central to the extensive process of institutional restructuring that is taking place in Greece under the state of emergency imposed in this time of crisis. Responding to EU crisis policy and debtors' demands, the country has committed to implement an adjustment program which mandates the adoption of fiscal consolidation measures as well as deep structural, market orientated, reforms that touch upon all dimensions of the institutional landscape existing before the crisis: wage-labor relations (or growth-enhancing structural reforms as defined in the Memorandum); fiscal policies, which besides imposing austerity measures and severe budget cuts, include the extensive privatization of state owned property, public assets and common goods; monetary and financial regulations; and forms of regulation enabling / mediating corporate competition. These structural 'reforms,' which must be implemented within specified timeframes, constitute essential conditionalities for the disbursement of the financial assistance to Greece by the European Financial Stability Facility.

Among the conditionalities included in the second Memorandum signed by the Greek government in 2012, *"Memorandum of Understanding on Specific Economic Policy Conditionality"*, were a series of measures calling for the facilitation of spatial planning which included the:

- simplification of town planning processes (including the reduction of needed time)
- update and codification of legislation on forests, forests lands and parks
- codification of legislation on forests
- the revision of regional spatial plans in order to make them compatible with the sectoral plans on tourism, aquaculture, industry and renewable energy, and
- acceleration of the completion of the land registry

To a large degree, the imposed measures seemed to respond to a pre-existing demand for restructuring the planning system to address and ameliorate some of its long enduring negative structural characteristics: legislative complexity (multiplicity of laws), ambiguous and conflicting regulations that greatly increased administrative discretion, lack of coordination, centralization of planning powers and very long processes for plan preparation, approval and amendment (YPEKA, 2012). However, different drafts of the Memorandum, prepared during the negotiation process, reveal the existence of alternative proposals calling for deeper reforms leading to the redefinition of planning's scope and direction by calling for:

- the reform of planning, which entailed the review and amendment of general planning and land use legislation with a view to ensure more flexibility in land development for private investment and the simplification and acceleration of land use plans
- the establishment of a One-Stop Shop for the licensing and permitting of various activities, and
- the simplification of environmental, building and operating permits.

The divergent mandates do not only reflect underlying differences of perspective in reference to the rapidly prevailing political position supporting the dominance of market processes. They, moreover, epitomize the importance that the regulation of land, as a factor of production, has for this neoliberal restructuring strategy in the sense that the facilitation of direct investments is considered the main (only) impetus to realize the country's new growth model which is based on real estate-related tourism, industrial scale development of alternative energy sources, logistics, agriculture, aquaculture, mineral extraction and health services[3].

Although, the process of regulatory restructuring that ensued and was legitimated upon the obligation to implement the prescribed conditionalities was at first characterized by these underlying contradictions regarding the content and scope of the 'reform', it has come to be defined by the gradual prevalence of the neoliberal dogma. Within this overall framework, the

---

[3] | The government's new growth strategy was largely based on the report "Greece 10 years ahead. Defining Greece's new growth model and strategy" prepared by McKinsey and Company in 2012 and commissioned by the Association of Greek Industrialists.

process has so far involved the production of over 30 pieces of legislation directly affecting the use and development of land that have been adopted or are in the process of adoption. Characterized by extremely brief public consultation and parliamentary review procedures and, oftentimes, surpassing the limits of constitutional legality – which in some cases has enforced the resubmission of legislation due to its annulment by the Council of State – this process has essentially resulted in the 'dismantling of the inherited institutional landscape' (Brenner and Theodore, 2002) affecting the use and development of land.

3. Development re-regulation

In addition to the piecemeal transformation of the spatial planning system which will be described in the following sections, the emergent institutional landscape includes an array of new policies and procedures affecting the use and development of land. Overall, these are, generally, oriented to overcoming the particularities of space production in Greece – i.e. small property holdings, land use configurations and protective status of natural capital – that have so far inhibited the construction of the new 'urban spaces of neoliberalization' (ibid) and more particularly, large scale urban and real estate development projects.

Built environment and urban form

With a declared intent to provide 'solutions' to the issue of building stock renewal and the re-investment of construction capital in built up areas, the amended universally applied Building Construction Code (L. 4067/2011) focused primarily on the increase of densities and building heights and the promotion of land consolidation. More specifically, according to the Greek Association of Architects, the new Code "... introduces and adopts the logic of real estate in cities. It rewards, by a 25-35% increase in floor area ratios, the development of large tracts of land in the already congested urban centers of Greek cities. In the attempt to reverse the declining of degraded areas, it offers a disproportionate increase of floor area ratios and height to the detriment of already built up areas. The logic of devaluing the existing building stock, as obsolete, by a land consolidation premium that produces buildings that are out of the existing scale and serves special interests, alters the urban environment, the quality of life of the inhabitants and the existing social and economic structure" (SADAS, 2012).

Respectively, the recently adopted Land Use Classification Code[4], moving away from the development of a hierarchical system of land use categories, it establishes a zoning system which restricts in a substantive way planning's power to formulate locally specific land use configurations[5]. By further intensifying a pre-existing policy of land use mix, the new land use zones provided for the: a) substantial intensification of commercial, institutional and office use in residential areas as well as the location and/or expansion of, potentially conflicting uses, i.e. parking lots for freight trucks and hospitals, that are anticipated to exacerbate in these areas the negative neighborhood effects characterizing Greek cities, that is, noise, traffic congestion and increased levels of air pollution, b) the formation of a multitude of mixed use districts directed towards the attraction of real estate related productive and entrepreneurial activities, i.e, trade zones, enterprise zones, logistics, tourism, technopoles, and c) the commercialization of public and open space in urbanized areas.

Streamlining of permitting procedures

In the name of combatting corruption, the new policies (Laws 4024/2011 and 4030/2011) deregulate and privatize the permitting process by greatly reducing state control powers and transferring responsibilities to architects / designers, supervising engineers and private controllers. As a result, the ensuing autocratic system grounded on the superiority of the moral ethic of the private sector, proclaims its distrust to the citizens and public servants, thereby failing to empower the inherited system through the promotion of transparency and accountability in public services. Furthermore, the updated fast-track procedures proclaiming the 'speeding

---

[4] After several drafts which were substantially differentiated in terms of content, the Land Use Code was adopted by Law in the same Bill as the reformed planning system instead of a Presidential Decree and was, thus, not subjected to a review by the Council of State.

[5] For example, in the residential use category, the Law promotes strip development of commercial and office use along the, mostly over-capacity, main road network by mandating the designation of roadside properties as urban activity centres while restricting residential use.

up and transparency in the implementation of strategic investments' are solely directed towards bypassing local resistances, i.e. by substantively limiting pre-existing public consultation timeframes and procedures thereby restricting the ability/power of competent public authorities to even express advisory opinions.

Consolidation of property rights

With the sole intent to increase state revenues, an extensive program formalizing illegal construction is still underway. Grounded on the particularities of the Greek property and real estate system, this policy, fundamentally fiscal in nature, detached the entire 'legalization' process from spatial development and planning policies while rendering acceptable the consequent degradation of both the natural and built environment. The invalidation of the first Law (L 4014/11) by the Council of State led to its subsequent amendment (L.4178/13) based on a distorted use of land bank and transfer of development rights concepts which essentially provide for an extensive re-allocation of development rights throughout the country.

Environmental deregulation

The initial focus of the, then, socialist government in the promotion of green economy in cities and the integration of European environmental directives into Greek Law[6], was soon re-directed towards the simplification of procedures for Environmental Impact Studies (L. 4014/2011 and) and lately, on the severe limitation and /or annulment of the protective status of primarily forests and other natural and environmentally sensitive areas by permitting the location of various economic activities such as tourism, industry, livestock farming and mining (Laws.4264/14 and 4258/14). The potential damage inflicted upon the core of the country's natural capital by two recent legislative proposals[7], one providing for new

---

6 | These included primarily the Laws for: Landscape Conservation (L. 3827/2010); Protection of Biodiversity (L. 3739/211); Management of the Marine environment (L. 3983/2011).

7 | Both of these proposals were openly supported by the Troika and the European Commission on the grounds that they constituted a Memorandum conditionality (Kathimerini, 2013)).

classification categories for forested areas and the other for the intensive development of the seashore, were repealed by the government, at least temporarily, because of issues of constitutionality and immense public opposition. In particular, the legislative proposal regarding the seashore – prepared and submitted for adoption by the Ministry of Finance instead of the competent Ministry of the Environment – provided not only for the intense development and commercialization of the sea, seashore, and the beach, but also for the abolition of their public use character[8].

Planning reform 1: "Deregulating" panning

The dismantling of the planning system was first achieved through the adoption of the regulatory framework providing for the privatization of state-owned property articulated in the seminal law entitled *Emergency Measures for the Implementation of the Medium Term Fiscal Strategy Framework 2012-2015* (L. 3986/11). By giving highest priority to the successful implementation of the entire privatization program, the law has been a core element of the new institutional landscape both in terms of its impact on spatial planning as well as on the consolidation of new forms of urban governance.

A fundamental provision of this law was the consolidation of a new "regulatory regime" that annulled statutory planning by functioning in parallel with it (Zifou, 2012). Having as a core objective to safeguard the sale or concession of public lands under investors' terms, the new regulatory regime has exclusive power over the processes of planning, permitting and selling of property. Summarized below are the constitutive features of this regime which denote essential aspects of the wider transformations of spatial planning policy that are taking place in the conjuncture of the crisis in Greece.

---

8 | Described as "the proposal that sacrifices everything on the investors' altar" ,it is the only piece of legislation that has mobilized immense public opposition and contestation reflecting the fact that the seashore and the beach have been established in peoples' consciousness as public goods that everyone should have free access to, a right also provided by the Greek constitution.

New decision making and permitting structures: The Hellenic Republic Asset Development Fund, S.A. (TAIPED), modeled after Treuhand[9], is established as the agency responsible for implementing the privatization program of the country. In accordance with the law, the Ministry of Finance has to transfer full ownership, possession and occupation of all public assets that are to be privatized to the Fund which is to be supported by a council of advisors, some members of which are appointed by EU member states, as well as technical, financial and legal, mostly foreign, experts. The Fund has the absolute control over the use as well as the management of the sale of the sites and functions, along with any other SA that it may establish to manage individual properties, as a 'one-stop-shop' agency responsible for the issuance of all the required planning and building permits. So far, a total of 412 properties located all over Greece and covering a land area of approximately 110 mil m^2 and 516.000 m^2 of building surface have been put up for sale – a great number of which includes environmentally sensitive areas (i.e. Natura 2000 sites), beachfront areas and/or archeological sites (Picture 1). As indicated by the present functioning of the Fund, apart from the lack of transparency and public accountability, this take-over of state control has not only established a type of neocolonial regime influencing urban dynamics and promoting land grabbing, it is also facilitating the opening up of the Greek land and real estate markets to global processes of capital accumulation[10].

---

9 | It is the agency responsible for the implementation of the privatization program of the former German Democratic Republic.

10 | The intricate ways by which this new regulatory regime allows the transfer of policies and the rearrangement of relations between national and supranational institutions is exemplified by the recent announcement of the Fund to hire Deutsche Bank, BNP and UBS to act as is consultants in order to comply with Troika's request for the speeding up of the formulation and adoption of the legal framework providing for the securitization of real property in Greece.

Picture 1: An interactive map showing 195 of state owned properties that are currently on sale by TAIPED whose privatization is estimated to have direct impacts on the physical environment.

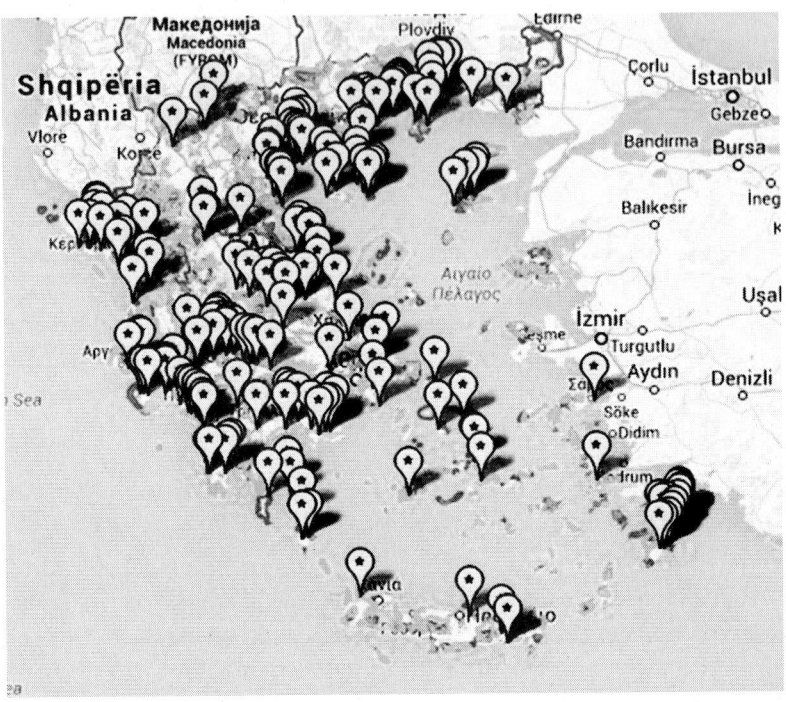

Source: Hellenic Ornithological Society (2014)

Establishment of new planning tools[11]: in order to provide the necessary certainty to investors and turn the properties into viable that is, profitable economic ventures, this regulatory framework introduces: a) proposed land use designations applied only to state owned properties consisting of mixed use zones oriented primarily to tourism and consumption, and b) a new planning instrument, the 'Special Development Plan', that specifies permitted land-use and development regulations for each property. The

---

11 | A similar regulatory framework has also been established for the development of public and private strategic investments (L 3894/2010).

plan is prepared by the Fund and adopted by ministerial decree[12] with the intent to determine each property's 'investment identity' in order to initiate the bidding process for its subsequent sale or concession. These plans are empowered to by-pass and amend statutory local land use plans and environmental regulations and to specify terms for the use and development of the seashore and the beach, which are conceded to the buyer / investor, thereby, annulling their public use character which is (was) a constitutionally vested right. This planning process has been widely contested not only for its total lack of transparency and public accountability but also for its reliance upon the 'logic of the market' that disregards any concerns for the integration of prospective developments into local environments and therefore their particular needs and socio-economic dynamics. A case in point, is the privatization of the 620 ha property of the former airport of Ellinikon in Athens (Picture 2), where contrary to the original designation of the site as a Metropolitan Park and despite the immense opposition expressed at the local level (Picture 3), the Special Plan provided for a mix of land uses – covering a total area of 1,7 mi m^2– that compose a mixed use enclave (picture 4) with an emphasis in consumption and catered to mainly upper income foreign buyers while excluding Athenians from the sea front of the city (Vatavali and Zifou, 2012; Castro et al., 2013).

---

12 | Only the non-obligatory opinion of the Regional Authority, submitted during the Strategic Environmental Assessment approval process, is taken into consideration for the issuance of the ministerial decree.

Picture 2: The site of the former Airport of Ellinikon in its urban setting

Picture 3: Protest against the privatization of the property

Picture 4: A conceptual master plan submitted for the development of the site

Securing the profitability of the investment: a significant provision of this Law is that the state is obliged to: a) provide the infrastructure needed to service the site, i.e., road network, and utilities, the construction of which must be given first priority despite the extensive budget cuts due to austerity policies, and b) pay the moving cost for all the activities, i.e. public services, public administration etc, that might be located on site. At the same time, the (neoliberal in origin) policy of exacting community benefits as a compensation for the impacts of the development on local communities is converted into an opportunity for the investors since it is connected with an increase of the permitted densities.

Planning reform 2: Consolidation of flexibility

After almost two years of elaboration, a new Planning Act was adopted amidst wide opposition – by parties of the Left and professional associations – regarding its content and ostensible consultation procedures[13]. Based on the widely held assertion dominating the public discourse since the inception of the crisis that land use planning constituted an obstacle to investments and, therefore, to economic growth (Kathimerini, 2012; Reporter, 2013, Mckinsey and Company, 2012), the new Act provides for the full scale restructuring of the spatial planning system. So, contrary to the original demand – and apparently to the conditionality as officially stated in the Memorandum – for the amendment of the 1990's planning legislation with a direction towards the update and simplification of planning processes (i.e. local plan preparation could take up to 7 years on the average), the reform is focused on dismantling the inherited planning system with an all defining objective: to embed flexibility, 'the watchword of the neo-liberal state' (Harvey, 2005), into planning. Flexibility which is achieved not by deregulation but through the construction of a new centrally-controlled planning system designed to accommodate the new economic, and political, landscape under terms that allow the unconditional (and subsidized in the case of public lands) materialization of all large scale investments. The emergent planning system is constructed upon the following fundamental elements:

---

13 | The new Planning Law was submitted for adoption in late June (2014), under a process of 'extreme urgency', in the Recess Section of the Greek parliament, which is composed of only one third of all MPs and allows the construction of parliamentary majorities and was immediately adopted after only a day's discussion in the competent parliamentary committee.

Economic determinism

A dominant feature of the emerging planning policy is that the economy is considered the only determining factor for the formulation of spatial strategies and subsequently, of plan content. This policy directive emanates directly from the Act which specifies that future strategies and plans, particularly the ones developed at the national and regional level constituting the guidance framework for local planning, must be informed by the National Economic Strategy, the Medium Term Framework for the Fiscal Strategy[14] (that is, the country's adjustment program) and the Public Investment Program without making any reference to other spheres of activity. The prevalence of this economic rationality denotes that the new 'paradigm' views planning as the mere spatial expression of the country's economic program as it is defined by the political economic context of the crisis. Although this direction may be considered a prominent planning trend under the regulatory conditions of neoliberalism (Allmendinger, 2001; Taylor, 1998) the absence of any reference to social and environmental goals and policy guidelines including relevant provisions of the Greek constitution illustrates a total lack of concern for achieving, or even striving for, environmental and social justice.

This proposition is verified, as far as environmental protection is concerned, in the following case involving the recent update of the (National) Spatial Plan for Tourism (L. 3155/2013), the objective of which is to provide guidelines for the spatial organization of tourism, considered to be a flagship sector of the economy. The update of the preceding Plan – adopted in 2009 right before the outbreak of the crisis – was presented as necessary in order to accommodate / comply with the government's new strategy for tourism prepared by the competent Ministry of Tourism. Reflecting to a large degree the proposals made by the McKinsey report, which estimated that the country's future tourist model may, potentially, include the construction of 30-35 new marinas and 25 integrated tourist resorts[15] (Pictures 5 and 6) with a total area of 4,5 million m² the Ministry's strategy provided for the

---

14 | A provision which clearly illustrates the 'temporal fixity' () of the measures adopted under the 'state of emergency'.

15 | New legislation is being prepared allowing the drawing of sale or lease contracts before the construction of vacation homes in order to enable the materialization of these developments.

immense growth of the sector with a focus on real estate related tourism[16], while it also defined relevant development regulations.

Pictures 5 and 6: Conceptual plans of integrated tourist developments on a Greek island

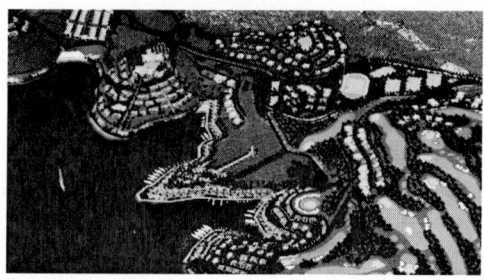

In turn, in conformance with the sectoral plan's guidelines, the Spatial Plan without any consideration for issues such as the capacity of environmental-technical-social infrastructure, natural resource depletion, or climate change, allows the indiscriminate location of tourist activities and tourist integrated resorts (Maps 1 and 2) all over the country, irrespective of local conditions and dynamics reflected in the plan area-categories (i.e. overdeveloped, urban, insular, mountainous, Natura 2000

---

16 | This post-colonial tourist development model associated with large multinational corporations, precarious employment and limited dispersal of tourism-related activity to local communities is greatly differentiated from the so far prevalent model in the country characterized by its integration into local economies and the small/medium scale invested (mostly Greek) capital.

sites) and in direct contrast to the provisions of the previous Plan which were, already, widely contested for their pro-growth direction.

Map 1: Designated guidelines for the spatial organization of Tourism*

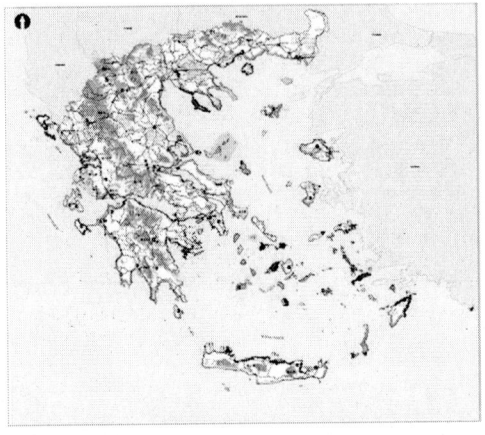

Map 2: Organization of the tourist port network**

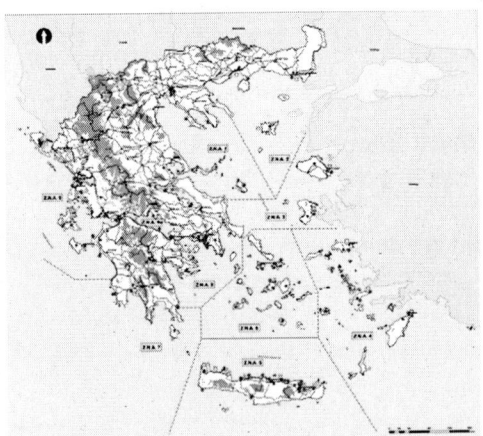

Source: Ministry of the Environment, Climate Change and Energy

* Colors and patterns denote spatial categories
** Includes marinas (red circles), hotel ports (purple) and anchorages (green)

Centrally determined policies

A second defining characteristic of the new planning system is the introduction of increased state control over plan content with the aim to ensure that land use regulation is firmly embedded in central government strategies to attract capital. This is primarily instituted through the establishment of a top-down hierarchical planning system[17] with no substantive feedback provisions, the main features of which include:

- the reduction of the "National (General) Spatial Plan" – originally intended to provide 'priorities and strategic guidelines for the integrated spatial development and sustainable organization of the national space' (L. 2742/99) – to a *National Spatial Policy* outlining the government's basic priorities and medium term goals for the spatial development of the country[18]
- the strengthening of the regulative function of sector-specific spatial plans prepared at the national level, in continuance of the pre-crisis planning policy and despite the Law's intent for these plans to take on a more strategic character. This provision greatly increases their command over the policy content of regional and local plans whose role is essentially reduced to qualify / specify the guidelines of national plans.
- the reduction to the absolute minimum of public deliberation procedures which, in the new planning culture, are viewed as the major factor for plan preparation delays.

The most controversial issue, however, relates to the power assigned to the Minister of the Environment, Climate Change and Energy (the competent ministry for spatial planning) to amend plans, including local plans, on the basis that the proposed amendments are, as they are vaguely referred to in the Law, "localized and non-essential".

---

17 | With the exception of the abolishment of metropolitan strategic plans, the basic structure of the system remains the same.

18 | Whereas the previous plan was adopted by Law, and therefore subjected to parliamentary review, under the new Law, the National Spatial Policy is approved by the Cabinet and its notification to the Parliament for discussion is not mandatory.

The prevalence of master planning

Apart from the exercise of central government's control over the content of local land use policies, the 'reformed' Act introduces two other features that in total result in the weakening, and in essence abolishing, the role of local planning (and in turn of local communities' capacity) in guiding development.

Firstly, despite the implementation of the local government restructuring program in 2010 involving power decentralization as well as extensive local unit consolidation resulting in a decrease in the number of municipalities by almost 1/3, central government retains its power over the preparation and approval of local plans which are, now, drawn for only a section of the municipality corresponding to the area of the old municipal units. Moreover, municipalities are given one month to express their opinion on local plan content after which the plan approval process proceeds by the competent Minister without regard on whether such an opinion has been submitted. Secondly, the Act embodies into the planning system, as a new type of local plan, the master plans which were recently introduced, as an exceptionality, for the development of state-owned properties and strategic investments. These plans, which may now be prepared for any type of large scale development, i.e. tourism, housing, enterprise districts etc., not only do not have to comply with the provisions of (municipal) local plans, as they are considered to be on the same hierarchical level, but they may also amend them.

The dominance of this fragmented, project-led approach constitutes a major retreat from the '90s planning policy aim to ground development control on a unitary land use plan, thereby severely limiting the earlier intention to provide a programmatic and guidance framework for local community development[19] while, at the same time, reinforcing urbanization trends that exacerbate urban sprawl.

---

19 | The development and programmatic framework for each municipality, i.e. population projections, development perspective/ vision, spatial organization etc., is now defined by the corresponding regional plan which is prepared and approved by the Ministry of the Environment, Energy and Climate Change.

4. Conclusion

The structural adjustment program imposed in this time of crisis in Greece, in the name of reducing public deficit and paying up the sovereign debt has placed land, and more generally space, at the center of the ongoing regulatory restructuring process, while it is facilitating the entry of global financial capital and its companion, international / globalized real estate in the Greek property market (thus, changing rapidly the so far dominant social and economic relations within the country). In this process of neoliberalization, the imposed market driven regulatory restructuring is forcing the dismantling of an already market supportive planning system which, however, by embodying the political view of 'social democracy', was oriented to a middle-class society and to the fulfillment of social cohesion goals. In its place, a new planning paradigm is established based on a different conception of interests, power and outcomes. Oriented solely towards promoting entrepreneurship and corporate competition, the new planning system is considered an instrument to combating the crisis, i.e. sovereign debt, unemployment, and capital accumulation, through urbanization and the exploitation of common goods and public assets.

The new regulatory landscape is institutionalizing two major changes which constitute both a long departure from addressing the long lasting structural problems of Greek cities and more generally of spatial organization, i.e. deficient public space, conflicting land uses, urban sprawl, as well as a substantive rupture with the so far dominant planning policy. The first change rises from the further concentration of planning power to central government and the emergent regulatory regimes, a policy that fosters the transfer of the debate and negotiations regarding space production from the public sphere to ministers' offices, elite power centers and teams of specialists and foreign experts. The adaptation of the former system of clientelism to the new political economy context is associated with the total restriction of public access to decision making and/or the absolute minimization of public consultation processes, and thereby raises serious concerns regarding the lack of transparency and democratic control. And while the inherited system could not claim much relation to communicative rationality – especially in terms of including notions of the 'other' – it nevertheless promoted planning as the arena for knowledge generation and the resolution of conflicts regarding spatial development. On the contrary, the new model dismisses any alternative development discourse while denying/ignoring any form of contestation and severely limiting the right of local communities to influence local trajectories, and even less, formulate locally-contingent strategies.

Secondly, the emergent development and spatial organization patterns emphasizing large-scale, mixed use planned developments, are based on the transfer of 'recipes' that have been implemented in developing or post-socialist countries thereby ignoring local particularities which are embedded in the, until now, dominant social relations. The aesthetic convergence and adoption of post-modern lifestyles highlighted by tourist-entertainment resorts, shopping malls and thematic parks raise serious questions regarding not only the future morphology of Greek cities, the countryside and the islands but also the effects of this new configuration towards the formation of divisions and spaces of exclusion uncharacteristic of Greek cities. Additionally, one has to wonder about the degree to which the development of these 'spaces of neoliberalization' are associated with the suppression of the role of middle class, small construction companies/ entrepreneurial capital and small size land ownership in space production processes, thus creating new socio-spatial inequalities.

Moreover, the absolute domination of economic rationality as a defining element of the emerging planning policy has so far been equated with the unconditional use and selling off / transfer of the country's natural assets and public lands. Thus, in the name of creating a favorable business environment, as a fundamental mission of the neoliberal state, a tremendous pressure is put upon the country's pristine natural environment, coastal areas and beaches undermining their quality, their value and as it seems, their public use character. At the same time, the equation of the public good with the fulfillment of fiscal objectives, economic entrepreneurship and competitiveness inhibits the so far redistributive role of planning while it legitimizes the socialization of costs and the privatization of profit. So, even though the consequences of the debt crisis and its associated policies are already evident in the new urban landscape and in peoples' everyday lives, i.e. poverty, vacancies, diminishing public services, homelessness and increasing housing foreclosures, the emergent planning policy is leading towards the re-creation of a speculative growth model which has been directly associated with the recent global economic crisis. In this conjuncture, when austerity politics have created conditions of humanitarian crisis in Greek cities, the new planning policy seems to not only defy objectives for social cohesion, and more generally social and environmental justice, but also to foster the division of land solely for profit instead of meeting human needs.

REFERENCES

Aglietta, M. (1979) A Theory of Capitalist Regulation: The US Experience. London: Verso

Allmendinger, P. (2001) Planning in Postmodern Times. London: Routledge

Amin, A. (ed.) (1994) Post Fordism. A Reader. London: Blackwell

Brenner, N. and N. Theodore (2002) Cities and the Geographies of "Actually Existing Neoliberalism". In: Antipode, 349-379

Castro, M., B. Garcia, F.Vatavali and M. Zifou (2013) Ultra-neoliberal urban development in Spain and Greece. The case of Port Vell in Barcelona and Hellinikon Airport in Athens. In: Geographies, 22, 14-29

Hall, S. (1988) Brave New World. In: Marxism Today, October: 9-24

Harvey, D. (2005) Spaces of neoliberalization: towards a theory of uneven geographical development. München: Decker and Bokor

Hellenic Ornithological Society (2014) http://ornithologiki.us7.list-manage1.com/track/ click?u=57eddb7e8d462b19fa2d8093eandid=bd9d84e6dcande=afd3c9a7c7 (last access: 24/9/2014)

Kathimerini (2013) Invest in Greece: Spatial planning is an obstacle to investments. In: Kathimerini – Greek daily newspaper, Business section, 7.11.13

Mantouvalou, M. and M. Mavridou (1993) Informal construction: one way street on dead end. In: Architects' Association Bulletin, 7, 58-71

Mantouvalou, M. and E. Balla (2004) Transformations in the land and construction system and planning stakes in Greece today. In: City and Space from the 20th to 21st centuty. Honorary volume for the Prof. A. Aravantinos, Athens: NTUA, Univ. of Thessaly, SEPOX: 313-330.

Mantouvalou M. and G. Patrikios (2008), Athens' narrative of regulation processes and models of urban growth. Paper presented in the 18th INURA meeting, Athens 3-10 October http://inura08.files.wordpress.com/2008/10/ mantouvaloupatrikios-athens.pdf (last access: 24/11/2012).

Peck J. and A. Tickell (2002) Neoliberalizing space. In: Antipode, 380-404

Peck, J., N. Theodore and N. Brenner (2012) Neoliberalism Resurgent? Market Rule after the Great Recession. In: The South Atlantic Quarterly 111/2, 265-288

Reporter (2013) Investor Mediator: lack of property rights and permitting procedures, the obstacle to development. Reporter, e-news, 8.11.13, www.reporter.gr (in greek)

Taylor, N. (1998) Urban Planning Theory since 1945. London: Sage

Vaiou, D., M. Mantouvalou and M. Mavridou (2000) Post war Greek city planning between theory and conjuncture. In: Proceedings of the 2nd Conference of the Society for the History of City and City Planning, Volos: 25-37

Vatavali, F. and M. Zifou (2012) Transformations of spatial planning in the time of crisis in Greece. The case of Hellinikon. Presentation in the Aegean Seminars, Syros, 4-7 September

Zifou, M. (2012) Planning policy in Greece in the conjuncture of the crisis: a critical perspective. In: Proceedings of the 3rd Hellenic Conference of Urban Planning and Regional Development, Volos

"The right to the city" in Athens during a crisis era

Between inversion, assimilation and going beyond

Vaso Makrygianni and Charalampos Tsavdaroglou

Ever since the book of Henri Lefebvre "The right to the city" was published in 1968 it served as a great inspiration for several scholars, researchers, academics and activists. Being the point of departure for various urban movements, it contributed to a wave of resistance and destabilization of sovereignty in many parts of the western world during the turbulent decades of the 60s and 70s. While it has become extremely popular or even fashionable, it often appears detached from its original meaning. Various forms of sovereignty used its revolutionary and innovative rhetoric in an attempt to grand radical contexts in their political agendas. Forty five years after the first publication of Lefebvre's book, the Athenian metropolis, a city in the (epi)center of the crisis turmoil, is governed by a municipal authority party that goes under the name of "Right to the City". The party adopted much of Lefebvre's revolutionary rhetoric, such as "the city as oeuvre", in order to form its political agenda and win the municipal elections of 2010 and 2014. Ever since, a political program is applied based on a rather distorted interpretation of "the right to the city".

In this chapter two approaches of "The right to the city" ('TRTTC' from now on) will be confronted. On the one hand the Lefebvrian notion of the 1960s and on the other hand Kaminis' (the Athens mayoral candidate) appropriation of 2010 and 2014. The first approach is considered as an effort to introduce the Marxian thought in spatial thinking in order to contribute to the emerging emancipatory movements, and the second as a fine example of distortion of contexts in favor of gaining power and promoting neoliberal policies.

In this direction, we unfold the political program of Kaminis and examine its applications versus its title and theoretical context. By examining urban policies and tactics that are applied under the cloak of "TRTTC" and form the everyday life in Athens we intend to demonstrate that divisions between form and content can often lead to the complete inversion of primal meanings. By lifting the veil of propaganda it becomes visible that the assimilation of radical contexts on behalf of municipal authority does not lead to emancipatory urban policies but aims to cover up sovereignty.

Bringing to surface neo-interpretations of Lefebvre's analysis, though, does not only enlighten the subversion of the original notions or highlight them as stolen contexts from sovereignty. In fact, not only is it a great opportunity to explore once again and rethink what Lefebvre was teaching and writing during the 60s but also a motive to question, think beyond and challenge it in the contemporary contexts of urban uprisings and revolts. Inspired by the work of several radical scholars like Harvey, de Souza or Pasquinelli we make an argument on the perspectives beyond the Lefebvrian notion and an attempt to approach Athens as an emerging rebel city. During the crisis years various struggles and acts of solidarity have been taking place in the city area, thus several spaces of resistance and commoning have emerged. In this regard, we deal with the transition from demanding the city to occupying the city as a contemporary space of resistance.

1. "THE RIGHT TO THE CITY": TWO CONTRADICTORY APPROACHES AND A SUBVERSIVE PRACTICE

1.1 "The Right to the City" and the Lefebvrian approach

In the late 60's Henri Lefebvre wrote his famous book the "The Right To The City". The publication of the book in 1968 coincided with the 100th anniversary of the publication of Marx's Capital, and came just before the revolutionary outbreaks in Paris, Prague, the rest of Europe and the US. "TRTTC" was influential for several radical scholars and urban movements like DIY urbanism in Sydney, Australia or the Right to the

City Alliance in NY,USA , to name but a few. One of the basic thesis and point of departure of Lefebvre (1996: 109) was that

"the city [is] *a projection of society on the ground* that is, not only on the actual site, but at a specific level, perceived and conceived by thought, [...] the city [is] the place of confrontations and of (conflictual) relations (...), the city [is] the 'site of desire' (...) and site of revolutions".

In the previous quote Lefebvre demonstrated the trialectical character of space as conceived, perceived and lived, which he farther analyzed in his later work "The Production of Space" (Lefebvre 1974). By verbalizing imaginary spaces which are crucial to every process of space alteration he widened not only the notion of space but also the possibilities to imagine and produce different spatialities. By introducing social relations as a mean of space production he questioned vividly both the hierarchical perception of city space in terms of production (according to which space was formed by the expertised authorities) and the perception of space as two dimensional or box container of life. Moreover, according to several scholars (Collinge, 2008; Soja, 1989; Shields, 1999) Lefebvre's analysis constituted a break to the former aspatial dialectic of historical materialism of orthodox Marxism. Lefebvre thematised space and suggested that the dialectic can be "raised up" from a temporal to a spatial medium. For our purpose, one of the most significant contributions of Lefebvre's point of view is that he identified the space and the city as a result of social class antagonisms.

In this regard, Lefebvres' concept of "TRTTC" challenged the notion of citizen. By bringing to surface people as protagonists of the production of city space and introducing a dialectical schema of space -production he gave a new meaning to citizenship. In his thought, citizenship is not defined by membership in the nation-state but is based on membership in inhabitance, thus on the everyday production of city space. As Purcell (2003: 577) notes "Everyday life (...) is the central pivot of the TRTTC: those who go about their daily routines in the city, both living in and creating space, are those who possess a legitimate right to the city (Lefebvre 1991a)". Though he didn't manage to escape from the notion of the white west man as the absolute subject he contributed vividly to the proclamation of emancipator strategies.

Furthermore, Lefebvre (1996: 158) clarified that "TRTTC" is not a typical right to nature and the countryside but "in the face of this pseudo-right, the right to the city is like a cry and a demand" and he (1996: 173-174) continued "right to freedom, to individualization in socialization, to habitat and to inhabit, (...) to the oeuvre, to participation and appropriation (clearly distinct from the right to property), are implied in the right to the city".

In his work, like so many other scholars of the decade of the 60s, he aimed not only to reach the analytical tools in order to understand the city but also to encounter all those forces able to change it. In his words the right to the city meant "a radical restructuring of social, politic and economic relations, both in the city and beyond" (Lefebvre 1996:34). As Marcuse (2010: 88) points out the right to the city is far more than the individual liberty to access urban resources and as Harvey (2008:26) adheres "it is a right to change ourselves by changing the city". Stavrides (2007:8) felicity described it :"Lefebvre, encountered in the city not only horror but also hope, not only orderliness but also disorder, not only the reproduction of the sovereign principles but also challenge, not only the normalization of routine but also the liberation feast."

1.2 "The Right to the City" and the sovereignty approach: a short discourse analysis

In 2010 the new party "RTTC", under the leadership of George Kaminis, a former ombudsman, participated in the municipal elections. In the first round of the November 2010 elections Kaminis' party came in second but managed to win the second round, gaining 52% of the popular vote against the conservative party of the former mayor, Nikitas Kaklamanis, mainly due to the support of the centre-left. Kaminis governed the city for the period 2000-2014 and in May 25th 2014 won the second round of the elections that assured him another 5 years of service. It is noteworthy that, for the first time, in 2010 a Nazi political party entered the town council, while in 2014 it came third with about 120.000 votes.

The manifesto of the party "TRTTC" focused on citizens, public space (mainly in terms of cleanness and security), private property, social services, green development and innovative entrepreneurship. Within this optic, Kaminis (2010a:5) considered the city as a "collective oeuvre created by the inhabitants, the visitors and everyone that lives and works in the city and creates its actual wealth". Moreover, he (2010b) adhered:

"I am referring to our common perception that life in the city essentially means an aggregation of rights. Rights that are nowadays under massive attack; from the right to mobility in public space without spatial and temporal limitations, to the right to work, to private property, to the freedom of creation. For all of us, 'demanding the city' means demanding our right to the city; all the rights for all human beings. We want and demand a civilized city, open to its citizens and open to the world."

Reading, however, in depth Kaminis manifesto we come across to several contradictions. First and foremost, the inclusion of as many as possible in "the collective oeuvre" that forms the city is indicative of the gap between form and content in Kaminis rhetoric. Obviously this invocation was made in order to target potential voters and to reinforce the pluralistic profile of the party. Kaminis himself was presented as "a citizen for the citizens" (Kaminis, 2010a: 2). Still, the way he conceived the notion of citizen involved several inconsistencies and contradictions. Though he referred to citizens, inhabitants, workers and students in general, he posed a clear distinction between indigenous and newcomer population. Likewise, in his political manifesto appears an underlying bias for young couples or students that should inhabit the city center and change its character, not only due to their economic status (the crisis hadn't completely unraveled when the manifesto was formed in 2010) but mainly because they are regarded as members of the city's "creative class". Kaminis adopted much of the government's rhetoric for "preferable citizens", a creative class that would inhabit the freshly gentrified areas of the city center.

However following Lefebvre (1991b:2342, translated in Kofman and Lebas, 1996: 34) the right to the city, complemented by the right to difference and the right to information, should modify, concretize and make more practical the rights of the citizen as an urban dweller (citadin) and user of multiple services.; it would also cover the right to the use of the center, a privileged place, instead of being dispersed and stuck into ghettos (for workers, immigrants, the 'marginal' and even for the 'privilege').

In total discrepancy, Kaminis endorses the analysis of the ghettoization of the city center and introduces security, urban development and entrepreneurship as a response. He is in accordance with gentrification processes, as we will show later on, that are promoted as the salvation of the so-called "city's decay" and brings forth cultural capital as the leading force behind real estate, while appears eager to attract both investments and highly skilled workers.

But the emersion of this "chimera", as Pasquinelli (2010) would describe the above strategy, determines also the relation between the city and the rest of the world. This relation with the "outside" is filtered thoroughly through the tourist industry. Athens is considered as the "face of the country" and therefore a highly important touristic destination. Though the rhetoric of the Olympic Games (2004) for a competitive city full of large-scale projects has faded, Kaminis brings forth once again the importance of the city image as a link to the outside. He unfolds a strategic of city-lifting, including small scale and neighborhood projects and targets to promote the city like a product ready for consumption. The Kaminis' city-commodity reflects the absolute subversion of the Lefebvrian city. The key words of the manifesto under the title "urban development" are: entrepreneurship, city identity and tourism (Kaminis 2010a:7). This constitutes an explicit contradiction to Lefebvre's critique for deification of the city image and its transformation to a commodity. Lefebvre's internationalism is surpassed by a universal industry of cities. Athens is praised by Kaminis as a tourist destination taking no account of Lefebvre's (1996: 70) criticism (of the 60s) while he wrote for the Athenian metropolis: "The monuments and sights (Agora, Acropolis) which enable to locate ancient Greece are only places of tourist consumption and aesthetic pilgrimage."

The 2010 right to the development of the city, in other words the right to a touristic city, is directly linked to entrepreneurship and for this reason Kaminis announced measures against excessive bureaucracy. In the memorandum context though, the overcome of any possible delays in order to facilitate investments or entrepreneurship is directly connected to new investment law the so-called "fast track"[1], a governmental tool that

---

1 | *"Acceleration and Transparency of Implementation of Strategic Investments"* or Fast Track Law (3894/2010) aims to abolish critical obstacles that have inhibited major investment in Greece. (...)This law streamlines the licensing procedure for Strategic Investments, making the process easier, smoother and more attractive. (http://www.investingreece.gov.gr/default.asp?pid=167andla=1)

was invented in order to skate over any legal difficulties or oppositions concerning private investments.Thus, Kaminis' "TRTTC" paves the wave for the "right" to fast track policies.

On the side, the selection of the name "TRTTC" by George Kaminis and his partners is neither incidental nor coincidental, but maintains direct links and references to Lefebvre's oeuvre. This assumption is strengthened by the fact that at least twelve candidates of his party (Kaminis 2010b) are architects or involved in space and art sciences. Unsurprisingly, Kaminis promotes the aestheticization of the "TRTTC" by cutting off quotes and propound them as romantic thoughts of his political manifesto. In this way, he identifies himself and his party by using the terminology of an ideology he has very little in common.

The adoption of radical raisons and contents has been diachronically the strategic for numerous power mechanisms. The lack of a critical engagement with Lefebvre's rhetoric has often led to an overstretching of the concept. On deconstructing Kaminis' manifesto, the ostensibly radical intentions are ultimately weathered. The patchwork of rights, from private property to public space, along with strong indications of neoliberal policies and governance, leave no doubt that there is no common space between Kaminis' «Δικαίωμα στην Πόλη» and Lefebvrian "Droit à la ville".

1.3 "The Right to the City" and the sovereignty practice

Following Lefebvre's analysis we consider space as a product of social relations, therefore, we examine the production of the Athenian space in relation to its inhabitants and visitors. In order to perceive the politics applied to the Athenian metropolis over the past four years we examine the way these policies 'position' the subjects- citizens in the city. With 'position' we are not implying that any authority is truly capable of positioning, thereby determining, the subjects, since they are self-determined and therefore position themselves in space according to their social relations. Mostly we refer to the intentions and practices of the authorities to act in the name of the inhabitants. In this direction, we use the dialectic schema of inclusion-exclusion, which help us understand the municipality's policies and the consequent urban space that is produced by them.

The municipality's declarations of population reclassifications, by bringing "the young and the restless" Greeks to the city center, directing migrants to ethnic markets and displacing "the decadents" to the outskirts are indicative of their intentions. Subsequently, not all the inhabitants are considered as equal citizens, some of them are not considered citizens at all, and not all of them have the same rights to the city. The Kaminis' "right to the city" is connected with race and class prerequisites and this constitutes one of the primary distortions of the Lefebvrian notion.

Kaminis (2010c) noted in one of his interviews: "Greece is a country in which-because of economic traditions-you cannot just make a sudden move, gather 5.000 people and take them to three concentration camps. This is not practically possible and does not comply with the fundamental coexistence principles of a coordinated community." However, since 2010 hundreds of police operations have taken place in Athens. According to statistics of Ministry of Public Order and Citizen Protection within seven months (8/2012-2/2013) 77.526 migrants were prosecuted, that means in most cases beaten, deported, arrested or abused. Since the operations was decided in the Ministry of Public Order and Citizen Protection (with the active support of the municipal police, though) Kaminis attributed the issue to the Prime Minister's office. Migratory populations are often thought to come from an outer sphere; therefore they are considered to have no actual connection, references or rights to the city they inhabit. Kaminis by transferring the migrant issue in another hyper spatial structure or even in a supranational level, he practically dislocates them out of the city. At the same time several concentration camps, the so-called "hospitality centers" by the authorities, have been created in Greece, one of them in the wider district of Athens. At the moment (May 2014), there is an open discussion for the transformation of a former hospital ("Agia Varvara") in west Athens (closed due to cuts in health that followed the advent of IMF in 2010) to a detention center.

The political formation of Kaminis explicitly targeted immigrants from the very beginning of his administration. In his (Kaminis 2011) words: "our policy concerning migration should aim to the social incorporation, to manage illegal migration and all illegal migrants that already inhabit our country. This population should come out to light and be recorded. All the illegal migrants should return to their home countries."Using the "illegal trade" as a pretext Kaminis separated the indigenous populations from the newcomers. The latter became the scapegoat of the recent crisis accused for the collapse of the commercial sector (Kaminis 2010c, 2011). As formulated by Kaminis (2011a) "the city center decays because of two things: illegal trade and manifestations." Significantly, the attitude of the municipal authorities, in 2011, towards one of the biggest hunger strikes that have taken place in Greece (300 migrants hunger strikers claimed legislation for migrants in Greece) was indicative. Kaminis washed his hands of migrants' demands by refusing to provide them accommodation during the strike and transposed any responsibility once again to the government.

The municipal authority has been making a furious attack against migrants indicating their expulsion from the public space of the city since they are considered as non-citizens. This massive pogrom in which Nazis, racists, state police and municipal police take part has had several victims, like Cheikh Ndiaye, an African street vender who died falling on the train rails in February 2013 while hunted by municipal policemen. Such politics express certain spatialities. The expulsion from public sphere means inevitably the alteration of city public space. For instance, since 2009 members of the Nazi party Golden Down have banned access to a public playground in a central migrant neighborhood, targeting in this way migrant's children. The playground remained locked until April 2014, a month before the elections.

Moreover, in December 2011 took place a vicious pogrom in the city center. Several sex workers, many of them were migrant women, were arrested and imprisoned for over a year. They were slandered of being HIV positive and accused of "transmitting diseases to the Greek family" (Loverdos 2012) by the Minister of Health. As the Minister (Loverdos 2012) distinctively declared "it is necessary to deport HIV positive prostitutes in order to stop being a threat to the Greek family (…), it is a problem of the Greek family as the disease is transmitted from the illegal migrant women, to the Greek client, to the Greek family." Kaminis disclaimed again any responsibility but he supported the minister indirectly. A few days later he signed a protocol of cooperation with the minister concerning "measures for the improvement of citizen's everyday life and the reassurance of a better living condition". The contemporary 'vagabonds' such as drug addicts or homeless that have been increasing rapidly the last few years live in a blurred routine. On the one hand the municipality created spaces to provide them food and sometimes shelter and on the other, a constant battle takes place in order to keep them out of tourists' sight. Numerous times they are exiled with police buses from the city center either to detention centers or abandoned in the national highway, in order to achieve a "clean and clear" urban environment.

Since 2010 (the year of the advent of the IMF), several groups and individuals have expressed openly a strict negation to the "Memorandum". Their spaces of reference have been targeted constantly from the various aspects of sovereignty, including the municipality. During the last two years several evictions of squats, occupied buildings and social centers have taken place in Athens. The eviction of the anarchist social centers-squats Villa Amalias and Skaramaga showed the stigma of zero tolerance to the voices of resistance. Though the municipal authorities once again renounced any responsibility by declaring that this was an issue held by the state police, they willingly decided to reclaim the buildings once they were evicted. In the case of Villa Amalia (a building squatted for the last 22 years in the center of the city that functioned also as a space of fight back to numerous fascist attacks to migrants) the municipality started renovation works a few days before the 2014 elections. Still, in the case of the municipal market of Kupseli, an abandoned local market occupied by citizens in a central neighborhood of Athens and transformed into a social center, the eviction came from a direct command of the municipality. Indeed, the eviction of such spaces and the dislocation and exclusion of certain people and ideas from the city equates with the production of a sterilized city environment friendly to Nazis and the police.

But the pinnacle of municipal policies that distorted ultimately the meaning of TRTTC was the eviction of Syntagma Square[2] occupation by the 'Indignados' and various other people. The 29th of June 2011 a big riot took place in Syntagma square. The next days the mayor (Kaminis 2011b) stated:

"The municipality does not oppose to the Indignados. The right to gather in public spaces and manifestate is supported by the Greek constitution. The Municipality respects, as it should, the right to peaceful protests. Still, there is a distinction between the right to manifestate, that could be on a daily basis in the same spot on special occasions (like the Indignados did) and the 'right' to camp in public spaces with all the consequent effects concerning the malfunction of the city."

---

2 | 'Syntagma' means 'Constitution'. Syntagma Square is the square in front of the Greek parliament.

And he (Kaminis 2011b) continued arguing that

> "It is inconceivable that those who name themselves Indignados think that they can occupy the central or any other square of Athens. The square should be clean, open and available to all citizens and inhabitants of the city with no exceptions or discriminations. This applies for all the squares of the city and especially for the first one."

In mayor's speech we distinguish once again the thrasos of sovereignty to determine the rules, the topography, the means of fight and behavior of the revolted (Makrygianni and Tsavdaroglou 2010: 52). What Kaminis described was the breaking of the former "spatial contract" of Syntagma square. The permanent occupation of a square constituted a break to the former temporary demonstrations. Until June 2011 there were two main tactics in the repertoire of protestors: occupations of public buildings and demonstrations. Both of them express the spatial contract, i.e. the "democratic" right to interrupt the urban normality and protest for a limited time in public space or in a public (State) building. Square occupations combine the two previous tactics and constitute a new spatial grammar in the syntax of struggles. In the words of Antonis Vradis: "the occupation of Syntagma Square (...) was a first attempt to break the spatial contract or to cancel it definitively" (Vradis, 2011:215).

Confronting the above with Lefebvre's rhetoric it seems rather ironic that while the later, inspired by the Paris Commune of 1871 flared the events of May '68, Kaminis' rhetoric contributed actively to the suppression of the Indignados movement and the wave of resistance that followed in Greece.

Nonetheless the policies of exclusion go hand in hand with certain inclusive practices. The rhetoric of the municipality reflects the dominion of the capital over city space and promotes a specific and restricted topology of rights. The production of the desired space derives from the exclusion of the "flagitious" and the concomitant inclusion of the "desired" through the promotion of certain plans.

In 2011 an architectural competition for the renewal of a central Athenian named "Rethink Athens" street took place. The competition was held on behalf of the private institution-foundation "Alexandros Onassis" and urged us to rethink the Greek capital in 'better' terms. The competition that was embraced warmly by the authorities and the municipality interpreted the city followed close Kaminis' scenario. The "creative class" should inhabit Athens, give her new breath and character along with an ethnic essence created on multicultural markets (that is one of the few places where migrants are welcomed). Thereafter, in April 2013 a new plan for Athens, "Re-launching Athens" with time horizon the year 2020 was presented by the mayor. This ambitious concept concerns large-scale gentrification projects in the city center like the construction of commercial and habitat infrastructures, the renewal of abandoned building, the pedestrianization of central streets etc. The plan's funding is based on the EU and private investors (it also entails the Jessica program and NSRF[3]).It is crucial here to notice the terms in which the municipality and certain spatial politics are related to the EU. "TRTTC" is linked to huge infrastructures which will alter the urban environment in favor of the capital and will inevitably abort the redundant population. In a similar spirit the "Re-activate Athens" initiative, that was presented a few months ago by various researchers, enjoyed the warm acceptance of the mayor.

Indeed what Lefebvre (1968: 84-85) was writing in 1968 for the planning developers seems rather insightful

"They conceive and realize, without hiding it, for the market, with profit in mind (…) they are no longer selling houses or buildings but planning. With, or without ideology planning becomes an exchange value…They will build not only commercial centers, but also centres of privileged consumption: the renewed city."

The production of the city space following Kaminis "rights" and guidelines come to direct opposition with the thought of the French philosopher. In Kaminis' ratio the city and especially the city image turns into commodity, a suggestion that is directly opposed to Lefebvre's principles. In Kaminis case the collective oeuvre of the inhabitants refers to the creation of pleasant scenery to host tourists. In this context they create new spatialities taking as guiding principles not only major projects but also small scale interventions in the daily life. The contemporary manufacturers familiarize with tools like "the everyday life", introduced from Lefebvre (1991a), but use them in order to include the city into the market and turn it to an antagonistic tourist spot on the map.

---

3 | National Strategic Reference Framework (NSRF) is the programming of European Union Funds at national level.

2. "THE RIGHT TO THE CITY": CONTRADICTIONS CROSSINGS AND CRACKS

2.1 Contradictions of the Lefebvrian 'Right to the city'

The more we unfold Kaminis project in theory and practice, the less commons it appears to share with Lefebvre's rhetoric. Nevertheless, these contradictions open spaces of controversies and urge us not only to read again "TRTTC" but also to think critically and go beyond. To do so, we first have to dive in deep waters of Lefebvre's theory and then emerge in the contemporary crisis' everyday life struggles.

One of the basic notions that Lefebvre used in order to evolve his thought is the perception of the city as "oeuvre". Lefebvre sought to define the "oeuvre" and the city, which are articulated in "TRTTC" through the Marx's categories of value: use value and exchange value. Lefebvre (1996: 124) argues that "if one wants to go beyond the market, the law of exchange value, money and profit, it is necessary to define the place of this possibility: urban society, the city as use value", and he (1996: 126) states later that the city "did not have, it has no meaning but as an oeuvre, as an end, as place of free enjoyment, as domain of use value". In the previous quotes Lefebvre seeks the characteristics of urban society and he is opposed to the categories of exchange value, money and profit. However we argue that he misinterprets the Marxian category of use value. Lefebvre tends to separate the two forms of value, use value and exchange value, and he attributes an ontological positive status in use value, thus the social antagonisms in their historical context, that he previously mentions, are lost. But as Marx conceptualizes the categories of value and labour (exchange value and use value as well as concrete-useful and abstract labour) Lefebvre's misinterpretation becomes clearer.

Marx in the beginning of the first volume of Capital presents the two factors of commodity: the use value and the exchange value and he argues that in the capital mode of production "in the form of society to be considered here they [use-values] are also the material bearers of ... exchange-value" (Marx, 1976: 126). According to Marx the use value is directly linked to the useful-concrete labour and "the usefulness of a thing makes it a use-value" (Marx, 1976: 126). Different useful labours differ from each other qualitatively and not quantitatively.

Following Marx's analysis (Marx, 1976: 128, 132-133) the qualitatively different useful labours produce use values, which are the bearers of exchange value. Furthermore exchange value, as opposed to use value, concerns the quantitative relations of commodities: "exchange value appears first of all as the quantitative relation, the proportion, in which use-values of one kind exchange for use-values of another kind. This relation changes constantly with time and place." (Marx, 1976: 126) The discovery of this double character of commodities, as use values as well as exchange values, as qualities as well as quantities, runs throughout the entire work of Marx's Capital. Illustrative is the following quote from the subchapter "Value-Form or Exchange-Value":

"commodities come into the world in the form of use-values or material goods, such as iron, linen, corn, etc. This is their plain, homely, natural form. However, they are only commodities because they have a dual nature, because they are at the same time objects of utility and bearers of value. Therefore they only appear as commodities, or have the form of commodities, in so far as they possess a double form, i.e. natural form and value form." (Marx, 1976: 138)

Marx claimed that use value comes from useful labor and later on explained where exchange value comes from. To do so, he analyzes the dialectical dual character of labor as concrete-useful labor and abstract labor. Marx shows that concrete labor produces use value and the abstraction of concrete labor that means abstract labor produces exchange value. In his words (1976: 129) "a use-value, or useful article, (...) has value only because abstract human labor is objectified or materialized in it." Marx (1976: 310-1) makes clear that while it is necessary for the commodities to have a concrete use value, however it is totally indifferent which exactly this use value will be. This finding is based on Marx's conception of abstraction

"the exchange relation of commodities is characterized precisely by its abstraction from their use-values(...)If we make abstraction from its use-value, we abstract also from the material constituents and forms which make it a use value. It is no longer a table, a house, (...) or any other useful thing. All its sensuous characteristics are extinguished. (...) With the disappearance of the useful character of the products of labour, the useful character of the kinds of labour embodied in them also disappears; this in turn entails the disappearance of the different concrete forms of labour. They can no longer be distinguished, but are all together reduced to the same kind of labour, human labour in the abstract." (Marx, 1976: 127-8)

Consequently, the capital mode of production is based on use value, which is abstracted, and aims in value (exchange value) and ultimately in surplus value. The outcome of Marx's analysis is that the conceptualization of commodity as something dual, is based on the dual character of labour, as concrete-useful labour as well as abstract labour; and "this point is crucial to an understanding of political economy" (Marx, 1976: 132)

Once we recognize this dual character, it becomes easier to understand the missteps of the Lefebvrian "TRTTC". Indicatively are the following quotes, in which Lefebvre separates use value and exchange value and then he unhistorically prettifies the use value and consequently the city itself:

"City and urban reality are related to use value. Exchange value and the generalization of commodities by industrialization tend to destroy it by subordinating the city and urban reality which are refuges of use value, the origin of a virtual predominance and revalorization of use" (Lefebvre, 1996: 67)

and

"The most eminent urban creations, the most 'beautiful' oeuvres of urban life (we say 'beautiful', because they are oeuvres rather than products) date from epochs previous to that of industrialization" (Lefebvre, 1996: 65)

Lefebvre follows a 'dangerous' path: First, he disconnects the use value from exchange value and he argues that the only form of commodity is the exchange value. Then, he unhistorically illustrates use value as a positive substance, which existed before industrialization, and creates only "beautiful" oeuvres. And finally, he connects the city only with use value, hence attributes the city with the same unhistorical positivity. As a result of this way of thinking, Lefebvre contradicts himself with his original thesis, that the city *is a projection of society on the ground*. While this thesis suggests that the use values and exchange values are determined at each historical time by the social class antagonism, Lefebvre's outcome is different.

He repeats the same argument several times in his book and constantly seeks for the moments that "the use (use value) of places, monuments, differences, escapes the demands of exchange, of exchange value" (Lefebvre, 1996: 129). Since he has disconnected use value from exchange value, then he seeks the lost ontological primacy of use value, "use value, subordinated for centuries to exchange value, can now come first again. How?" Although his thought it was extremely visionary on the concepts of city and space, he is however trapped in the supposed confrontation between use value and exchange value.

Ultimately, he builds his theoretical framework "TRTTC" on the postulation of use values and defines as the revolutionary subject for this purpose the working class. In the words of Lefebvre:

"the right to the city (…) the proclamation and realization of urban life as the rule of use (of exchange and encounter disengaged from exchange value) insist on the mastery of the economic (of exchange value, the market, and commodities) and consequently is inscribed within the perspectives of the revolution under the hegemony of the working class" (Lefebvre, 1996: 179).

2.2 From "the right to the city" to the occupation of the city

Lefebvre's analysis in "TRTTC" has been adopted by numerous urban and environmental movements, NGO's, also often co-opted by state institutions with respect to housing and mortgage regulation (Brenner et al., 2009; Leontidou, 2010; Mayer, 2009). Their common feature is the postulation of urban use values i.e. affordable housing, free spaces, open-green areas, parks, bicycle lanes and generally public goods (education, health, energy etc.). The movements and agencies for the right to the city criticize the neoliberalism or the capital relationship only in the form of exchange value, and they ignore how the commodity value is produced as a unity,. The result of this tactic is that the produced or claimed use values, at the same time when they are defined and claimed they are transformed and abstracted to exchange values, hence serving as a like a necessary fuel for the circulation of commodities, as an inseparable unity of use value and exchange value. According to de Souza (2010:316-317) for these agencies the political-philosophical and social-theoretical premises could be resumed as follows: "As much social justice and environmental protection as possible, of course; but please let us be realistic, the time of utopia has passed". As he (2010:316) felicitously points out, the right to the city has the meaning that

"neoliberalism obviously is refused, but not capitalism as such (i.e. (...) [it] should, in the best of all cases, be replaced by a sort of "left-Keynesianism", which could in turn be supplemented by alternative, "solidarity"-oriented economic [micro] circuits)(...) a "participative democracy" must be achieved, and this usually means the following: representative democracy must be supplemented and "corrected" by "participation" (that is, representative "democracy"(...) ."

In contrast with the traditional movements for the right to the city, the last years we are witnessing a rising tide of urban revolts and mobilizations. In the 'Reclaim The Streets' movement of the late 90's, in the uprising of Parisian banlieue in 2005, in Oaxaca 2006, in Athens 2008, in London 2011 and in the recently occupied squares of Cairo, Madrid, Athens, US, we recognize that the rebels do not claim and do not postulate the city from the sovereign power but rather they occupy it and tend to transform it.

What was typical of the last years' urban conflicts in the Athenian metropolis was not a defensive stance against State violence but a constant offensive against all that resembled the presence of sovereign power. The struggles and revolts brought to light the rebel space and gave birth to a plethora of spaces and practices in the perceived-conceived-lived space. Furthermore they left dynamic spatial legacies that are used and enriched in every new moment of resistance. Several initiatives and movements focused to answer the crucial question of social reproduction. In Athens, more than fifty local decentralized neighborhood assemblies were created, while in all over Greece more than one hundred started organizing communal gardens, collective kitchens, give-away bazaars, barter structures, self-studying and social tutoring. Furthermore, autonomous labor grassroots base unions emerged, as well as unemployed networks, immigrant networks, agro-collectives and social structures as social self-organized health centers, social kindergartens and social groceries. The recent uprisings were accused of having no demands and no representatives to negotiate concrete claims, or better concrete use values. We claim that the passage from the famous slogan of the 60's "be realistic, demand the impossible" to the slogan of the recent Occupy movement in US "occupy everything, demand nothing" (see Deseriis and Dean, 2012) formulates a different culture of struggles and signifies a new era for the emancipator movements.

References

Brenner, N., Marcuse, P. and M. Mayer (2009) Introduction. In: City, Special Issue 'Cities for People, not for Profit', 13(2/3), 176–184

Collinge, C. (2008) Positions without negations? Dialectical reason and the contingencies of space. In: Environment and Planning A, 40, 2613-2622

De Souza, L. M. (2010) Which right to which city? In defence of political-strategic clarity. In: Interface: a journal for and about social movements, 2/1, 315-333

Deseriis, M., and J. Dean (2012) A Movement Without Demands? http://interactivist.autonomedia.org/node/39512 (last accessed 15 May 2013)

Harvey, D. (2008) The Right to the City. In: New Left Review, 53

Kaminis, G. (2010a) The Right To The City: 9 priorities for Athens, Athens: [manifesto of campaign trail] [in Greek] Retrieved from: www.gkaminis.gr (last accessed 15 June 2013) [in Greek]

Kaminis, G. (2010b) The Right To The City: the list of candidates. [in Greek] Retrieved from: http://ekloges-liondas.blogspot.gr/2010/10/blog-post_5376.html (last accessed 30 June 2013) [in Greek]

Kaminis, G. (2010c) Interview. In: Lifo, 13/10/2010. [in Greek] Retrieved from www.lifo.gr[in Greek]

Kaminis, G. (2011a) Speech in environmental committee of the Greek Parliament (15/3/2011) [in Greek]

Kaminis, G. (2011b) The cleaning of Syntagma-Parliament square, Press Release 1/8/2011. [in Greek] Retrieved from http://www.cityofathens.gr/node/13560 (last accessed 15 June 2013) [in Greek]

Lefebvre, H. (1996[1968]) Writings on Cities. Oxford: Blackwell

Lefebvre, H. (1991a[1947]) Critique of everyday life. Verso: London

Lefebvre, H. (1991b[1974]) The Production of Space. Oxford: Blackwell

Lefebvre, H. (1991a) Les illusions de la modernité, Maniéres de voir 13, Le Monde Diplomatique, 14-17

Loverdos, A. (2012) Checks on all brothels. Newspaper To BHMA 30.4.2012 [in Greek] Retrieved from: http://www.tovima.gr/society/article/?aid=455467 (last accessed 15 June 2013) [in Greek]

Makrygianni, V. and H. Tsavdaroglou (2011) Urban Planning and Revolt: A Spatial Analysis of the December 2008 Uprising in Athens. In: A. Vradis and D. Dalakoglou (eds) Revolt and Crisis in Greece: Between a present yet to pass and a future still to come. AK Press./Occupied London, 29-57

Marcuse, P., (2010) Rights in Cities and the Right to the City? In: A. Sugranyes and Charlotte, Mathivet- Habitat International Coalition (HIC) Cities for All :Proposals and Experiences towards the Right to the City, Santiago

Marx, K. (1976 [1867]) Capital, Vol I. New York: Penguin

Mayer, M. (2009) The 'right to the city' in the context of shifting mottos of urban social movements. In: City, 13(2/3), 362–374

Mayer, M. (2012) The Right to the City in Urban Social Movements. In: N. Brenner, P. Marcuse and M. Mayer (eds) Cities for People Not for Profit: Critical Urban Theory and the Right to the City. New York: Routledge

Ministry of Public Order and Citizen Protection (2013) Valuation of the police operation "Xenios Zeus". Athens 06.02.2013 Retrieved from www.astynomia.gr [in Greek] [in Greek]

Onassis Foundation (2011) Rethink Athens. Retrieved http://www.rethinkathens.org/

Pasquinelli, M., (2010) Beyond the Ruins of the Creative City: Berlin's Factory of Culture and the Sabotage of Rent.In: KUNSTrePUBLIK (ed.) Skulpturenpark Berlin Zentrum, Berlin: Verlag der Buchhandlung Walther König

Shields, R. (1999) Lefebvre, Love and Struggle: Spatial Dialectics. New York: Routledge

Soja, E.W. (1989) Postmodern Geographies: The Reassertion of Space in Critical Social Theory. London-New York: Verso

Stavrides, S. (2007) H. Lefebvre: The emancipatory perspective of the oeuvre-city. Introduction in H. Lefebvre The Right to the City. Athens: Koukida [in Greek]

Vradis, A. (2011) Breaching the Spatial Contract. In: C. Giovanopoulos and D. Mitropoulos (eds) Democracy under Construction. Athens: A/Sinechia publications [in Greek], 211-218

State repression, social resistance and the politicization of public space in Greece under fiscal adjustment

Maria Markantonatou

The article discusses the politicization of public space in Greece since the outbreak of the crisis and under the program of fiscal adjustment. In particular, it discusses the ways in which public space became a fundamental field of political action for different social forces; on the one hand for the governments that imposed the austerity policies since 2010 and on the other for those who resisted such measures with protests, rallies, solidarity initiatives etc. In the first case, austerity and fiscal discipline were combined with policies of law and order and symbolic policies of "cleaning" the urban space of people considered as "threatening" (immigrants, HIV positive women, drug users). In the second case, several forms of resistance to austerity emerged which utilized public space as a field of social struggle with the state and those political forces that imposed austerity within a post-democratic framework of political decision making. As it is argued, this twofold instrumentalization of public space is reminiscent of Karl Polanyi's concept of the "double movement", illustrating a – more intense in times of crisis – conflict between the needs of the economy and those of the society.

1. The Social Impact of the Austerity Agreements

The main priorities of the agreements ("Memoranda of Understanding") signed between the Greek governments and Troika (ECB, EC, IMF) since the outbreak of the crisis in 2009 have been the reduction of public deficit, the shrinking of the public sector, plans for the privatization of the remaining publicly owned enterprises and state assets as well as a series of closures of public organizations and mergers, for instance through the so-called "Kallikratis plan", which dictated the merger of local communities in order to form larger administrative units. But, most importantly, the austerity policies aimed at the deregulation of labour through the "internal devaluation" strategy. Within four years such a strategy instituted rapid reductions in wages, pensions and benefits from 20% up to 50%, a barrage of emergency taxes and the reduction of the personnel at the public sector, for instance through the measure of "labour reserve" (a form of dismissal of employees) or the "one to ten" law, dictating that, in the public sector, only one person can be hired for ten retirements.

The austerity measures have put the Greek economy in a recession spiral and caused severe blows to labour and labour rights. Regarding collective agreements, it has been decided that enterprise-wide agreements will override sectoral and national collective agreements. This has set the basis for regulations favoring individual bargaining. Also, the notice period for dismissal and the amount of severance pay were reduced, the mass layoff limit was increased and the regulations concerning "unfair dismissal" were loosened. These measures widened the reach of labour flexibilization and precarization, as it is shown, for instance, by the rise (in the first two years of the crisis) in uninsured labour from 22.6% to 30.4% of the labour force in the private sector, an increase even more intense among immigrant workers (SEPE 2012).

Under these conditions, unemployment has skyrocketed, reaching 28% in November 2013 (Eurostat 2014), with long term and very long term unemployment, as well as female and youth unemployment reaching shocking highs. The pauperization of the population was rapid. In only one year (2010-2011), the median income and poverty threshold fell by 8% but, despite this, the population under that threshold increased still further, from 19 to 21% (Eurostat 2013). A series of small and medium enterprises, which have traditionally constituted the core of the Greek economy could not stand recession, lack of liquidity and increased taxes. As a result, more than 65.000 of such enterprises have closed down only in the first months of the crisis (Mylonas 2011: 8) and this number has since been multiplied.

Although the austerity measures have spatially disparate effects on incomes, affecting the least developed regions most (Monastiriotis 2011: 330), a general image prevails. It is that of cities and urban centers being strongly hit by the crisis due to the dramatic cuts and staff reductions in local government that have severely undermined urban and municipal infrastructure and caused the degradation of living standards for local communities and populations. In addition, emergency taxes have had indirect effects for the urban environment, as in Memorandum I it was decided that the price of heating oil should be equal to the price of diesel fuel. This meant a 40% increase in prices for consumers and a drop in consumption of heating oil by 75% in winter 2012 (Dabilis, 2013). Consumers turned massively to the use of electrical heating appliances and wood for their fireplaces and stoves. This led to a dramatic increase of smog and suspended particles by 200% in urban areas (ibid.), with such effects as allergies and respiratory problems, as well as, in some cases, fatal accidents.

At the same time, familialistic strategies of home provision to younger members, which traditionally constituted a fundamental means of social reproduction supplementing poor social protection and a weak welfare state in Greece, are now shaken, as more and more jobs are lost, wages no longer suffice for hundreds of people to repay their loans, and pensions are drastically reduced. In such a setting, houses are abandoned or lose the value they had some years ago, while homelessness has increased dramatically (Alamanou et. al., 2011). Next to the "traditional" homeless, mainly consisting of poor, socially marginalized unemployed, and the "hidden" immigrant homelessness, now stands a new generation of "neohomeless", including persons with a middle or higher educational background, with a former satisfactory standard of living and previously, of a medium social level.

Overall, the crisis and the austerity program have caused a serious social deregulation in the country with the number of people committing suicide increasing (Kentikelenis et. al., 2011), households being strongly hit by pauperization, the youth being unable to enter the labour market, thousands of people migrating to other countries, and the majority of the population suffering income decreases and a rapid degradation of living standards, within a post-democratic, technocratic governance based on the attempt to set market needs and priorities above the societal ones. Unsurprisingly, these austerity policies and the shock-therapy since

2010 have caused a wave of different forms of social resistance not only by official trade unions that reacted by means of hundreds of strikes[1], but also by various, heterogeneous social groups that participated with massive numbers in a series of demonstrations and rallies. Some of the most characteristic forms of resistance, manifested at the urban public space, are summarized in the following section[2].

2. Resisting the Austerity Program

For the manifestations of social resistance, public space did not simply serve purposes of visibility and representation, but became the arena of "radical politics" (Kallianos 2013: 549). Streets did not merely operate as spaces for the self-awareness and the political socialization of citizens, but as spaces of confrontation with the state, where "the hegemonic Other" was contested and "where most of the battles were fought" (ibid.: 554-555). One of the most important moments of social resistance to austerity was what became known as the "movement of the squares" that made its debut at the end of May 2011, in front of the Parliament building at Syntagma square. Within a few days, protests, popular assemblies and sit-ins spread to other districts of the capital and other cities with the explicit aim to deter the vote of the Midterm Fiscal Strategy (a package of austerity measures to cope with unmet fiscal targets of the previous year).

During a general strike on June 15, 2011, the protesters managed to retain control of Syntagma square, despite heavy police repression sufficiently severe to be criticized by Amnesty International (2011a). This kind of resistance strengthened the dynamics of the protest. However, the next general strike of June 28-29, 2011, and the encirclement of the Parliament called for by the Greek "Indignants" did not prevent the approval of the Midterm Fiscal Strategy and the protesters, once again,

---

1 | For instance, only in 2011, there have been 91 strikes in the public sector and 240 in the private sector – mostly within firms but also across professional categories or whole sectors or branches of the economy (Katsoridas/Lampousaki 2012).

2 | For instance, the rally that took place in Athens during the general strike on 19.-20.10.2011 has been estimated to be the largest in the last forty years (Katsoridas/Lampousaki 2012).

faced violent repression and clashed with the police (see Amnesty International 2011b). The movement faded a month later, but open popular assemblies continued to operate in other districts of Athens and other cities across the country until at least the next year (Pantazidou 2012: 12).

At the same time, several other practices were set in motion, such as the occupation of social spaces (e.g. the continuation of the public national TV broadcaster by its staff, and transmission via the internet, after the government announced its closure and the dismissal of hundreds of employees, leading to continuous protests outside the broadcaster's central premises for many weeks; the occupation of the local general hospital at the district of Kilkis and its re-opening on the basis of self-management and free health care); grassroots initiatives and informal citizen networks to provide relief from some of the effects of the crisis (e.g. social kitchens for the cooking and distribution of free food to unemployed, homeless, immigrants etc., social clinics and social pharmacies established by doctors, nurses and pharmacists as a response to the dramatic degradation of the public health system due to spending cuts, closures or merger of health units, services of free tutoring etc.), and local exchange networks (e.g. exchange of services or products, either mediated by new virtual currencies or directly in a barter-like fashion or in the form of give away, free of charge initiatives) (for an overview of the new initiatives, movements etc. see Filopoulou 2012, Wainwright 2013, Malkoutzis 2013, Oikonomides 2013).

Notably, since the outbreak of the crisis, the tendency to present various problems, economic or social, as problems of "security" against a series of heterogeneous "threats" has intensified. For the Eurozone elites, the Greek "disease" had to be cured by the program of fiscal discipline, in order to avoid "contagion" of the "virus". For the justification of the treatment, several narratives were used, e.g. about Greece as a rent-seeking society living beyond its means (Markantonatou, 2013). But the politics of stigmatization were equally implemented at the domestic level, with public space serving as a field of state repression. As specific social groups and individuals such as migrants, HIV positive women and drug users were defined in different contexts as "threats" to society, the arguments about the need for fiscal adjustment were combined with strategies of law and order and securitization, for which the rhetoric of scapegoating and social stigmatization were used. Some of the ways in which the program of fiscal adjustment and austerity was combined with politics of law and order are described in the following section.

3. Governing public space by scapegoating

Since December 2008, when three weeks of protests and unrest spread throughout the country after a 15-year-old high school student was shot dead by a policeman, policies were implemented to empower the police forces, by increasing their number and establishing new units. By 2010, a new special corps was formed, often consisting of former military staff with a nationalist orientation. This explains to a certain degree the political preferences for the neo-Nazi group 'Golden Dawn' within the police force (To Vima 2012a), as well as the tolerance towards actions of racist activism of several so called "residents' committees" in certain areas of Athens (e.g. closing down a playground visited by migrants, anti-migrant patrol groups, attacks towards offices of ethnic communities etc.) (see Kandylis and Kavoulakos 2011: 158-159). Since the outbreak of the crisis, this tolerance became compatible with the hardening of the official migratory policy, as shown, for instance, by the construction of a 12,5 kilometer fence along Greece's North borders in order to prevent migrants entering the country, or by the increase of the percentage of foreign prisoners in Greek prisons, rising from 48% in 2008 to 63% in 2012 (Ministry of Justice 2014).

In the conjuncture of the economic crisis, in which the government's power to decide on the most important dimensions of economic policy shrunk drastically, the rhetoric of national sovereignty and internal security was revived, as shown, for example, by the central role that migration politics had in the 2012 pre-electoral campaign. This was, actually, the case not only for the neo-Nazi political group 'Golden Dawn' with their slogan "to clean the filth [the migrants] from the city", but also for the social democratic party PASOK which, for instance, linked the risk of robberies to the poor living conditions of immigrants and the supposed threat posed by the latter to public health (Xenakis and Cheliotis 2013: 301). Similarly, the right-wing's Nea Demokratia pre-electoral campaign was based on the demand, as the party's president, A. Samaras (see Vima 2012b) put it, to "take our cities back from migrants". His campaign was also based on two promises; the first was to "deport immediately all illegal migrants", and the second, to renegotiate the Memoranda austerity agreements. While the latter was hardly realized or even discussed after the elections, several measures were taken for the former.

Indeed, some months after the election of Nea Demokratia as a leading governmental party, the so called "Operation Xenios Zeus", ironically named after the ancient Greek God of hospitality, was carried out in several Greek cities. Within one year, more than 80.000 migrants were detained and transferred to empty factories, military camps and police stations for paper checks and interrogations. After being subjected to several processes of identification and control, migrants were released, until the next unannounced "stop and search" check. Notably, Human Rights Watch (2013) criticized the Xenios Zeus operation for police brutality and stressed that finally only 6% of those inspected were illegal immigrants, despite the government's polemic language against "illegal migration".

As Agamben (2005: 14) has described in detail, the tendency towards the generalization of the security paradigm as a technique of governance is characteristic of today's societies. In the case of Greece, the new emphasis on social control, law and order and policing has been part of the broader agenda of the "state of emergency" that has been more or less implicitly declared during the crisis by the different governments that imposed the austerity policies. In specific cases, the state of emergency mobilized the exercise of a biopolitical power for heterogeneous aims and combined for instance medical care for public health with a need to "clean the city" from people defined as threatening or morbid. According to the government's narrative, this kind of "cleaning" would benefit tourism and entrepreneurial activity and, supposedly, the Greek economy. The basic function, however, of the state of emergency was social disciplination and the making of social order in times of unrest.

Characteristically, during the May 2012 pre-electoral campaign and amidst one of the most serious financial crises of the last decades, there was a wave of arrests of HIV positive sex workers, broadcasted live on television. While authorities had hardly been interested in the issue for many years, there was suddenly an intense campaign of demonization of the HIV positive women held in custody who were described in several mass media as "dirty", "sick" and "dangerous" and were further blamed for the image of decadence of the Athens city center. According to A. Loverdos, Minister of Health at that time, these prostitutes "had to be deported immediately", because "they harmed the institution of family". Some days before the crucial 2012 elections, he stated that "the virus is transferred from the illegal woman directly to the Greek family" (see PICUM, 2012). Photos, names, age, land of origin and details about the womens' and their parents' life histories were shown in newspapers and on television, while a series of police press releases warned about this new "state of emergency".

The method of penalization of HIV positive women was soon extended to other groups of people that were considered as threatening. "Operation Thetis", a joint action between the Greek police and the Hellenic Center for Disease Control and Prevention of the Ministry of Health conducted in 2013 and named after the Greek goddess of Justice, targeted drug users in a spirit similar to that of "Operation Xenios Zeus". Drug users were treated as a kind of urban virus to be cured by the police in cooperation with several agents of public health. Aim of the operation was "to gather drug addicts who wandered in the city center and transfer them to police's concentration infrastructure in order to conduct a census", as well as to "clear" the city center from people who were "using drugs in public" (see OKANA, 2013). In this frame, hundreds of drug users were arrested and taken to distant detention centers where they were obliged to take a medical examination, and then were released (see Exiles in Balkans, 2013).

One more strategy of the governments that imposed the austerity measures, especially of the conservative Nea Demokratia, was to present several leftist forms of protest as equally "extreme" and "dangerous" for the political system and democracy as those tactics of the neo-Nazi group Golden Dawn. This "theory of the two extremes", as the term was established in the Greek mass media discussion, suggested that both leftist and neo-fascist political forces attempted to challenge the state's authority and put the country in a course of political destabilization. As racist physical violence exerted on migrants by neo-fascists was equated with leftist protests against austerity, the government attempted to appear as the sole guarantor of the country's constitutional order and political stability.

This is also how the police operations against squats were justified. The Minister of Public Order and Citizen Protection, N. Dendias, required the police to "reoccupy squats" and stressed that "law and order is neither a governmental agenda, nor a political slogan, but it is a constitutional obligation and right of every Greek citizen" (see Ta Nea, 2013). In this period, from late 2012 to the end of September 2013, police raided and closed down various squats in the cities of Athens, Thessaloniki, Patra and Ioannina. Dozens of people were detained and many of them arrested. Since then, the government of Nea Demokratia has been using this "theory of the two extremes" not only as an argument against the major leftwing opposition, but also as a means of social disciplination against protesters, squatters and others who were presented in the public discourse as people in conflict with the law, causing anomie and challenging the constitutional order, similar to the actions of the neo-Nazi Golden Dawn.

4. Concluding Remarks

Karl Polanyi used the term "double movement" to describe a conflictual interplay or tension between economy and society that he understood as inherent in market liberalism. He defined the "double movement" as "the action of two organizing principles in society, each of them setting itself specific institutional aims, having the support of definite social forces and using its own distinctive methods" (Polanyi 2001: 138). The first organizing principle, economic liberalism, was supported by entrepreneurial classes and aimed at the establishment of a self-regulating market. The second principle concerned social protection for all those disadvantaged by the market and aimed at the conservation of man, nature and society. Polanyi set the double movement in the historical context of 19th century's liberalism when a "Great Transformation", as he called it in his homonymous book, took place. This transformation started with a marketization process that followed the abolition, in 1834, of the Speenhamland system that had managed to keep wages low by means of allowances proportional to the price of wheat. With the abolition of Speenhamland and the Poor Law reform, the poor were entitled to an allowance, only if committed to the workhouses, which in the meantime, had become places of social coercion and immiseration. These measures, which led to an unprecedented pauperization, aimed at the establishment of a competitive labour market no longer at a local level, but at a national one and set the basis for the expansion of capitalism. According to Polanyi (ibid: 3), this 'great transformation' ended with the "collapse of the nineteenth century civilization", as he put it, during the 1930s crisis.

However, the gradual deregulation of the welfare state and the attack on labour rights since the mid-1970s disproves Polanyi's view that the vision of a self-regulating market was over with the 1930s crash. Four decades of neoliberalization have shown that the vision of self-regulating markets has not been exhausted. This is observable also in the frame of the Eurozone, having a neoliberal orientation already since its establishment.

Especially since 2010, when measures were deployed, ranging from the socialisation of bank losses to the imposition of austerity packages and fiscal discipline in several countries of the Eurozone and more intensively in Greece, this neoliberal orientation broadened. The Eurozone's elites did not challenge the doctrine of the self-regulating market, the consequences of which have been described by Polanyi. On the contrary, these elites rushed to deepen its institutional setting as shown, for instance, by the Six Pact in October 2011 or the Fiscal Compact in December 2011, which dictate automatic sanctions in case of non-compliance with the Eurozone's rules of fiscal discipline.

If Polanyi's concept of the "double movement" is understood as an ideal-type, it can then be set in the historical conjuncture of the crisis in Greece, in which it acquires a clear spatial dimension. For market supporters and political forces imposing fiscal discipline, public space served as a strategic means to promote an unprecedented neoliberal shock-therapy through strategies of social disciplination. For those social groups hit by the crisis and those dependent on the remaining welfare state and with no other option than to resist the austerity measures, public space became an arena of conflict and struggle with the state as well as a field for social solidarity. The forms of social resistance in Greece, though heterogeneous or fragmented as they often have been, express in their complexity, mutatis mutandis, what Polanyi described as the "realistic self-protection of society" and are to be added to the overall history of the "universal 'collectivist' reaction against the expansion of market economy (...)" (Polanyi 2001: 157).

How a "double movement" develops further in the Greek context, as the crisis in unfolding, or how such a counter-movement is to be interpreted are open questions. Whether forces struggling for more market liberalization, labour flexibilization and welfare deregulation will prevail, and under what conditions, over those fighting for social rights and democracy depends on social struggle and pressure put on the state. As an outcome of the crisis, public space is being politicized, although this does not mean it did not have a political dimension before the crisis. On the contrary, public space has always been political. In the conjuncture of the crisis, however, public space has become one of the most crucial and urgent stakes for conflicting social actors, a site where the demands of those resisting are articulated in order to emerge as the fundamental responses to the crisis and neoliberal austerity.

REFERENCES

Agamben, G. (2005) State of Exception. Chicago: University of Chicago Press

Alamanou A., E. Stamatogiannopoulou, O. Theodorikakou and K. Katsadoros, K. (2011) 6th European Research Conference, Homelessness, Migration and Demographic Change in Europe, Pisa, 16th September 2011, available online at: The Configuration of Homelessness in Greece during the Financial Crisis

Amnesty International (2011a) Greece urged not to use excessive force during protests (press release PRE01/301/2011), June 16th 2011, available online at: http://www.amnesty.org/en/for-media/press-releases/greece-urged-not-use-excessive-force-during-protests-2011-06-16, 30.7.2013

Amnesty International (2011b) Tear gas fired as Greek police clash with Athens protesters (press release PRE01/324/2011), June 29th 2011, available online at: http://www.amnesty.org/en/for-media/press-releases/tear-gas-fired-greek-police-clash-athens-protesters-2011-06-29, 30.7.2013

Avgi (newspaper) (2013) Kedikoglou insists on the theory of the two extremes, 18.05.2013, available online at: http://www.avgi.gr/article/322376/epimeneistin-theoria-ton-duo-akron-o-simos-kedikoglou [In Greek]

Dabilis, A. (2013) High oil prices drive Greeks to burn wood, South Eastern Times, 18.01.2013, available online at: <http://www.setimes.com/cocoon/setimes/xhtml/en_GB/features/setimes/features/2013/01/18/feature-03>

Eurostat (2013) People at risk of poverty or social exclusion: Statistics Explained, 2013, available on line at: <http://epp.eurostat.ec.europa.eu/statistics_explained/index.php/People_at_risk_of_poverty_or_social_exclusion>

Eurostat, Unemployment Statistics, Main Statistical Findings, 2014, available online at: http://epp.eurostat.ec.europa.eu/statistics_explained/index.php/Unemployment_statistics

Exiles in Balkans (2013) Greece: After Zeus, Thetis, 09.04.2013, available online at: http://exilesingreece.over-blog.com/article-greece-after-zeus-thetis-116947636.html

Filopoulou, L. (2012) The resistance movement in Greece: challenges and alternatives, Corporate Europe Observatory, April 10th 2012, available online at: http://corporateeurope.org/publications/resistance-movement-greece-challenges-and-alternatives

Human Rights Watch (2013) Xenios Zeus and the True Meaning of Greek Hospitality, 09.07.2013, available online at: http://www.hrw.org/news/2013/07/09/xenios-zeus-and-true-meaning-greek-hospitality

Kallianos, Y. (2013) Agency of the street: Crisis, radical politics and the production of public space in Athens, 2008-2012. In: City: Analysis of Urban Trends, Culture, theory, Policy, Action, 17/4, 548-557

Kandylis, G. and K. I. Kavoulakos (2011) Framing urban inequalities: racist mobilization against immigrants in Athens. In: The Greek Review of Social Research, special issue 136 C, 157-176

Katsoridas, D. and S. Lampousaki (2012) Strikes in 2011, Institute of Labour of the General Confederation of Greek Workers: Studies, 37, 2012, available online at: http://www.inegsee.gr/sitefiles/files/meleti37.pdf [in Greek].

Kentikelenis, A., M. Karanikolo, I. Papanicolas, S. Basu, M. McKee and D. Stuckler (2011) Health Effects of Financial Crisis: Omens of a Greek Tragedy. In: The Lancet, 378, 1457-1458

Malkoutzis, N. (2013) The Debt Crisis in Greece: Birth of a New Civil Society? In: W. Puschra and S. Burke (eds.), The Future We the People Need, Friedrich Ebert Stiftung, New York office, available online at: http://library.fes.de/pdf-files/iez/global/09610-20130215.pdf

Markantonatou, M. (2013) Diagnosis, Treatment and Effects of the Crisis in Greece: A "Special Case" or a "Test Case"?, Max-Planck-Institut für Gesellschaftsforschung, Cologne, Discussion Paper, Nr. 3/13

Ministry of Justice (2014) General Statistics for Prisoners 2003-2012, available online at: http://www.ministryofjustice.gr/site/el/ [In Greek]

Monastiriotis, V. (2011) Making geographical sense of the Greek austerity measures: compositional effects and long-run implications. In: Cambridge Journal of Regions, Economy and Society, 4, 323–337

Mylonas, H. (2011) Is Greece a Failing Developed State? Causes and Socio-economic Consequences of the Financial Crisis. In: K. Botsiou (ed.) The Global Economic Crisis and the Case of Greece. Berlin: Springer, 77-88

Oikonomides, T. (2013) The Squares Movement: Combining Protest and Solidarity. In: W. Puschra and S. Burke (eds.) The Future We the People Need, Friedrich Ebert Stiftung, New York, 2013, available online at: http://library.fes.de/pdf-files/iez/global/09610-20130215.pdf

OKANA, Greek Organization Against Drugs (2013) OKANA's press release regarding Operation Thetis, 07.03.2013, available online at: http://www.okana.gr/2012-01-12-13-29-02/deltia-typoy/item/355-deltiotypouepixeirisithetis [In Greek]

Pantazidou, M. (2012) Treading New Ground: A Changing Moment for Citizen Action in Greece. Civil Society @ Crossroads Project, 2012, available online at: http://www.pria.org/docs/A-Changing-Moment-for-Citizen-Action_Greece.pdf

PICUM, Platform for International Cooperation on Undocumented Migrants (2012) Minister of Health blames undocumented women for HIV infections and calls for their deportation, available online at: http://picum.org/pt/noticias/boletim/31644/#news_31597, 17.1.12

Polanyi, K. (2001) The Great Transformation: The Political and Economic Origins of Our Time. Boston: Beacon Press Books

SEPE (Labour Inspectorate) (2012) Hellenic Republic, Ministry of Labour, Social Security and Welfare, Statistical Data on Labour Inspectorate Activity, Press release DT_2012-07-18_SEPE (in Greek), 18 July 2012, Athens, available online at: http://www.ypakp.gr/index.php?ID=press_releases

Ta Nea (newspaper) (2013) Dendias: Constitutional Obligation of the Greek Police to Reoccupy Squats, 29.08.2013, available online at: http://www.tanea.gr/news/greece/article/5037682/dendias-h-el-as-tha-synexisei-to-syntagmatiko-ths-kathhkon-na-anakatalambanei-toys-xwroys-poy-teloyn-ypo-katalhpsh/ [In Greek]

To Vima (newspaper) (2012a), Police men voted massively once again for the Golden Dawn, 19.06.2012, available online at: http://www.tovima.gr/society/article/?aid=463063 [In Greek]

To Vima (newspaper) (2012b), Speech of A. Samaras, 07.04.2012, available online at: http://www.tovima.gr/politics/article/?aid=452514 [In Greek]

Xenakis, Sappho, Cheliotis and K. Leonidas (2013) Spaces of contestation: Challenges, actors and expertise in the management of urban security in Greece. In: European Journal of Criminology, 10/3

Wainwright, H. (2013) Tapping the resistance in Greece, Znet, May 22nd 2013, available online at: http://www.zcommunications.org/tapping-the-resistance-in-greece-by-hilary-wainwright

Portugal

Planning and governance in the Portuguese cities in times of European crisis

João Seixas and José Carlos Mota

This chapter aims at analysing the impacts of the European crisis and its main responses in Portuguese city-regions; and to examine the correspondent development of spatial planning instruments and public policies for urban development. There are proposed several insights to an already widely open discussion. Particularly on how territorial dimensions – and namely the urban realms – show to be relevant to the interpretation of the European crisis and its consequences; over its vast and differentiated spatial impacts as well on the conflicts resulting from the intersection of the reactions of the different political stances (Hadjimichalis, 2011; Werner, 2013).

These are being particularly painful times for Southern European territories and societies; due to the conjunction of the financial crisis that perceivably started in 2008, and the following European and several nation-states political responses. The main political reaction was to put in place austerity measures that deeply disrupted social, economic and territorial tissues; driving attention towards if the crisis is not anymore – if it ever was – mainly due to public and financial reasons – having instead multidimensional and structural sociopolitical bases.

To analyse the territorial performances and responses here under subject, two political and administrative levels were considered: a functional regional one, where the focus was on the Metropolitan Area of Lisbon and the Intermunicipal Community of the Region of Aveiro; and a municipal one, where the focus was on its correspondent inner cities, Lisbon and Aveiro. These two regions represent two somewhat similar and differentiated realities. Both cities have relevant scientific and technological system units and high foreign exposure (economic, social and cultural internationalization) and can be seen as interesting examples of innovative approaches towards crisis impacts.

In analysing the impact of the European crisis, key indicators were considered: unemployment, poverty, social deprivation, political instability, cuts, public debt of local authorities and the central state; this being sought to realize the extent of the crisis impacts as well as resilience and responsive factors.

For analysing the instruments, main public policies for development and spatial planning were considered at the regional level (in particular the guidelines for European funding periods 2007/2013 and 2014/2020) as well as the municipal level (urban regeneration or socio-economic programs). Furthermore, focusing was made on the integration of different local actors and the way they were mobilised to tackle the crisis. Finally, urban planning instruments and its changes were also under analysis.

1. Portuguese cities and urban development in times of European crisis

1.1 Contexts[1]

The 2008 financial crisis marked the beginning of a profound change in Portuguese society and politics. Portugal was already suffering through the first decade of the century, major shocks that had a profound impact in its ability to compete internationally: for adopting a strong currency, the Euro; for suffering the impacts of global liberalisation and on Chinese exports on traditional Portuguese export markets; for receiving the oil and energy shocks since mid-2000. All this lead to the so-called "lost decade" (as it was commonly termed by media) for Portuguese economy; none withstanding several focuses of innovation and neo-modernity in the country. From 2000 to 2010, Portuguese GDP grew at an annual average

---

[1] | This section, as well as the sections that analyze Lisbon region in its geographical and sociopolitical developments since 2008, owns much to the data collection and correspondent analytical work made by Simone Tulumello, Susana Corvelo and Ana Drago. The authors wish to strongly thank their work and permission in this use.

rate of only 1%; and the country seems to have been answering to these shocks through a progressive shift towards an economic model grounded on low wages – and growing inequality – rather than investments in sectors with high added value (Reis and Rodrigues, 2011).

The Troika's (the EU, the IMF and the European Central Bank) therapy consisted mainly on a supposedly neo-classical or neo-liberal agenda for the country. It included the obligation towards drastic cuts in public spending and public investment as well as in restructuring and liberalisation policies. State administration, public services and public salaries were to be strongly reduced, as well as public spending in fundamental areas as health, education, poverty and inequality reduction and unemployment benefits. A mix of tax increase was imposed over work and pensions revenues as well on consumption. A vast privatization program was implemented in strategic economic sectors as transport, energy and communications, postal services, airports.

The main social and economic effects of the "adjustment program" carried out from the bailout in 2011 cannot be understated: since then, Portuguese GDP felt 5,9% and is expected to fall again in 2014. In 2013, private consumption has returned to the levels of 2000, public consumption has fallen to the figures of 2002. As far as (both public and private) investment rates are concerned, there is no memory (i.e. no statistical data) of such a collapse. In the first trimester of 2013, the net investment in Portuguese economy was 20% lower than in 1995 (Abreu et al., 2013). From 2011 to 2013 national available income dropped 4%, whereas work income suffered a significant reduction of 9,7%[2]. These figures can be interpreted as a lowering-wage pressure typical of a recessive economy, but were certainly induced both by government continuous wage cuts in public sector since 2010, and the effects of massive unemployment.

1.2 The crisis in the Lisbon region

The focus is here given to the Lisbon Metropolitan Area (LMA) recent performances on economic, territorial and social dimensions, and on interpreting the effects of the Eurozone crisis and its political reactions, through correspondent data analyses. First of all, evidence will confirm that exist a strong relationship between the performance of the metropolitan

---

2 | Elaboration of authors on data Pordata (www.pordata.pt/).

region and the national context. But further on: it will be proposed that within this correlation, there were developed two markedly different impact periods; and maybe a third one, recently starting.

As relevant concentrational territory, it is no surprise that LMA recent evolution has been strongly affected by the economic crisis and subsequent austerity measures, both by European and national politics. Nonetheless, this happens in apparently contradictory ways. When taking into account the years prior to and after the beginning of the implementation of austerity measures (since mid-end of 2010), the Regional Development Composite Index, on its competitiveness component, shows a slight improvement pattern, clearly contradicted by cohesion and environmental quality effects, which affect the overall index, with clear downward consequences. A more careful analysis helps to understand this apparent competitiveness recovery. All variables – per capita GDP, qualified personnel, exports growth, RandD intensity or the prevalence of knowledge intensive activities – in LMA outperform country's average, are less reactive taking into account the LMA specialization profile[3], where an internal market dependence is markedly balanced by the exports profile; thus giving a sense of growth while the behaviour of macroeconomic variables is not so positive.

During what here is called the first phase of the economic crisis (2007/8-2009/10), a moderate growth occurred in the LMA, as economy started to contract. The predominance of service sectors and tourism activities in the region seemed to contribute to balance economic depressors which started to become evident after 2008. But during a second phase, just after 2010, performance differences showed to be quite evident, with both cohesion and environmental components starting to lower and the overall regional index being mostly affected.

---

3 | According to its GVA, the Lisbon Region specializes in services, transport and logistics, energy and environment, tourism, chemical, electronic and mechanical industries.

Table 1 – Regional Development Composite Index

		RDCI	Competitiveness	Cohesion	Environmental Quality
Portugal		100	100	100	100
Lisbon Metropolitan Area (LMA)	2011	105,33	113,26	103,99	98,01
	2010	106,48	113,93	104,64	100,20
	2008	106,79	113,18	106,57	100,00
	2006	107,21	113,01	107,78	100,27

Portugal: 100. Data from INE

The analysis of further economic performance variables helps to understand the real effects of the economic crisis and then of the austerity measures: major private and (especially) public investment drops, while the austerity discourses grew together with cuts in public spending to supposedly restore competitiveness. In these senses, the numbers are quite expressive: Gross Fixed Capital Formation drops by almost 20% from 2008 to 2011. Around 65.000 companies (17, 6%) have disappeared between 2008 and 2012, shifting the survival rate under national average.

The LMA is today a densely urbanized system, however considerably fragmented and with difficult capacity to a clear multipolar capacity; this being the result of several decades of urbanisation economies prevalence. This is quite noticeable on the levels of growth in terms of inhabitants and dwelling stock. According to the last census, between 2001 and 2011, a 6% population growth was reflected into a growth of the built area of around 14, 2%. Being the real estate and construction sector one of the first to suffer with the crashes and the crisis anticipation movements, as can be clearly seen on the significant drop on building sale contracts. After a sustained growth in the early 2000s, construction works dropped by half in a few years (2007 to 2012) in the Lisbon area and Setúbal peninsula (southern part of the metropolitan region). It is to be said that the 2007/8 financial breakdown intervened in processes already ongoing: building sale contracts stop growing in 2006, because of the burst of the construction bubble and growing effectiveness of planning regulations.

Figure 1 – Construction and real estate in LMA

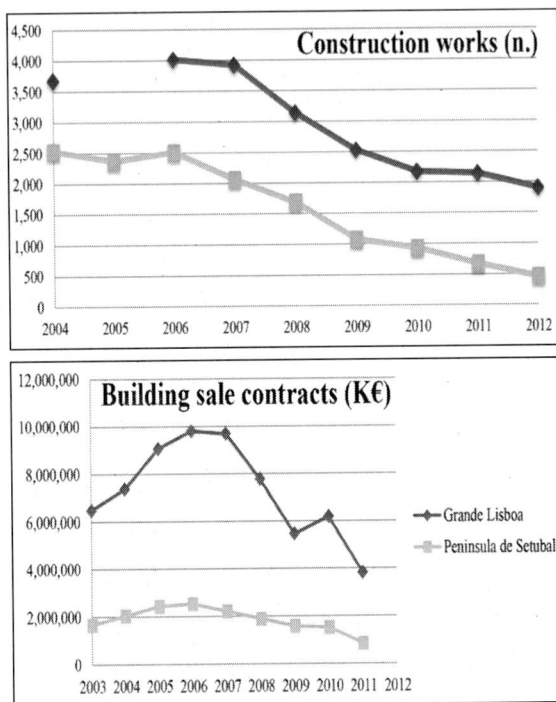

Data from INE

At the same time, mortgage insolvencies were rising by 49,5% from 2009 to 2013. The political discourse of recent years, both at European level and by the Portuguese government since 2011, underpinning the blame of Portuguese economic and fiscal crisis on families for their excessive indebtedness, can largely be explained by the lack of an overall public housing policy for decades. In 2010 housing loans accounted for 80% of family indebtedness, and homeownership was encouraged by tax benefits and a state-subsidized credit system for house purchase that lasted for more than 30 years until 2010. This pervasive system created a specific articulation, linking state policies, family investments/indebtedness, and credit-financial institutions (Santos, 2013).

LMA is a highly qualified region in European average terms, concentrating the biggest university poles in the country, the highest number of RandD centres and a considerable number of innovative companies. With a 16,8% of inhabitants having high education degrees (against 11,8% national average), and a slight increase in young people population, it is nonetheless an ageing region with birth rates dropping and where over the last ten years, the elderly (65 years old and more) rose from a 15,4%, to a 18,2% weight in the overall population, already considering the balance of a fairly young immigrant population. These trends are just as significant as we look at labour market figures and their aggravated behaviour throughout the crisis development. In fact, the effects of the crisis and political responses are deeply clear here, with a reduction of ~180.000 employees between 2008 and 2013. Even though the region accompanies the country's trends, the aggravated effect in LMA is evident when taking in consideration the unemployment figures. The unemployment rate in the LMA more than doubled in the 2008-2013 period (from 7,9% to 17,3%), a growth than became steeper since the 2011 bailout, confirming the depressing effects of austerity politics in macroeconomic variables. Particularly, youth unemployment rate grew from 16,9% in 2007 to 22,7% in 2010; then booming to 42,4% in 2013. The numbers of registered unemployment at public employment services figures, which gives a monthly picture and allows capturing trends more quickly, is also consistent with these findings: registered unemployment in LMA started to rise at a low pace just after 2008, growing drastically after 2010/11, when cut off measures by central government started.

Figure 2 – Unemployment rate and beneficiaries of Social Integration Income (SII) (No.)

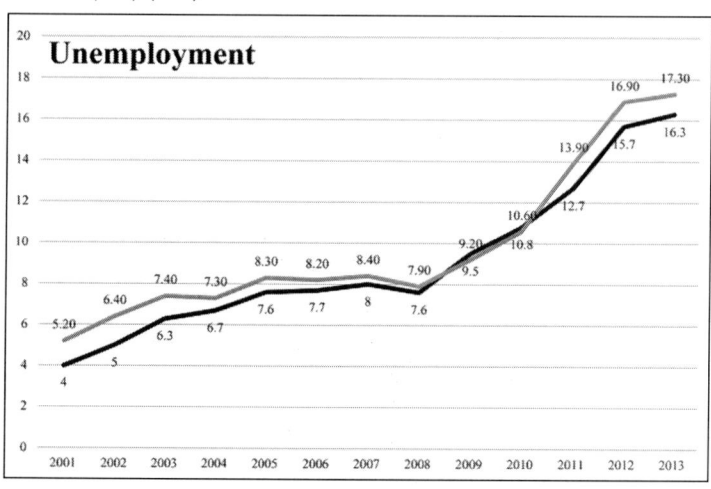

Data from INE; II/MSESS (http://www4.seg-social.pt/estatisticas)

Other relevant analysis concerns income inequalities and poverty rates. Poverty risk rapidly grew since 2009, rapidly inverting a slightly positive trend traced since the beginning of the decade by steady social policies. According to the 2013 EU Statistics on Income and Living Conditions survey on 2012 income data for Portugal (no regional poverty data are available), 18,7% of the population was at risk of poverty after social transfers, against 17,9% in 2009. The growth is much more significant using a time-anchored rate[4]. The 'at risk of poverty' rate for the unemployed population in the country was of 40,2% in 2012, a rise of almost 4 points when compared to 2009. Under the austerity agenda, a renewed rise of asymmetry in income distribution since 2010 has reverted the trends of the last decade. Considering the beneficiaries of the Social Integration Income (social security benefit for poorer families) in LMA, there has been a strong increase (approximately 66%) in the first phase of crisis. Since 2010 onwards, however, the austerity measures[5] produced a drastic reduction in these figures, in paradoxical contrast with the contextual rise in unemployment.

The austerity measures and the lowering of wages and family income also strongly affected one of the most important dimensions of urban life: mobility. The urban mobility and transportation effects of the crisis are particularly serious in a quite unstructured urbanised region like LMA is. Lisbon metropolis is characterised by huge daily commuting and semi-polycentric travels; with for instance its main core, Lisbon-city (with a population of circa 600.000 residents) having normally a daily duplication of its inhabitants. Between 2008 and 2010, the numbers of urban and suburban travels in LMA public transports have been considerably stable; but then a 23% drop was to be experienced for the 2010-2012 period. This sharp reduction of travellers happens when the purchasing power loss

---

4 | At-Risk-of-Poverty rate is statistically dependent on a percentage of the national average income. When national average income is reduced, as it has happened in the present context, the at-risk-rate income is reduced as well. To avoid this misleading effect, some experts have experimented a "time-anchoring" analysis, using 2009 national average income as benchmark (see Rede Europeia anti-pobreza, Portugal, http://www.eapn.pt/documentos_visualizar.php?ID=322).

5 | The measure, called "condição de recursos" and imposed by the first national austerity package (known as PEC 1) in response to the EU demands, imposed cuts on beneficiaries with property ownership evidence, through fiscal analysis.

effect is aggravated with cutbacks in public metropolitan transport offer; paralleled by significant fare increases (~24%, 2010-2012) decided not by local but by central government.

Table 2 – Poverty and Deprivation Indicators (EU-SILC 2010-2013)

	2009	2010	2011	2012 (estimated)
At Risk of Poverty Rate before Social Transfers (%)	43,4	42,5	45,4	46,9
At Risk of Poverty Rate after Social Transfers (%)	17,9	18,0	17,9	18,7
Time-anchored At Risk of Poverty Rate (reference income=2009) (%)	17,9	19,6	21,3	24,7
Severe Material Deprivation (%)	9,0	8,3	8,6	10,9
At Risk Of Poverty Population (%)	25,3	24,4	25,3	27,4
Gini Coefficient	33,7	34,2	34,5	34,2
Inequality on Income Distribution (S80/S20)	5,6	5,7	5,8	6,0
Inequality on Income Distribution (S90/S10)	9,2	9,4	10,0	10,7

Data from INE/Eurostat. Po: estimated value

Finally, migration flows were also analysed; as mirror for socioeconomic capabilities of the territory under question. From 2010 onwards, there is a complete inversion of migration trends in the LMA: immigration flows fall drastically – the values of 2012 being half of those in 2009 – whilst emigration – especially among young people – rises abruptly in only 3 years. In 2012, it was three times higher than in 2009, forming a negative demographic balance for the first time in the decade.

Having analysed in this section the impact of economic crisis in LMA through a set of socioeconomic and urban indicators; some relevant conclusions can be made. Regional and local data evidences on the Lisbon Region, suggests that rather than a simplistic 'crisis approach', a series of differentiated causes and consequences have followed the global financial breakdown. Two main temporal phases are to be highlighted. In the first phase the long-wave of the structural financial and ecological crisis affects strongly the economic areas mostly dependent on urbanisation and space production. In this phase, and as main urban and diversified hub for the country, the LMA seems to show some resilience; albeit increasing internal polarization. The second phase, marked by the implementation of national austerity policies, and then with renewed vigour with the 2011 bailout; configures the widening of the impacts over vaster areas of the social and urban and metropolitan fabric. The effects are now particularly strong over middle-classes, public employees, as well as increasing pressures on poverty-risk and elderly populations. The correlation between the austerity measures and the social impacts of the crisis are evident; and here more in-depth analyses will be necessary in order to accurately discern the main drivers and its effects.

However, a third phase now seems to be showing. The recent migration trends, boosting drainage of not only poor as well as younger and skilled people, prefigures a potential third crisis-effect to come, in the form of a skills and demographic depression. Nonetheless, the statistical data available is not still complete for a clear picture of the complexity of localised trends.

1.3 The crisis in the Aveiro region

Starting from the general framework of the region of Aveiro, an effort was made to understand the consequences of the crisis and the austerity policies of recent years (2008-2013) for the social, economic and urban dynamics and to identify the most worrying signs. Looking at the region of Aveiro in the national context, it can be noted that this is the sixth most populous Intermunicipal community (which roughly corresponds to a NUTS III and therefore is an intermediate level between the regional administration and the municipalities), with about 380,000 inhabitants. It is followed by the Ave, Cávado, Tâmega, Setúbal Peninsula and the Algarve, excluding the metropolitan areas of Lisbon and Porto.

This territory has a pattern of scattered land use, developed around the lagoon area of the Ria de Aveiro. It is served by a good road, rail and port infrastructure, connecting it to the main urban centres (Porto and Lisbon), Europe (A25) and the world, which enables a good overall economic performance and exporting capacity (Dispersed City Project, UA/DGOTDU, 2009).

Figure 3 – Populational Density by NUTS III in Portugal

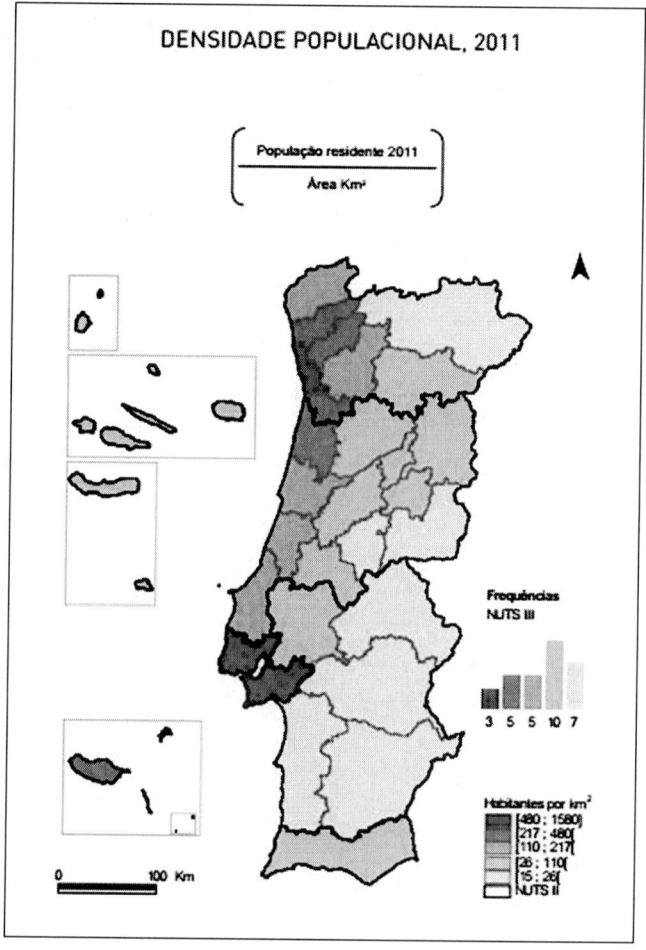

Source: INE, Censos 2011

Analysing the period between 2001 and 2011, the amount of built houses has increased 19%, which is higher when compared to the national average (which was 17%) or the increase witnessed in Greater Lisbon region (15%). Much of this trend in the region is a consequence of the construction of single family housing in single-storey buildings, which occurred mainly in suburban parishes with above average construction rates between 2001 and 2011 (EDT 2014-2020, CIRA, 2013). The amount of vacant housing between 2001 and 2011 has increased 50% in Aveiro region (12% of the total housing), which is well above the average in Lisbon region (26% increase, 13% of the total housing) and Portugal (35% increase, 13% of the total housing).

The mobility pattern in the region is characterized by a predominance of trips done by personal transport (53%), which is similar to National and European average values. The motorisation rate is 502 vehicles/1000 inhabitants and has increased 42% (2003-2012), at a much higher rate than the national average (26%). The fact that 40% of these trips lasted up to 5 minutes suggest that there is a significant margin for developing alternative modes (PIMTRA, 2012).

Regarding mobility patterns, Baixo Vouga (the NUTS III which approximately corresponds to the Intermunicipal Region of Aveiro) has a relevant particularity, is the Portuguese sub-region where most people use bike regularly – this value is eight times higher than the national average – 3.9% vs 0.5% (Census 2011). In the Murtosa municipality, which is part of this sub-region, this figure is even higher (17%) and comes closer to Danish than to Portuguese average values. Further, the importance of bike use in this territory can be assessed by the bike industry located in Águeda (another municipality of the region) and the public bike system of Aveiro (BUGA), which was the first to be implemented in Portugal and one of the first in Europe (in 2000). Furthermore, more than half of the population has a bike at home (535 bicycles per thousand inhabitants), which is higher than the average rate of motorization of the region's municipalities. Although this propensity for bike usage is not directly linked to the crisis, it provides conditions for developing other measures of urban policy.

In the region, 80% of the total population lives within 250 meters of a road served by collective transport. Still, it has a modal split for the collective transport of about 4.7%, well below the national average of 22%, but close to that found in regions with similar pattern of settlement. Nevertheless, in the main urban centre (Aveiro) the values are lower than expected. The ones using public transport (road) are mainly women (60%), young people (46%) and seniors (20%) (PIMTRA 2012).

In the case of municipal public road transport, in the period from 2005 to 2010 there was a decrease in the number of passengers. In 2011 there was a very sharp drop in all public transport availability indicators, with fewer vehicles/km and places/km, reflecting the troubled finances of the municipality and the transportation company (Municipal Mobility Plan of Aveiro, CMA, 2011).

Figure 4

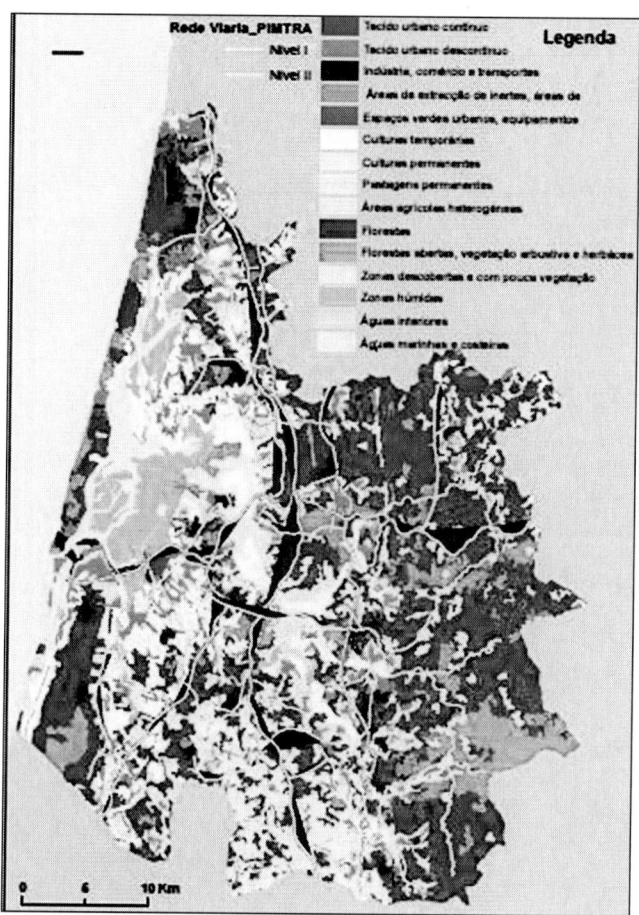

Source: UA, PTD 2014-2020

Focusing the analysis on productive fabric, it can be concluded that the region's companies are mostly micro, small and medium sized, represent about 6.7% of the national companies (INE, 2009), and are strongly export oriented, particularly in industries such as footwear, automobile components, habitat, ceramics, bikes, agro-food, moulds, electronics and telecommunications with two distinct sectors: one more connected to primary products (focusing on early segments of the value chain) or unqualified labour (such as furniture or wood); and one based on greater product differentiation and that has a significant export potential and dynamism (metallurgy or ceramics) (Augusto Mateus, 2005).

This pattern explains its national relevance, representing 15% of the national GVA (Gross Value Added), the third region of the country, after Porto and Lisbon, and one of the major exporting regions of the country, representing 13% of the total national exports and amounting to EUR 4.7 billion, with a rate of coverage of imports by exports of 81.6%, while in the country this figure reaches almost 140%.

Figure 5

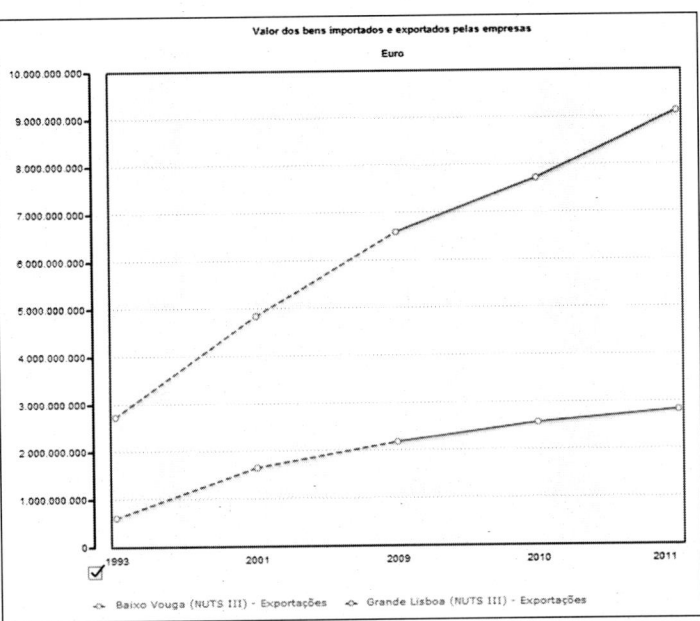

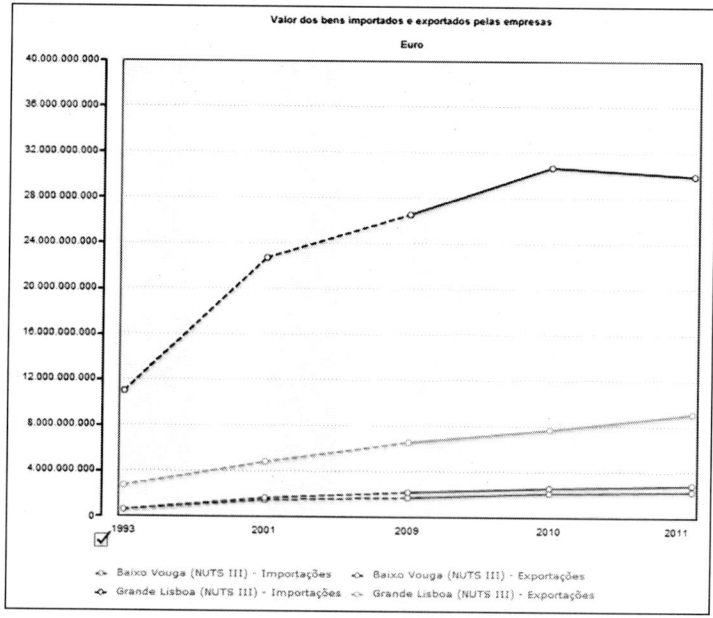

Source: PORDATA (http://www.pordata.pt/Municipios/
Ambiente+de+Consulta/Gr%C3%A1fico)

The good performance of the region's companies may be related to their innovative capacity, measured by the fact that 10% of the total national companies certified to ISO 9001 and 14000 belong to the region of Aveiro (AIDA Yearbook, 2013).

Despite the crisis and the high number of dissolved companies (273 companies), which peaked in 2009 and was particularly high in the commercial sector but also in accommodation, catering, transport, storage and repair of vehicles, the number of companies created was even higher, with a positive balance of 41, which far outweighs the national balance. The sectors that have a better balance (between those created or dissolved) are related to health and social support, finance and insurance activities and consulting, scientific and technical activities (EDT 2014-2020 CIRA, 2013). According to the Aveiro Region Territorial Development Strategy 2014-2020 (CIRA, 2013) there is currently a "reconfiguration of the productive fabric of the region with a significant number of bankruptcies in traditionally important sectors, particularly manufacturing, and the emergence of firms in sectors with more embedded knowledge, such as scientific and technical consulting".

Despite this generally positive economic environment, the significant increase in unemployment in the region, between 2001 and 2011 the unemployment rate in the region increased considerably above the national average (there are about 20,500 unemployed people), makes it possible to infer that "the businesses that are being established are far from creating the same amount of jobs than those who have disappeared" (EDT 2014-2020 CIRA, 2013).

Recent data shows that unemployment in the region rose from 6.8% to 8.2% (2008-2012), compared with 7.0% and 9.6% at the national level in the same years. It peaked at 17.6% (in January 2013) and is currently at 14.6% (April 2014). Another serious problem is youth unemployment which currently reaches 37.7% nationally (February 2014), with the highest values in the mainland in the Lisboa e Vale do Tejo region (45.5%) and the lowest values in the mainland in the Centre region (31%).

One of the main investments of the region has been the qualification of its human resources. It hosts important units related to RandD and the Scientific and Technological System of national and international relevance, in particular the University of Aveiro, one of the most country's most renowned universities, ranked as the "66th best university in the world with less than 50 years and the best English" (Times Higher Education Ranking 2013), PT Innovation (the national research centre of Portugal Telecom, which is being merged with the Oi group in Brazil) and the headquarters of the ICT cluster (62 member companies, which represent an aggregated turnover of 365 million Euros, employ around 3617 employees, most of which have a higher education degree (over 70%) (INOVARIA Auditors Report, 2012). Although the effort and the overall training levels have increased substantially in recent years, "the regional labour market has not been able to absorb this labour-force at the same rate, generating qualified unemployment "(EDT 2014-2020 CIRA, 2013).

In response to the difficulty of integrating this labour force, there has been an increased emigration, especially of young active population. With no data on migration in the region, it is estimated that since 2008 about 500.000 Portuguese nationals have left the country, which is similar to the migrations levels of the 60, and exceeds the amount of births. A recent study by the Centre for Emigration, based on national censuses of 2001 and 2011, from the Eurostat, notes that the migration to the

UK has quadrupled in this century (Centre for Emigration, 2014). This phenomenon, beyond the problems related to the loss of skilled working-age population, also has a serious impact on the birth rates, since it is also the most fertile population that migrates the most.

In parallel to the above mentioned problems, the region has also been witnessing an increase in the number of RSI (Social Security) beneficiaries. Between 2007 and 2010 this value rose from 6,860 to 10,117 (an increase in 47,5%), reaching a share of 29.66 RSI beneficiaries per 1000 working aged population in 2010 (or 2.73% of the resident population), while the national average increased 42.6% increase in the same time-span, reaching 58.45 beneficiaries per 1,000 working aged population in 2010 (or 4.99% of the resident population) (EDT 2014-2020, CIRA, 2013).

These results show that the region of Aveiro revealed considerable resilience to the impacts of the economic crisis, due to its emphasis in innovation, exportation and training of human resources.

2. URBAN POLITICS, PLANNING AND GOVERNANCE IN PORTUGAL

2.1 URBAN POLITICS, PLANNING and GOVERNANCE IN PORTUGAL

2.1.1 Planning Context

Although spatial planning at the municipal level has been practiced since the seventies of the last century (the first legal act which created the Municipal Master Plans dates from 1977), the institutionalization of planning in Portugal is still relatively new – the Law for Spatial Planning and Urbanism (1998) completed recently fifteen years.

The building of planning instruments at the national, regional and local levels embodying the Territorial Management System is not yet finalized: the National Program of the Spatial Planning Policy (PNPOT) was completed (approved by the Cabinet Council, discussed in the 1st quarter of 2007 in the National Parliament), the Regional Programs of Territorial Planning (PROT) is at an advanced stage of preparation but not yet concluded and the third generation of the Municipal Master Plans is still in preparation (awaiting the completion of PROTs review).

Despite the political and technical effort made in the last decades in matters of planning, the outcomes are mainly reflected in a planning praxis that is very focused on the development of spatial land use plans; a limited financial and organizational capacity of local governments to implement the planned actions; a relationship of distrust between the central government, local authorities and various social and economic agents that are active at the municipal level; and a contradictory and even conflicting guidelines given to the municipal spatial planning, without intermediate structures for consultation (at the regional level).

The practice of preparing plans in the last years has been characterized by a fragile and minimalist agenda focused on controlling urban growth through a statutory and normative approach, without considering issues such as competitiveness, sustainability or social cohesion. The prevalent methodology followed a rigid and bureaucratic procedure, which is very time consuming and lacks institutional and stakeholder debate and the outcomes showed a weak operative capacity, worried with the legal procedures which underlay the administrative approval of private projects, but lacking financial support for public proposals. As a consequence, there emerged an inefficient and rigid planning system characterized by plans with limited social, economic and spatial impacts.

The practice of spatial planning revealed itself inadequate regarding the growing needs of municipalities and struggled with a diverse set of overlapping and, often, contradicting problems. While completing basic infrastructure, local authorities must be able to manage the social, cultural, sports and educational facilities and initiate tasks related to the promotion of economic development but frequently failed to accomplish this.

The emergence of spatial strategic plans in Portugal in the mid-nineties allowed answering some of the new needs of municipalities, with some methodological innovations – including the creation of Strategic City Planning Offices, which encouraged participation, the discussion of the goals to pursue, the necessary measures to achieve them and mechanism to monitors their implementation. Unfortunately, the various generations of strategic plans showed a tendency for justifying projects with no real "urban strategy", but specific, targeted actions, without consistent links between them (Pereira, 2000).

A growing disenchantment of citizens and public and private stakeholders emerged from this planning practice. This disenchantment was related, on the one hand, to an increased difficulty in accessing the 'public sphere' to discuss planning proposals and to find «common causes», which induced an individualistic climate, and, on the other hand, to a low capacity of municipalities to implement the proposed plans.

The National Strategic Reference Framework (QREN) 2007/2013 launched a new set of instruments for spatial planning which was not provided by the fundamental law of territory management (LBOT) – the "Policy for the Cities". One of these instruments developed – "the Partnerships for Urban Regeneration" (PRU) – aimed to support actions to revitalize intra-urban spaces, supported by a structure of Local extended partnerships (DGOTDU, 2008). This instrument was particularly innovative in its formulation, both because of the diversity and relevance of its concepts and of the philosophy that it advocates – building partnerships and, specially, being demanding regarding design and implementation. Recently collected data allows us to understand the true scale of the challenge. There are, at this time, about 182 approved partnerships, most of which are located in the North (50%) and Central (30%) regions, which account for a total investment of one billion euros (with ERDF contribution of about 60%). Thirty per cent of the initiatives (about 56 cities) have an investment of over than EUR 8 million (Total EUR 600 million).

Even though it has a very significant budget and expected impact, a systematic evaluation of the program's merits has not yet been made. The case analysed in this chapter shows relevant evidence pf the difficulties to clarify the goals and to translate them in concrete, coherent and useful proposals.

The start of a new cycle of spatial planning is thus dependent on the new financial support program 2014-2020 to introduce a new set of challenges highlighting the articulation of territorial dimensions ("territorial qualification") and strategic dimensions ("competitiveness and innovation").

The challenges faced today by spatial planning are related to the operationalization of concepts and principles, a result of an increasing gap between theory and practice, between expectations and results.

2.1.2 Urban Politics and Governance

The practice of urban politics, planning and governance at the municipal level has shown some of the most innovative answers to the crisis. Unfortunately, municipalities are facing a severe financial problem, as a consequence of general public indebtedness. Nevertheless, they have one of the smallest budgets in the EU countries, spending less than 10% of the total public investment.

As part of the TROIKA memorandum, the Government was invited to develop "a consolidation plan to reorganize and significantly reduce the number of these entities":

"3.43. Reorganise local government administration. There are currently around 308 municipalities and 4,259 parishes. By July 2012, the government will develop a consolidation plan to reorganize and significantly reduce the number of such entities. The Government will implement these plans based on agreement with EC and IMF staff. These changes, which will come into effect by the beginning of the next local election cycle, will enhance service delivery, improve efficiency, and reduce costs.
3.44. Carry out a study to identify potential duplication of activities and other inefficiencies between the central administration, local administration and locally-based central administration services. [Q4-2011] Based on this analysis, reform the existing framework to eliminate the identified inefficiencies. [Q2-2012] Portugal: Memorandum of Understanding on specific economic policy conditionality" (3 May 2011)

In addition to reducing the number of parishes, less municipal enterprises and less managerial positions in local authorities, saving 9.2 million €/ year, TROIKA has failed to impose any kind real reform in Local Government.

2.1.3 New Urban Policy Instruments

Another instrument created at the beginning of the crisis in 2008, still under the previous government, shows a concern of the central government with the need to stimulate a set of new ways of thinking about the performance of local government – Policy for the Cities – Polis XXI, previously referred.

The Partnerships for Urban Regeneration (PRU) was one the instruments of the Polis XXI aiming to "respond to increasingly complex challenges faced by cities, overcome the weaknesses of the national urban system and transform our cities into effective engines of development of the regions and the country".

The design of this instrument posed several challenges to the way public policies concerning cities are generated. These challenges have been systematized by the former Secretary of State of the Cities, João Ferrão. The first challenge relates to the fact that "public policy in general must address the needs of citizens, helping to strengthen the collective ability to adapt to structural changes (especially in times of crisis) and create opportunities (development) not only to companies, but for people, organizations and territories." The second states that "the relevance of a PRU or a town policy only exists if it can bring added value to the local sectorial policies" This implies that it "has to produce a (new) territorial intelligence that perceives the relationship between different systems and promotes an integrated vision among some of the local policies (eg, mobility, culture, environment and health)". The third states that the "quality of the instrument depends on the quality of the overall vision for the city, where it falls, and the quality of the partners and the relationships that is established between them." The fourth states that "citizens' participation in this instrument should not be just a mere bureaucratic requirement that is fulfilled at the end of the process" and should have "mechanisms for public scrutiny to how the PRU's processes are being conducted." It was also said that "for participation to occur, it is important to create moments and take appropriate methodologies" with "courage and boldness" in this matter. The last challenge suggests that "municipalities must realize that times have changed and that the methodologies for carrying these instruments also have to change," making it critical to "create (regular) opportunities to discuss collectively and produce ideas for the future of the city (creation of collective learning processes)".

2.2 Sociopolitical changes in the Lisbon region

Between European and national austerity pressures; and multiple local and civic differentiated responses, Lisbon region clearly shows a complexity – when not a contradictory – political landscape; both within and beyond the crisis contexts. The section is set out around three themes: local government capacitation and national reforms; local government responses; new civic profiles of socio-political empowerment.

The first picture to expose considering Portugal's territorial politics is the secular limitation of sub-national territorial powers – or what it might be called a secular 'austerity localism', driven by central politics. The country remains one of the most politically centralised societies of Europe – being the second non-micro EU country (after Greece) with the lowest proportion of sub-national public expenditure decisional competence (i.e. regional and local public expenditure) –, which accounts for around 15% of public expenditure, well below EU27 average (~25%) (Dexia and CCRE, 2012). Moreover, the regions themselves (accounting for around 4,5% of public expenditure) have no politically autonomous governments, rather deconcentrated bodies of the national government (Nanetti et al., 2004). This severely centralized pattern is the main scenario for a constant weaknesses of local administrations, coupled with chronic issues regarding fiscal and financial support of its own existence (Seixas and Albet, 2012). Furthermore, the weak resourceful capacities are now being even more curtailed by the fiscal stress induced by not only the economic crisis but above all by the reduction of national transfers promoted since 2010. As a result, municipal budgets within the AML have seen, with few exceptions, steep reductions since 2009/2010 – in the order of 20-30% in three/four years.

In addition to local budget cuts, the national government has been carrying on fiscal and administrative reforms of local powers in the frame of austerity policies. Firstly, a strong suppression of municipal economic and real estate taxes is to be envisaged for 2018. Secondly, the Law 22/2012 about administrative reorganization of municipalities is targeted to expenditure cuts through the elimination of 27% of parishes. Seemingly on other hand, there was envisaged a decentralisation process, through the transference of public competences from central Estate to municipalities, and from these to the parishes – but this movement not being accompanied by a minimum reinforcement of resources.

The administrative reorganization of the parishes throughout the whole country, decreed by the central government in 2013, is a clear demonstration of the very specific austerity strategies followed on the territorial political spaces, developed by very closed central political communities and lacking a minimum of democratic and governance capacity. Municipal assemblies were asked to elaborate in 90 days a proposal for internal reorganization in respect of the parameters established by the law. The national association of parishes has contested the reform, advocating that the reorganization should have been grounded on voluntary aggregations rather than semi-automatic demographic parameters (ANAFRE, 2012). Several civic protests arose throughout the country. Of the 18 municipalities in LMA, 14 deliberated against the administrative reorganization and two (Sesimbra and Sintra) did not submit any proposal within the given terms. As a result, the working group established at the national parliament imposed administrative restructuring to 14 municipalities (in two cases the former parishes have been kept). The sole municipalities of Lisbon (the main centre of the metropolitan region) and Amadora elaborated alternative proposals. The municipality of Lisbon was working since 2009 on an administrative reform and could thus previously forestall the national law – with its pressing temporal terms. The Lisbon-city reform has been grounded on a study developed by a multi-disciplinary scientific team (Mateus et al., 2010) and the reduction of parishes (from 53 to 24) is being implemented as one of the elements for the all-round enhancement of governance quality, where crucial is the transference to the parishes of several competences: management and maintenance of public spaces; permissions and licences; project and management of proximity services; promotion of cultural and social programmes. This municipal reform has undergone a consultative process which received more than 7.000 contributions. Overall, paralleling its own objectives of urban politico-administrative qualification, the Lisbon-city administrative reform as also placed itself as a 'protestant reform', against the centralised and austerity-driven national territorial reforms.

The Law 75/2013 was a further centralised step towards attentive reforms of local power, with four aims: decentralization, strengthening of municipal power, backing of voluntary associations of municipalities, promotion of territorial cohesion and competitiveness. Metropolitan boards – Lisbon and Porto, instituted in 2003 – and municipal associations (instituted in 2008) are nonetheless kept as coordination bodies without actual competences and elected boards (Crespo and Cabral, 2010). This law envisages the delegation of competences from the national towards the local and inter-municipal level; however the only transferences actually prescribed are those from municipalities towards parishes. The creation of regional bodies with actual competences remains outside the horizon, the discourses about "decentralization" not resulting at all in any evident measures.

Beyond the reactions to politico-administrative reforms, the implementation of participatory instruments can also give a good exemplification of the complex patterns of institutional local responses towards contemporary urban governance challenges in LMA. Most common instruments are Agendas 21 (implemented in 5 municipalities of the metropolis) and participatory budgeting (see below), plus a number of other consultative tools such as public debates (Almada, Setúbal, Barreiro), digital tools for citizen/government communication (Lisbon, Cascais). Deliberative participatory tools are nowadays active in 5 municipalities – Amadora, Cascais, Lisbon, Oeiras, Vila Franca de Xira. Participatory budgeting is the most diffused tool (9 municipalities out of 18 have been implementing it) although with some lack of consistency in its application. Some municipalities had to cut budgets in recent years (Lisbon and Cascais); other have not been constant through the years (Odivelas, Oeiras, Sesimbra); in further cases, the so-called "participatory budgeting" have been consultative tools only (Alcochete, Palmela). In sum, the AML mirrors the recent Portuguese history of participatory budgeting, characterised by a lot of experimentation with some inherent "instability" (Alves and Allegretti, 2012).

The analysis of Lisbon sociopolitical recent tendencies concludes by focusing on changes in the profiles of civic participation and citizenship practices. As far as political-electoral patterns are concerned, the last three rounds of municipal polls (2005, 2009 and 2013) show a consistent trend of growing disaffection to politics, especially in 2013 where the number of voters dropped by more than 7% in comparison to 2009 elections. Contextually, blank and spoilt votes have showed a boom in 2013, reaching 8% of total. Moreover, a significant growth of independent parties is to be highlighted a phenomenon almost non-existent until 2009. Overall, the traditional parties lose significant portions of their constituencies in the reference period: the centre-right coalition experienced an out-and-out breakdown in 2013 – in correlation with the national discontent for austerity policies implemented by national government – but the votes did not move towards other classical political forces. The only exception was the centre-left Partido Socialista in Lisbon-city, driven by the boom of consensus for the strategies of Mayor António Costa and his team – whose party received the absolute majority in the municipal board and in the municipal assembly; as well as in the boards of 17 out of 24 parishes. Meanwhile, the May 2014 polls for European Parliament have confirmed the trends for reduced participation and fragmentation of constituencies in LMA.

The growing disaffection to politics seems to be mirrored by an emergence of new profiles of civic participation and protest. In 2006, the landscape of civic dynamics in Lisbon – formal grass-root organization and further forms of mobilization and intervention – was considerably small, although in expansion (Seixas, 2008). An enquiry conducted in 2009 (main results in Mateus et al., 2010) highlights the emergence of new sociopolitical cultures, mainly amongst most educated and younger classes but widening in denser urban areas. In times of crisis and austerity politics, some signs of a renewed civic participation are evident on two grounds. On one hand, protests against austerity measures promoted since 2011 by non-party organizations – such as Que se Lixe a Troika![6]–, although not comparable with the protest energies of similar Spanish and Greek movements, have been the biggest mass protests in history of democratic Portugal. On other hand, a number of alternative urban movements were born. To mention just a couple as exemplary of the growing civic dynamism: Habita[7] is the first network to offer advice and support to dwellers against evictions-without-rehousing on shanty towns and against rent's rising in council housing; Plataforma Gueto[8] promotes immigration inclusion and analysis of laws and policies, provides assistance to families victims of police violence and agoraphobia trends in several peripheral areas of Lisbon.

2.3 Sociopolitical changes in the Aveiro region

We tried to identify the nature of local and regional policies developed in recent years – covering a timespan which starts at the end of the last European support framework (2007-2013) and the start of the new period (2014-2020) – and how they tried to answer or mitigate some of the previously identified social, economic and spatial impacts.

The Intermunicipal Community of the Region of Aveiro (CIRA) is an association of municipalities roughly corresponding to the NUTS III of the Baixo-Vouga and was created under the Law 45/2008, of the 27th August. It succeeded the Association of Municipalities of the Ria (AMRIA) and the Greater Metropolitan Area of Aveiro (GAMA) as an association of municipalities for general purposes. The quality of the work developed and the way local actors have been involved, probably led to it being selected as a case study within a PILOT STUDY Intermunicipal communities (CIM) produced by the Government in 2012 that led to the definition of the statute that created the new legal concept of Intermunicipal communities (Decree n 75/2014 of the 13th of May).

---

6 | See http://queselixeatroika15setembro.blogspot.pt/.
7 | See http://www.habita.info/.
8 | See http://plataformagueto.wordpress.com/.

Focusing the attention on the last seven years, since 2008, we identified two cycles of financial support for the CIRA's activity: 2007-2013 and 2014-2020. The 2007-2013 cycle was conceived even before the onset of the crisis and therefore could not anticipate some of the encountered problems. However, some concerns as to how the region should think about the future – facing potential problems or challenges – were present in the design of planning tools.

The first milestone was the establishment of a protocol between the CIRA and the University of Aveiro in the design of a collaborative strategy for the development of the region (2007-2013) that aimed to support contractual agreements for the management of European funds with the government. Coordinated by a Pro-Dean of the UA for regional development, the document aims to establish a commitment for the future of the region, deepening institutional cooperation to face a new and complex socio-economic and political context.

The design of the Territorial Development Plan – PTD 2007-2013 – was developed with the intention to incorporate new concerns and guidelines for Regional Policy and Cohesion, the «rational use of EU funds in order to promote innovation based competitiveness and regional growth and to create more and better jobs» combined with the response to three challenges: take advantage of the opportunities of the new agenda for the region; increase and measure the impact of region's programs; create new mechanisms for the management and 'agency' of local and regional policies (PTD 2007-2013).

Figure 6 – Strategies PTD Baixo-Vouga 2007-2013

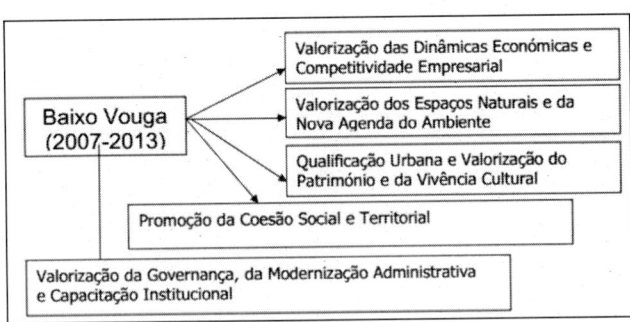

Source: PTD BAIXO VOGA 2007-2013

With this strategy, it was intended to manage funds of over € 100 million for projects in the various municipalities on a contractual base established by the Central Government.

An assessment of the implementation of the financial period concluded that, at the level of the Central Region, the Baixo-Vouga sub region (NUTS III) is among those with the highest volume of investment, and also has a fairly high per capita investment. Most of the investment is concentrated in the public sector (92%), 70% of the investment is made in equipment and 23% in infrastructure, and the immaterial investment is quite limited (EDT 2014-2020 CIRA, 2013).

Silva et al (2013) remember the innovative nature of this university's approach in its involvement with local authorities in the region, stating that it "entails a peculiarity in that this collaborative relationship represented a significant departure from a confined perspective of academic-industry relationship based only on consulting and was focused on a wider scope for technology and knowledge transfer" (Pires et al. ,2012), thus being an "innovative partnership: joint ownership of the Territorial Development Plan (UA and CIRA)" where the "University becomes a partner in the design of regional development policy".

The difficulties of the case were attributed to "local governments' weaknesses in understanding the "new language" and requirements of the (new) European regional policy approach (Lisbon and Gothenburg Agendas)", "local governments' difficulty in sharing the leadership of this process", "(assumed) unawareness regarding the work developed by the University of Aveiro", "difficulties related to the co-definition of the agenda" (Silva et al, 2013).

Beyond the PTD, several initiatives were developed for deepening the collaboration between universities and municipalities of the region. One of those was an application to the national programme Urban Networks for Competitiveness and Innovation (RUCI) aimed "to build, consolidate and/or enable collective dynamics of urban development of the network of cities and major settlements in the region of Aveiro". The proposal suggested three new agendas: a cultural agenda, promoting a cultural programming network, which articulates all municipalities of the region; a sustainability agenda, responding to the challenges of climate change and operationalized through an agency for sustainability and competitiveness, which is active in the areas of water and energy efficiency applied to buildings and public spaces and intended to replicate its results in the lives of citizens and communities; an entrepreneurship agenda, that aims to create a culture of innovation and entrepreneurship, with an emphasis on social entrepreneurship.

Figure 7 – RUCI

Source: 2010

It turns out that the approval of the program (2012) and the beginning of its implementation (2014) took a few years, so many of the projects and programs have not had the desired impact. An analysis of similar programs in other regions identified some problems, including the difficult articulation between actors at the sub-regional level, lack of regional orientation and a devaluation of immaterial over physical initiatives.

Recognising the problems and the emergence of new challenges for the programming period 2014-2020, a new Strategic Plan for Territorial Development 2014-2020 is under development, in liaison with the regional strategy at the NUTS II (CCDRC) level.

According to Teles and Santinha (2013) the new strategy for the region is based on the "common belief in the advantages of cooperation; the capacity for a co-agenda setting, supported by peer and inter-institutional trust; a new approach to knowledge co-production to foster a coherent territorial identity" and a focus on "regional specialization" maximizing the impacts of EU funding. The programme will present five core domains: Innovation and entrepreneurial context, natural and endogenous resources, community capacitation and inclusion, territorial identity and governance and public services.

Figure 8 – PTD 2014-2020

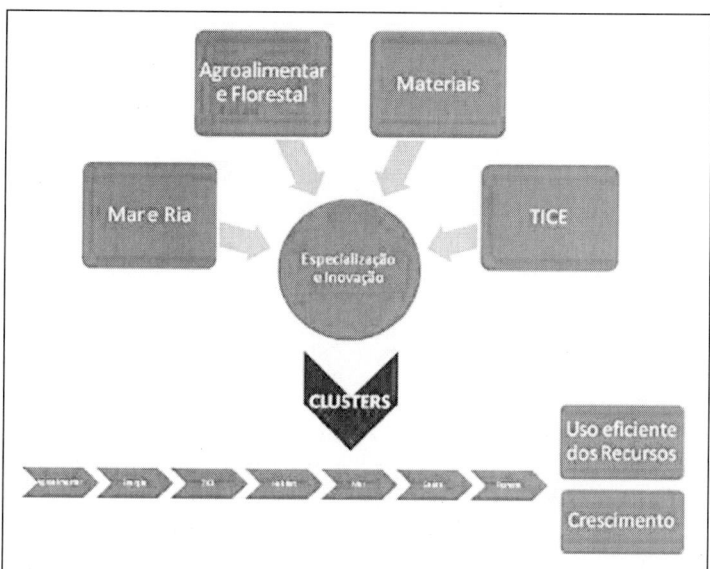

Source: CIRA

Santinha and Teles (2013) draw attention to the risks of starting the process with little information and uncertainty about its development, but remember the challenges of enabling regions to define their way to design a strategy for growth and innovation.

3. Urban politics, planning and governance – Lessons from the cities of Lisbon and Aveiro

3.1 Lisbon city anti-crisis and local reform proposals

Quite different local governments – including in its partisan and ideological components – in LMA have been trying to develop reinforced policies and new governance and institutional practices in order to respond to main crisis urban problematic. Amongst those, the municipality of Lisbon-city has been a political space where a large scale and strategic response has been developed since long. This has been happening thanks to a considerably stable political community since 2007, guaranteed by a centre-left government. The efforts towards sustained reform and political empowerment have been shaped around keywords such as "innovation" and "participation". In addition to the aforementioned administrative reform and participatory tools, the analysis of four policy areas is able to show the approaches of local power. Firstly, participatory budgeting and Agenda 21 are a piece of a wider attention to grass-root planning and social innovation, complemented by some rent support schemes and BIP/ZIP programme about priority intervention neighbourhoods[9]. The BIP/ZIP promotes micro-actions for urban regeneration through neighbourhood participative budgets funded with yearly competitive processes: although an innovative scheme is designed, the still scarce allocated funds (1 M€ a year, around 0,25% of municipal budget) cannot fully impact on the regeneration of deprived areas.

Secondly, Lisbon municipality's strategies to foster economic activity and employment were also developed. Several urban entrepreneurship support schemes have been launched, namely for business incubators, incentives to new businesses, support of retail initiatives. It is worth mentioning how important have been the EU cohesion policies within

---

9 | See http://bipzip.cm-lisboa.pt/.

this frame, and particularly the urban regeneration programmes funded through the Portuguese 2007-2013 framework for Structural Funds. The strategy of designing urban policies to attract international flows of tourism, although not new and growing in its contradictions between the priorities towards local life has been also at the core of the efforts of the municipal government. Globally, there can be seen that in the first phase Lisbon-city has suffered the impact of global tourism recession; emerging as an important tourist destination among Europe's cities in the following years. Town councillor for planning has recently launched the proposal for a non-tax area for hotels in the city downtown and a major investment is programmed for upgrading Lisbon Cruise Terminal in order to be able to respond to bigger fluxes of arrivals. Commerce, new services (bus, bike rental, tuc-tuc) tourist shops and restaurants are popping up in the centre and historical areas – and the local press has announced proudly the 2013's "tourism Oscar" awarded to the Portuguese capital for "City Break On a Budget" (Amadeus and WTM Travel Experience Award).

Thirdly, a new emphasis on building rehabilitation and urban regeneration has been envisaged as a cornerstone planning policy around investor-friendly actions, fiscal and edification incentives. As a result of thirty years of demographic contraction, a significant volume of vacant dwellings (around 50 thousands) is found in Lisbon-city, most particularly in its historical centre. Political discourses have since the 1990's emphasized the need for a public policy that would encourage building's rehabilitation, but for a long time that was not visible at all. With the crisis major and initial impact in the construction sector, and namely in the sprawl continuity, rehabilitation of derelict buildings has become a more tangible activity, both for public and private strategies. Just recently, central Government has introduced new regulation to lower technical requirements and to reduce rehabilitation costs in over 30%. In addition to stimulus to requalification of private dwellings, Lisbon municipality has elaborated a strategic plan for the requalification and management of council housing – around 30.000 flats – with the final aim to alienate the stock in few decades (UrbanGuru, 2011). However, and given the credit crunch which has been affecting middle-class families and their housing strategies, political critiques have addressed the risk that real estate investors only will be able to respond to the challenge, and that gentrification trends are to be expected in the next future in Lisbon centre – also as a consequence of tourism friendly policies.

The drivers of sociopolitical change here debated show a complex sociopolitical framework made of responsive, contradictory and clashing trends. Two main trends show to be restructuring urban politics in Lisbon. By one side the central state policies, most particularly when sustained by the 2011 Troika bailout and the support of EU main cupules. And by other side the local – or maybe better said, the urban – political actions and reactions, these founding some support on inner structures of the EU itself (like the cohesion policies), as well as on fast growing components of the society and its stakeholders (like universities, sociocultural institutions, and even corporate associations). As far as institutional processes are concerned, a clash between the harsh top-down austerity curtails; and the bottom-up urban evolution dynamics; is clearly ongoing and developing, through a complex frame of multi-scalar intersections. The historical and now renewed pressures for austerity localism in Portugal are colliding with local empowerment and resistances, shifting urban regimes towards a still unknown future. Furthermore, a steady evolution of grass-root activism and civic participation adds further pressure both on top-down and bottom-up institutional drivers.

3.2 Aveiro local urban policies

On another level, the average size of municipalities have sought to respond to the new challenges of contemporary economic and social development with some innovative measures, in some cases with good results, others not so much. The municipality of Aveiro, the capital of NUTIII Baixo-Vouga, has sought to develop an effort to promote economic development with very encouraging results. Leveraging the experience of involvement in the European Network FIN-URB-ACT and after two years of working together with local and regional around fostering entrepreneurship and support SME actors, drew up a plan for local action, designated "Aveiro Entrepreneur" (http://www.aveiro-empreendedor.pt/).

This project went through creating a strategy for promoting an innovative, entrepreneurial environment in the municipality of Aveiro with action in five priority areas: support for small and medium enterprises; entrepreneurship in higher education; promotion of entrepreneurship in schools; promoting an entrepreneurial culture and communication.

The program led to about 490 different actions, involving more than 100 thousand people, drove the launch of different technological platforms (sea, materials, smart communities, bicycle and mobility) and innovative measures to promote entrepreneurship.

The main results achieved where centered in creating agile channels for dialogue and joint working between local authority, university and economic agents, which resulted in the facilitation the design of collaborative projects. Furthermore, the realization of events (incubation programs, training and capacity building initiatives, talks – like TEDx Aveiro) and the proximity of the funding partners (public and private) and expeditors process led to the creation of an environment conducive to generating ideas and business climate, either in technology or in more traditional domains, with an impact that overflowed the boundaries of the region. Finally, working with schools in education for entrepreneurship, with the involvement of teachers and students, allows foreseeing the creation of a new culture of entrepreneurship.

Despite these relevant results, some difficulties and limitations where identified, particularly in networking, as a result of different interests and stakes and also the lack of time to assume a long-term involvement; in the territorial scale, that has shown to be limited for the nature of issues involved; and finally, in the lack of information for an adequate perception of the real needs of enterprises complicates the design of actions.

Beyond this effort to support economic activity, the municipality was involved in a major urban regeneration project – The Sustainability Park (PDS) funded by the National Strategic Reference Framework (NSRF 2007-2013).

The project was assumed as a Partnerships for Urban Regeneration (a program of the National Policy for the Cities), approved in early 2009, involving 15 local and national partners and a budget of nearly 14 million euros, subdivided by 17 subprojects. The project aims at establishing a greenway crossing a significant part of the city centre (199.106 m2), articulating a set of facilities and promoting an innovative environment for residents and tourists under the umbrella of the sustainable development concept. Intended to «affirm the city as a place of innovation, competitiveness» through a spatial intervention with renewed interest to residents and visitors.

The idea behind the project was the qualification of an entire green space surrounding several old neighbourhoods of Aveiro and the creation of a space of contact with nature and good environmental practices, somewhat in line with the concept of "Design for Sustainability" (FIG.7).

It was understood that two elements were needed to strengthen the application. First, a motto – sustainability – implying that it was not a mere physical rehabilitation project of a green space or a set of green spaces. Second, content that gives consistency to the concept, where the involvement of the University of Aveiro (UA) as a key partner was crucial.

The initiative intended to be more than just «another sustainable project» but one that «would serve as a model to be replicated in other areas of the city». The promoters also state that «the redevelopment and revitalization of the defined area, which is integrated in the largest continuous green area of the city, would be key to promoting urban sustainability and attractiveness», which proves crucial to sustain the policy of promoting a quality environment in the city and the welfare of its citizens.

The Local Authority considered that each of the projects within the scope of the Action Programme «assumed importance and relevance to achieve the objective of creating a multifunctional space and is followed a complementary and integrated rationale». Thus, the project was intended to function as an educational experience that "communicates and disseminate knowledge" through the promotion of seminars and publications. According to the project's promoters, a document will be produced ('Aveiro 2020 – a sustainable strategy') which will bring together "all learning resulting from this process and facilitate the replication of results in other areas of the city of Aveiro".

In face of such a complex initiative, some problems arose. First, the green corridor concept proved to have questionable planning options – a pedestrian bridge over the central channel of the city, renewal of an old garden – without a spatial planning framework and clear understanding of the key issues to be addressed. Second, the proposals had no mechanisms for public scrutiny and participation was seen as a mere bureaucratic requirement. Finally, there were several difficulties to put the new sustainability agenda in practice (traditional projects with "green label").

The PDS thus proved a project with a good and relevant theme – promoting sustainability in the context of urban regeneration – but having physical proposals, which were not coherent with the objectives. The adoption of the term in this context – the program for regeneration partnerships, funded under the NSRF – demanded a more careful identification of the object, the selection of places and themes that should be comprehended, as well as a more rigorous definition of the overall objectives, as well the objectives of its individual components.

The complexity of the exercise, which was basically understood as another public financial transaction, was neglected when the context was more demanding failing short of the need, stated by João Ferrão (2011), for more assertive and clearly identified problems and a more coherent set of local public policies, in this case linking mobility, energy, environment and culture.

Several of the proposals were defined on the basis of rhetoric and not supported by evidence and planning studies. For example, the need for a very visual impact pedestrian bridge was justified by "a long felt need" and it was expected to serve many users with great savings of time, while none of these statements were sustained by any facts or concrete data. On the contrary, there was some empirical evidence that contradicted the assumptions. Other proposals – the destruction of an old neighbourhood garden and a proposal to build a road in the middle – where defended with the argument of the need for public space betterment. In both cases, a strong public participation social movement occurred contesting the proposals and suggesting alternatives but where successively ignored.

Since this was a project concerned with sustainability, with ambitions to become exemplary and that could count on partners with extensive experience in the field, one would expect that the interpretation of the concept and its implementation would be particularly careful, in its social, economic, environmental and spatial dimensions. What happened was the opposite. There are several examples of dubious interpretation of the concept, both in what regards the social dimension of the concept – the lack of respect for history and memory of old neighbourhoods and the central channel – or the environmental dimension – total destruction of the existing tree structure in an old garden.

Civic reaction to various interpretations of the concept had a significant educational effect on the importance that the community was giving to the "memory, identity and respect for the place (no fundamentalist or conservative stance)", the "importance of an overview of the proposal's (studied and planned) risks and opportunities" and the fact that the intervention on (sensitive) places are to "earn extra caution (debate, and consensus requirements) and not be at the mercy of any 'enlightened technocrat'".

The information for the implementation of an ambitious project like this was not enough, lacking specific evidence on the subject (territory and the demands of the proposal – sustainability concept), and therefore did not lead to a properly informed planning exercise, leaving the designer the freedom to find answers to unasked questions. Two of the most problematic proposals have earned such a broad disapproval from those who would most benefit from them that it became clear that care was not taken to previously hear them on their problems and needs. In a way, this shows the perverse effect of funding programs that require a high level of precision in the definition of concepts and projects and establish a minimum level of review and control or flexibility, leading to a precipitation in the definition of objects and reasoning of the planning exercise in the project.

Still, even on these issues there were relevant achievements motivated by civic action, in particular the relevance of the value of sensible use of public resources, a critical attitude towards cheap money from Brussels and the consequences of becoming hostage to 'opportunism'. In particular, the weak mechanisms for assessing coherence become worrying from the point of view of the effectiveness of public policy, undermining the successful conduct of these operations. In fact, they allow incomprehensible acts of mismanagement of public funds and an inability to take advantage of existing potential for the production of innovative and exemplary public policy, particularly for Aveiro and for issues related to sustainability.

Both projects fall under two different postures of stakeholder involvement towards building transformative agendas, whether environmental or economic. The most successful practices show the importance of dialogue to identify shared understanding, to create a climate of trust between partners which allow a change of mind-set and create opportunities for social, economic transformation, essential during a crisis agenda.

4. Challenges for Spatial Planning in Times of Crisis

The previous analyses, considering the impact of the crisis in both Lisbon region and Aveiro region, reveal in a first stance two different institutional realities – high and medium-density with distinct economic and socio-political contexts and institutional responses – in the first case strongly dependent from the center (Lisbon) in the second (Aveiro) a more multi-municipal approach. These instances illustrate the multiplicity of public policy approaches to respond to crisis: organizing politic-administrative reform (in Lisbon), planning new agendas for the future (Aveiro Region 2014-2020), promoting entrepreneurship (Lisbon and Aveiro) and developing urban regeneration projects (PDS).

But in a second stance, the analyses permit the inference of most relevant findings and correspondent critical analysis. The urban scenarios are primordial places where social, economic and cultural dynamics are driving towards deep restructuring of sociopolitical patterns. The analysis of both geographical and sociopolitical trends in Lisbon and Aveiro during the course of the European crisis and its mainstream political austerity measures, as well of its more localized – or should we say glocalized – urban responses; show not only that there are different phases and crisis effects and drivers; but also that a clear geopolitical knowledge and planning conflict seems to be widening.

The evolution of main indicators in Lisbon and Aveiro Regions show that there have been developing three considerably different crisis-impact phases. The first phase impacted strongly on the urbanisation driven economies and its most dependent sectors and territories; the second phase is impacting widen throughout most of the urban territories of the metropolis – namely on the 'social transfers' poorer classes but as well as on middle-classes and public employment; the third phase is approaching now and derived from the skills and demographic depression, due precisely to the lack of systemic economic and labour opportunities. On one hand, the relevance of national pressures – and hence of European politics, at least in the Portuguese case – is quite evident in the dual evolution of the crisis around early economic impacts of the economic burst, as well as on the socio-economic impacts of the austerity policies. And on the other hand, a confrontation is clearly growing between these austerity pressures and the developing sociopolitical local dynamics; which at the same time still lie in unstable capacitation grounds; none withstanding being reinforced by a steady civic capacitation.

As stated in previous analyses (Leontidou 2010; Nel.lo, 2001; Chorianopoulos, 2002), for many southern European urban areas there has been a distinctive path of development and restructuring, as well as distinctive modes of governance, at least throughout a major part of the XX century. Causing not only specific urban production processes (strongly understood in major trends like the peri-urbanisation of vast Mediterranean urban and coastal areas), but also curtailing city qualification and competitiveness itself. Today, the hyper-positioning of urban geographies and human daily realities is bringing a complete set of dilemmas and challenges to Southern European cities (Seixas and Albet, 2012). This is an already complex panorama that the present crisis pressures seem to be widening even more; as the Lisbon metropolitan evolution since 2008 to present is showing.

Regional policies are an important tool to respond to territorial dynamics, especially in a context of crisis. Different institutional dynamics where identified with diverse settings and speeds. In the first case, the metropolitan context reveals a significant weight of autonomy of the capital. In the second, a context of medium-density region, there is a strong effort in deepening inter-municipal policies based on a strong relationship with the university as key partner for conceiving public policies.

The first results of the regional efforts reveal the potential of local and regional partnerships, particularly with regard to "share materials and information resources, have more innovation capacity, foster mutual learning, have more status and peer recognition, and to share costs and risks" (Mota, Luis and Rosa Pires, A, 2013).

In the case of Aveiro, the development of a framework for partnership between the university and the region characterized by mutual respect, understanding and trust, involving selected partners who share interests with clear roles and guidelines of the institutions founded on clear and open communication platforms (Mota, Luis and Rosa Pires, a, 2013) were key to the design of a shared agenda and for a coherent framework of action which increased the possibility of funding and execution.

Local policies have a different regional reach, although the cases – Lisbon and Aveiro – are of completely different sizes. Both cases show the importance of innovative measures undertaken by both local authorities to support entrepreneurship – strong relationship with the local authority and the university sector and business concerns with the proximity of institutional support.

Administrative reform Lisbon clearly reveals the importance of a smart political negotiation and the ability to intervene in territorial delimitation with a concern of allocating competences. The example of national administrative reform recommended by the Troika, did not follow this rule and simply add the parishes.

The response to new public policy approaches, related with the sustainability agenda in the context of urban regeneration, proved to be more problematic. In the case of Aveiro, an ambitious environmental public policy program, in line with the stakes of the European Union and the societal challenges – energy efficiency and climate change, in a context of scarce resources and economic crisis, showed a problematic methodological and conceptual approach, without a clear identification of problems to answer, the necessary technical skills and to produce responses, the lack of evaluation of consistency of results with objectives, and absence of communication with potential users, facilitators or managers.

In response to the emergence of non-consensual proposals and understood as undermining the collective interest emerged an intense civic dynamics, reflection, critique and protest over the three years of project development; at the lack of response from the local authority, unusual in the national tradition of low participation.

The importance of participation shows that although citizens mainly express themselves when a lot is at stake for them personally, evidence shows that they do get involved in such processes when: they have more access to information; learn about the problems and potential solutions; notice that there is a common share of ideas amongst the community and their voices can be heard (Mota e Santinha, 2012).

Both cases also reveal that in times of crisis and in lack of public and overall financial resources, there is growing the potential for civic action by exploring and mobilizing social resources (knowledge, time, mind) to contribute to both alternative and more effective local public policies, which requires appropriate reflection on how to inspire these policies in response to problems and societal challenges.

References

Abreu, A.; Mendes, H.; Rodrigues, J.; Gusmão, J. G.; Serra, N.; Alves, P. D.; Mamede, R. P. (2013). A Crise, a Troika e as Alternativas Urgentes, Tinta da China, Lisboa

AIDA, 2013. Anuário da AIDA. Aveiro

Alves, M. L. and G. Allegretti (2012). "(In)stability, a Key Element to Understand Participatory Budgeting: Discussing Portuguese Cases". In: Journal of Public Deliberation, 8(2), article 3

ANAFRE (Associação Nacional de Freguesias) (2012). Proposta de Lei nº 44/XII/1.ª (GOV) – Aprova o regime jurídico da reorganização administrativa territorial autárquica. Parecer. Available at www.anafre.pt/freguesias-associadas/reorganizacao-administrativa/parecer-anafre [Accessed June 2014].

Calvache, M., Teles, F., Rosa Pires, A., Silva, P. (2013) Universidade e Território: os desafios da inovação de base regional. Apresentação oral na Conferência «Europa 2020: retórica, discursos, política e prática». II Conferência de Planeamento Regional e Urbano, VIII ENPLANT e XVIII Workshop da APDR. Universidade de Aveiro

Chorianopoulus, I. (2002) Urban Restructuring and Governance: North-South Differences in Europe and the EU Urban Initiatives. In: Urban Studies, 39(4), 705-726

CIRA (2012) Plano Intermunicipal da Região de Aveiro (PIMTRA). Aveiro

Crespo, J. L. and J. Cabral (2010) The Institutional Dimension to Urban Governance and Territorial Management in the Lisbon Metropolitan Area. In: Análise Social, 197, 639-662

Dexia and CCRE (Conseil de Communes et Régions d'Europe) (2012) Subnational Public Finance in the European Union. Summer 2012. Available at www.ccre.org/docs/Note_CCRE_Dexia_EN.pdf [Accessed June 2014]

DGOTDU and Universidade de Aveiro (2009) Projecto da Ocupação Dispersa. DGOTDU. Lisboa

Hadjimichalis, C. (2011) Uneven Geographical Development and Socio-spatial Justice and Solidarity: European Regions after the 2009 Financial Crisis. In: European Urban and Regional Studies, 18(3), 254-274

INOVARIA, 2012. Relatório Contas. Inovaria. Aveiro

Leontidou, L. (2010) Urban Social Movements in 'Weak' Civil Societies: The Right to the City and Cosmopolitan Activism in Southern Europe. In: Urban Studies, 47(6), 1179-1203

Mateus, A.; J. Seixas and N. Vitorino (eds.) (2010) Qualidade de Vida e Governo da Cidade. Bases para um Novo Modelo de Governação da Cidade de Lisboa. ISEG, Lisboa. Available at http://www.reformaadministrativa.am-lisboa.pt/fileadmin/MODELO_

GOVERNACAO/Documentos/ISEG_governacao_abril2010.pdf (Accessed June 2014].

Mateus, Augusto and Associates (PM and A) (2005) Territorial Competitiveness and Economic and Social Cohesion (Vol. III) – Thematic study for the preparation of the NSRF, Lisbon

Mota, J.C. (2014) "Planeamento do Território: Metodologias, Actores e Participação. Tese de Doutoramento, Universidade de Aveiro

Mota, J. C. and G. Santinha (2012) Social media and civic engagement: discussing the case of Aveiro, Portugal, E-Practice 16

Mota, L. and A. Rosa Pires (2013) The challenges of managing partnerships in regional development projects. Apresentação oral na Conferência «Europa 2020: retórica, discursos, política e prática». II Conferência de Planeamento Regional e Urbano, VIII ENPLANT e XVIII Workshop da APDR. Universidade de Aveiro

Municipal Mobility Plan of Aveiro, CMA, 2011

Nanetti, R. Y.; H. Rato and M. Rodrigues (2004) Institutional Capacity and Reluctant Decentralization in Portugal: The Lisbon and Tagus Valley Region. In: Regional and Federal Studies, 14 (3), 405-429

Nel.lo, O. (2001) Ciutat de Ciutats. Editorial Empúries, Barcelona

Reis, J. and J. Rodrigues (eds.) (2011) Portugal e a Europa em Crise. Para Acabar com a Economia de Austeridade. Lisboa: Actual

Santos, A. C. (2013) Temos Vivido acima das Nossas Possibilidades? In: J. Soeiro, M. Cardina, and N. Serra (eds.) Não Acredite em Tudo o Que Pensa. Mitos do Senso Comum na Era da Austeridade. Tinta da China, Lisboa, 17-30

Seixas, J. (2008) Estruturas e Dinâmicas do Capital Sócio-cultural em Lisboa. In: M. V. Cabral, F. C. Silva and T. Saraiva (eds.) Cidade and Cidadania – Governança Urbana e Participação Cidadã. Imprensa de Ciências Sociais, Lisboa, 177-210

Seixas, J. and A. Albet (eds.) (2012) Urban Governance in Southern Europe. Ashgate, Farnham

Silva, P, F. Teles and A. Rosa Pires, (2013) Learning from the past: can we unveil a winning formula for networked governance under European Union regional policy?. Apresentação oral na Conferência «Europa 2020: retórica, discursos, política e prática». II Conferência de Planeamento Regional e Urbano, VIII ENPLANT e XVIII Workshop da APDR. Universidade de Aveiro

Teles, F. and G. Santinha (2013) The transition to the next programming period 2014-2020: discussing the Strategy for Growth and Innovation of Aveiro Region. Apresentação oral na Conferência «Europa 2020: retórica, discursos, política e prática». II Conferência de Planeamento Regional e Urbano, VIII ENPLANT e XVIII Workshop da APDR. Universidade de Aveiro

UrbanGuru (2011) Programa de Intervenção Estratégica no Património Habitacional Municipal e nos Devolutos Municipais. Relatório final. CML, Lisboa. Available at http://habitacao.cm-lisboa.pt/documentos/1323729521D4qVS7sl3Eu87LY5.pdf

Werner, R. A. (2013) Crises, the Spatial Distribution of Economic Activity, and the Geography of Banking. In: Environment and Planning A, 45(12), 2789-2796.

Authors

Nuria Benach is an urban geographer at the University of Barcelona. Her research focusses on the discourses of urban change, cultural diversity in public spaces and critical spatial thinking. Most recent publications: (2014, edited with A. Walliser) Urban Challenges in Spain and Portugal. London: Routledge; (2012) Richard Peet. Geografía contra el neoliberalismo. Icaria; (2012, with A. Albet) Doreen Massey. Un sentido global del lugar. Icaria and (2004) Public spaces in Barcelona, 1980-2000. In: T. Marshall (ed) Transforming Barcelona. London: Routledge.

Frank Eckardt is professor for urban studies and social research at the Bauhaus-University Weimar. He holds a PhD in political science and works in the study programs of urban planning and architecture. His main research is focused on social and political questions with regard to the social inequalities, cultural diversity and democratic governance of cities. Recent books: (2014) Lehrbuch Stadtforschung. Wiesbaden: Springer; (with A. Bourdin and A. Woods) Die ortlose Stadt. Über die Virtualisierung des Urbanen. Bielefeld: transcript; (2013) Zur Aktualtität von Mike Davis. Wiesbaden: Springer.

José Miguel Fernández Güell is an architect and urban planner from Madrid Technical University. Master of Science and PhD in Urban and Regional Planning from Texas AandM University. He has worked as a consultant for the Inter American Development Bank, the European Commission and the United Nations Industrial Development Organization. Presently, he is a full-time professor at the Urban and Regional Planning Department, Madrid Technical University. His areas of research interest are strategic planning for cities and foresight studies.

Maria Cristina Gibelli is an associate professor of urban policies, plans and projects at Politecnico di Milano since 1983 and an adjunct professor of urban and regional policies at Bocconi University of Milan (1995-2007). She actually works on strategic spatial planning for urban regions, urban sustainability and costs of urban sprawl with a comparative perspective. On these topics, she worked for the Milan Municipality, the Lombardy Region, the Italian Presidency of the Council of Ministers, the French DATAR. Recent publication: (with R. Camagni and P. Rigamonti) Urban mobility and urban form: the social and environmental costs of different patterns of urban expansion. In: Ecological Economics; (with E. Salzano) (2004) NO SPRAWL, Firenze: Alinea.

Francesco Indovina is a *professor* in "regional and urban system analysis" at the department of planning of the Istituto Universitario di Architettura di Venezia. Since 2004, he retired from work. Since 2004, he is a contract professor at the Faculty of Planning of the University IUAV of Venice and of the Faculty of Architecture, University of Sassari. Since the end of '60es, his research goals moved permanently to regional disciplines with a social and economic approach, particularly focussed on industrial plant location, housing, transportation and infrastructures, methods and goals of regional planning. He is editor of the book collection "Studi urbani e regionali". Recent publications: (2009) Dalla città diffusa all'arcipelago metropolitano, and (2013) La metropoli europea – una prospettiva. Milano: Franco Angeli editore.

Vaso Makrygianni holds a diploma in architecture and is a PhD candidate in Urban and Regional Planning in Aristotle University of Thessaloniki, Greece. In her research, she explores emancipatory practices of migratory populations and spaces of resistance in Athens during the crisis era. Her interests include socio-spatial analysis and urban planning, feminism and gender studies, social movements and radical geography.'

Maria Markantonatou is a lecturer in political sociology at the Department of Sociology, University of the Aegean, Greece. She is currently working on the crisis in Greece. Recent publications: (2013) Fiscal Discipline through Internal Devaluation and Discourses of Rent-Seeking: the Case of the Crisis in Greece. In: Studies in Political Economy; (2012) The State and Modes of Regulation in Greece from the Post-war Period to the 2009 Financial Crisis. In: Journal of Balkan and Near Eastern Studies; (2012) The Social Consequences of the Financial Crisis in Greece: Recession, Insecurity and Welfare Deregulation. In: International Journal of Anthropology.

José Carlos Mota is a lecturer at the Department of Social, Political and Territorial Sciences of the University of Aveiro. Since 2004 he joined the Department has a lecturer and researcher and in 2014 completed his PhD on Methodologies to promote participation in Spatial Planning. He has been involved in several spatial planning research projects with a focus on collaborative planning and civic engagement. Member of 'task force' that developed the following scientific and civic platforms: 'Global City 2.0' – a city civic movement's world map (http://www.globalcitynetwork.org/); Community Project Amigos d'Avenida in Aveiro (http://amigosdavenida.blogs.sapo.pt/). José is currently involved in the launch of a new RandD platform concerning Soft Mobility and the Bicycle (http://www.ua.pt/ptbicicleta/).

Javier Ruiz Sánchez, PhD, is an architect and Professor of Urban Planning, Universidad Politécnica de Madrid. He combines academic and research with professional activity as planner and urban designer in several scales. His research line focuses on analyzing relationship between comprehensive and sectorial planning and effective urban development, evolving nature of cities and regions, and cities and regions as complex systems, and also on conflict, difference and gender experiences in urban design. He has lectured or given courses in several universities and institutions in Europe, Latin America and Asia, and led research projects and European networks on urban planning or gender financed by public programs.

João Seixas is a professor and researcher on urban geography and urban studies at the University of Lisbon. Invited professor in the Federal University of Rio de Janeiro and the Autonomous University of Barcelona. Commissioner of the Strategic Charter of Lisbon. Since 2000, coordinator of several projects in the fields of urban studies and urban regeneration (both scientific as empirically applied). Most recent books: (2012) Urban Governance in Southern Europe. London: Ashgate; (2013) A Cidade na Encruzilhada. Porto: Afrontamento; (2014) Governação de Proximidade. Lisbon: INCM.

Charalampos Tsavdaroglou is an urban planner and PhD Candidate in Urban and Regional Planning, School of Architecture, Aristotle University of Thessaloniki (Greece) and his thesis title is "Commons and Enclosures, dialectic approach of Space". He has an MSc (2009) in Management of Resources and Development Projects, Faculty of Engineering AUTh (Greece) and a Diploma (2004) in Rural and Surveying Engineering, Faculty of Engineering, AUTh (Greece).

Álvaro Sevilla-Buitrago is an Associate Professor of Town and Regional Planning, Technical University of Madrid. Blending critical sociospatial theory and urban history, his academic research is focused on the social history of planning and the evolution of the territorial formations of capitalism. His recent work has also analyzed the historical and contemporary dialectics of urban commoning and urban enclosure. Recent publications: (2015) "Outraged spatialities: the production of public space in the #spanishrevolution", ACME: An International E-Journal for Critical Geographies (fc); (2014) "Central Park against the streets: the enclosure of public space cultures in mid-nineteenth century New York", Social and Cultural Geography 15:2, 151-171; (2014) "Urbs in rure: historical enclosure and the extended urbanization of the countryside", in Brenner, N. (ed.), Implosions / Explosions. Towards a Study of Planetary Urbanization, Berlin: Jovis, 236-259.

Alberto Violante holds a temporary research post at the National Institute of Statistics. He took his PhD at the University of Milan Bicocca and he was RNT fellow at the Department of Social Policy in Helsinki. He published a book about Rome's urban development (La Metropoli spezzata, 2008), many articles on urban issues and was recently part of a project of research about Urban Shrinkage (How Urban Shrinkage Impacts on Patterns of Socio-Spatial Segregation: The Cases of Leipzig, Ostrava, and Genoa, 2014 with others).

Maria Zifou is adjunct faculty at the Dept. of Planning and Regional Development, University of Thessaly. Her current research focuses on the crisis and the restructuring of spatial planning and urban policy in Greece. She has also conducted research with a focus on the critical evaluation of planning policy, spatial development policy and rural land use planning. She has extensive professional experience as urban planner in Greece and Florida, USA

Edition Kulturwissenschaft

Regula Valérie Burri,
Kerstin Evert, Sibylle Peters,
Esther Pilkington,
Gesa Ziemer (Hg.)

Versammlung und Teilhabe

Urbane Öffentlichkeit und performative Künste

2014, 344 Seiten, kart.,
29,99 €,
ISBN 978-3-8376-2681-0
E-Book: 26,99 €,
ISBN 978-3-8394-2681-4

■ In Auseinandersetzung damit, was Demokratie heute ausmacht, gehen gesellschaftliche und künstlerische Diskurse oft Hand in Hand. Urbane Öffentlichkeiten und performative Künste verbinden sich in der Frage nach neuen Formen von Versammlung und Teilhabe: Wie treffen Kollektive Entscheidungen, wer ist an diesen beteiligt und wie entwirft sich gesellschaftliches Engagement in die Zukunft?
Das erste künstlerisch-wissenschaftliche Graduiertenkolleg in Deutschland versammelt in diesem Band Forschungsergebnisse, in denen wissenschaftliche Analyse und künstlerische Forschung ineinander greifen.

www.transcript-verlag.de

Urban Studies

Alain Bourdin, Frank Eckardt, Andrew Wood

Die ortlose Stadt
Über die Virtualisierung des Urbanen

2014, 200 Seiten, kart., zahlr. Abb., 25,99 €,
ISBN 978-3-8376-2746-6
E-Book: 22,99 €,
ISBN 978-3-8394-2746-0

■ Kommunikation ist die Zukunft der Stadt: Räumliche Grenzen weichen auf, Entfernungen werden virtuell überwunden. Ein anregendes Buch über das Leben in der neuen, »ortlosen« Stadt.

»*Stadtsoziologen, Geographen, Architekten und Medienwissenschaftler sollten dieses Werk ganz weit oben auf den Bücherstapel legen.*« (Damian Paderta, Kritische Ausgabe, 19.12.2014)

»*Ein buntes Kaleidoskop mit Hunderten bedenkenswerter Einfälle. Allen stadtforschenden Disziplinen und Professionen zu empfehlen. Das Buch gehört unbedingt in die Hochschulbibliotheken von Sozial- und Medienwissenschaften, Architektur und Stadtplanung.*« (Lilo Schmitz, www.socialnet.de, 19.08.2014)

»*Ein anregendes Buch*«
(Simone Kraft, Magazine on Art and Architecture, 5/2014)

»*Anspruchsvolle Lektüre*«
(Nicole Bindreiter, Kunst und Kirche, 54/2014)

www.transcript-verlag.de

Urban Studies

Jörg Gertel,
Rachid Ouaissa (Hg.)

Jugendbewegungen
Städtischer Widerstand und Umbrüche in der arabischen Welt

2014, 400 Seiten, Hardcover, zahlr. z.T. farb. Abb., 19,99 €,
ISBN 978-3-8376-2130-3

■ Reclaim the Streets! Ein Buch über die Jugend- und Protestbewegungen in den Städten der arabischen Welt unter den Vorzeichen des arabischen Frühlings. Der Band beleuchtet ihre alltäglichen Handlungsspielräume im Rahmen wirtschaftlicher Zwänge und staatlicher Kontrolle sowie ihre Rolle in politischen Ordnungen. Die Beiträge zeigen, wie Widerstand und neue Initiativen die aktuellen Gesellschaftsentwürfe verändern und wie neue Vorstellungen von Heimat verhandelt werden.

»*Die Studien vor Ort bieten einen differenzierten Blick auf das breite Spektrum des Jugendlichseins in den Städten der arabischen Welt. Dadurch werden die unterschiedlichen Bedingungen für die Proteste deutlich, die unter dem einheitlichen Begriff ›Arabischer Frühling‹ verschwinden.*«
(Peter Nowak, neues deutschland, 22.10.2014)

www.transcript-verlag.de